D0934879

COACHING FOR MEANING

COACHING

FOR

MEANING

The culture and practice of
coaching and team building

Vincent Lenhardt

Translated by
Malcolm Stewart

First published as 'Les responsables porteurs de sens: Culture et pratique du coaching et du team-building' by Vincent Lenhardt 2nd edition
© INSEP CONSULTING *Éditions*, Paris 2002, 18 Malesherbers – 75008 Paris, France.
All rights reserved.

First published in Great Britain in 2004 by
PALGRAVE MACMILLAN
Houndmills, Basingstoke, Hampshire RG21 6XS and
175 Fifth Avenue, New York, N.Y. 10010
Companies and representatives throughout the world

PALGRAVE MACMILLAN is the global academic imprint of the Palgrave Macmillan division of St. Martin's Press, LLC and of Palgrave Macmillan Ltd. Macmillan® is a registered trademark in the United States, United Kingdom and other countries. Palgrave is a registered trademark in the European Union and other countries.

ISBN 1–4039–0225–9

This book is printed on paper suitable for recycling and made from fully managed and sustained forest sources.

A catalogue record for this book is available from the British Library.

A catalog record for this book is available from the Library of Congress

10 9 8 7 6 5 4 3 2 1
13 12 11 10 09 08 07 06 05 04

Printed and bound in Great Britain by
Creative Print & Design (Wales), Ebbw Vale

CONTENTS

List of Figures

List of Figures

List of Figures

What could appear simpler and more common place than the subject of this book? In our increasingly complex society, made up of interdependencies and growing uncertainties, accelerated and variable changes, there is scarcely a male or female manager who does not ask him or herself questions. First, there are the 'how' questions. For example: How do you motivate a team in synergy? How do you bring out and sustain the personalities which, through the process, are discovered, confronted and sometimes confronting the best interests of the community and development of each individual? How do you create change? How do you grant a level of autonomy which will ensure that growth is possible but will also allow crises to be overcome and possible setbacks to be by-passed? How do you fully live the responsibilities to be endorsed, in this solitude from the exercise of power without forbidding oneself at any time the possibility of doubt or change? There are 'how' questions, but also questions that are more insidiously fundamental that relate to the 'why': Why limitless production; growth which by its very nature must be incomplete; a pursuit of outperformance that is viewed as one of the fine arts; a leadership nourished by constant will power? In brief, simple questions about the meaning of things. With another question upstream of all others: How do we bring them the answers without ceasing to exercise what is the very essence of our responsibility?

Although Vincent Lenhardt's book may use the simple and everyday as its point of departure, it contributes fundamentally to our ability to go beyond these subjects. For he offers us a true thought process in order to progress in this search for the 'how' and the 'why'. It is an approach that passes first through the mediation of those special consultants who are capable of supporting managers along their paths, who help them and their teams to move beyond the paradoxes of solitude and division in which they are so often trapped. It also helps them to discover and construct real places of communication, of analysis, of what blocks and what transforms the relationships at work, of research into what is in play in the game of technology, products and markets, as well as in the game of strategies and stakes that punctuate the lives of companies and individuals. It is also an approach that is learnt and acquired through the progressive mastering of models of analysis, enabling one to read and to understand the phenomena we observe and of which we are an integral part, and also to tackle other ways of reading, eventually made possible by other levels of consciousness and personal development. No scientific pretensions in that. Rather, the sharing of an immense experience which simply authorises us to say: 'Everything happens as if reality could reveal itself this way, describe itself this way and be read this way; and, because being able to read also constitutes a way of understanding, reality can probably be foreseen in this way.'

The theme gains its legitimacy from the very life story on which it is based. It is a rare and unique pathway of personal research and experimentation, of practice and consulting, of renewed support to numerous senior executives and multiple teams whose way of working, of handling change, of stimulating relationships, of researching the individual and collective identity hiding behind the game of personalities have been profoundly modified. The transferability of his experience depends on the reader's involvement and his willingness to work in order to make the proposed analyses his own or, by relying on these, to create other analyses in his own words and in his own style. On this note, this work is in no way presented as a revelation. It is rather a presentation of the stages in reflection, of phases in understanding, like a sequence of intellectual or even spiritual exercises that help one to take up one's own trademark, to place oneself in relation to others and in relation to oneself and to orient and conduct one's actions. It does not promise efficiency at bargain prices, nor how to change oneself in five lessons, but encourages an attitude of research, elucidation, exchanges and a particular culture fashioned from growing transparency and autonomy.

This book is addressed first to consultants whose profession is to support managers and their colleagues in the search for a greater integration of their values and their managerial activities. Those who help managers to live out their responsibilities to the full (coaching) and their teams to develop simultaneously their effectiveness and their harmony (team building). It is moreover to these consultants that he addresses himself regularly; to those companions on the road who prove indispensable when one comes up against the impossibility of overcoming the contradictions of permanent urgency, the vicious circles of the games that participants play and the opaqueness of transactions. But precisely because it is presented as a guide to reading, as a collection of models and of reference points for action, it also concerns those who are at the centre of the chessboard, those men and women whose job it is to act, lead, choose and decide. That is to say, those whose first responsibility is to direct, create and transmit the meaning into the actions in their professional lives and relationships, to make daily life and work deeply significant and unique. To this end, two chapters seem especially important for the integrated management that Lenhardt proposes. On one hand, there is the chapter that deals with the different degrees of autonomy. This is because that capacity is essential to anyone who wishes to lead life as a player and an author; and because it is already progress to know at which stage of identity one finds oneself. On the other hand, there is the chapter on team building, this integrated part of general management that enables a number of men and women to become a group, then a team – a united team at the heart of which, the problems of one person are, at the same time, those of everyone in the team, and are treated as such. In this coherent team, changes, growth and results take their true place in what might be described as a culture of both individual and collective meaning.

The reader should not be surprised to find that he may have to make several attempts to comprehend the maps of how to interpret reality that are presented here. The extreme precision of the analysis, often well beyond that which is normally encountered, together with the multiplicity of concepts that are enriching, provided that one takes the time to absorb them, demand an attentive approach – perhaps a threefold approach. A first reading, in order to obtain a complete overview of everything that is offered here to assist in the work of coaching and of team building, coaching's collective extension. Then a second reading to be guided through the progression of chapters, reflecting on their relationships and interfaces, asking ourselves what they question and evoke in us, being urged on by a new way of being fully professional and fully oneself, whether as consultant or manager. It is at this point that one will be able to assimilate fully the different methods and tools, the technical aids, the performance indicators, set out here as signs of experience and sharing, and which can become operational guides for internal or external intervention. Finally, we reach the practice that underlies all of the preceding information and without which nothing is authentic. It will lead in all probability to a third reading: the one which enables, thought models, to become deeply held attitudes, that is, the mental structures that are the basis and the framework for action.

Moreover, if it seems difficult to find a meaning or a coherence in each of our actions, we must remember that the important thing in the journey is not so much seeing the star, but first finding the direction of the star. Because he who creates meaning in the daily round, in the society in which he lives, even if he has the impression that it is only a 'small meaning', experiences and helps others to experience that the meaning of the 'All' is found in the direction of the small. He then knows that he is on his way, even if he does not know where the search will lead him.

PIERRE CASPAR
Professor at CNAM

Ten Years after the First Edition, Evaluation and Perspectives

At the time of the publication of the second edition of this book, ten years after its first appearance in 1992, I believe it is useful to place this stage of proceedings both retrospectively over the last ten years and in the perspective of my sense of the future.

Coaching: a Catalyst in the Development of Collective Intelligence?

Coaching is increasingly present in the media and in the world of business. At the same time, there is still much to be done for this profession to achieve its reference points and a clearly identified image.

Let us try to sharpen its contours. The expression covers both 'a field' and 'an approach'.[1]

- It is a field in as much as it addresses in particular the human side of the enterprise as individuals or teams, or even at a more global level, all those who play a part in the organisation.

- It is equally an approach, in the sense that it represents a philosophy and an anthropology of specific attitudes, particular behaviours and finally the procedures in a firm. I have developed this second aspect at length in this book.

Apart from that, coaching is a generic approach capable of reaching and creating an impact at all levels of the organisation and of modifying its genetic code. Thus does coaching become one of the major factors (though certainly not the only one), if not the actual motor for the development of collective intelligence in the organisation.

I asserted in several recent articles, and somewhat provocatively, that given the number of needs to be taken into account, there would ideally be

a ratio of 'one coach for every fifty inhabitants'.[2] In fact, coaching stems
from a process of education that touches every living being in society;
this process aims at instigating in each individual an intuitive and relational
aptitude leading to the development of:

- Self-esteem;

- Ontological and relational security;

- The capacity to listen to and hear one's real needs and to deal with them;

- The capacity to take charge of oneself, to move into a dynamic of
  co-responsibility and to be in a position to generate the same in others.

On this point let me remind you of the phrase that Victor Frankl used,
when addressing a group of Americans: 'You have constructed in the East,
the statue of Liberty. There remains a continent to be crossed and a statue
to be constructed in the West, the statue of Responsibility.'

In our society, which is from now on necessarily global, each one of us
owes it to himself to construct in heart and head an authority assuring control of his own freedom and to join in coherence with the development of
the common good.

The events of 11 September 2001 in their inescapable drama do not allow
us to forget this.

In fact, coaching and the method of intervention linked to it create a 'posture', which each participant owes it to himself to adopt as an individual and
as a member of the collective. Its function is to integrate the different vehi-
cles for development and to contribute to the creation of coherence and
meaning both within each individual and in relational interfaces. In this
way, coaching can play a major integrative role in the recursive logic underlying organisations and society itself: the part generates the whole and the
whole generates the part. In the same way, the human being is in society
and society is in the human being. Looking forward, we have a 'holomorphic'[3] vision of the identity of the players: each has the shape of all and is
responsible for both the global and the local.

What is New since 1992 (10 Years after the First Edition)

First the Environment

- A big question that has been raised in recent times is to say whether
  coaching is a fashion or a serious trend. I have had occasion to write on

this subject elsewhere. For me, the needs of the individual and/or the collective, which have been latent until now, are becoming increasingly explicit; in the cracks, fractures, the chaos experienced in society and in companies, these needs are shifting into explicit demands.

▪ In face of this still fairly confused evolution, the response on the contrary has been quite explicit. All kinds of consultancy firms (specialising in human resources, recruitment, outplacement, change, etc.) have very recently come to understand that coaching is a response that is both useful and satisfactory for the personal dimension of these requests, even when it is sometimes only a dressed-up or made-up version of an already existing practice that does not directly arise from coaching. Apart from its fashionable and ephemeral elements, it seems to me that in each case we are in the presence of a serious trend, a very significant one in fact, that sees the emergence of a 'meta profession' at the heart of all the help-related professions and which therefore represents a profound and unstoppable trend which can contribute to the lasting development of people and of institutions.

▪ This need concerns all the players in a company, even if it is senior management that has been able to benefit from it up to now. From now on, we see middle management having access to this offer and formulating explicit requests. In addition, the development of executives cannot be satisfied by merely setting up training (being often ill-suited to the pace of operational life), through seeking solutions from consultants (off-the-shelf solutions are not the answer because the solution must be of co-elaborated with the person) or through the support that senior management may offer. The extrinsic solutions brought to the director must be connected with an intrinsic elaboration experienced by the manager himself.

The foregoing illustrates well the difficulties faced by those in charge, as a sports coach[4] close to me said: 'Sportsmen at least have time for preparation before the match and recuperation after it. Managers function in real time and under permanent stress.'

Coaching correctly permits a customised support, matching the constraints and the rhythm of the manager. It invites him to find his own solutions by providing him with the room, support and breathing space necessary to achieve it. Finally and above all, it allows him to emerge from his solitude.

The figures are there to prove it. The figures for the increase in the number of coaches in the United States, doubtless many more than there are in Europe in this area, show us that the number of coaches and the turnover realised by this profession are far from having reached their peak.

What Concerns me Now

Since the first articles in 1988, at a time when no one spoke of coaching in France, we have covered considerable ground.

In 1989, following a conference attended by 50 people in my own small professional premises in the twelfth arrondissement in Paris, 22 people immediately signed up for the training I was proposing (coaching and team building), organised over 20 days. Since then, that training has taken place very regularly almost without publicity, apart from word of mouth and some presentations at conferences. The package that I created in 1992 and published through Sonothèque Média (four 90-minute cassettes and a 100-page booklet to accompany them) became the first edition of this book. It appeared in the small world of consulting as an atypical and even bizarre publication.

By 2002, I had trained more than 500 coaches through these 20-day periods spread over a year (in seven sessions) and 20 classes have undergone certification.

In addition, I have led important missions to small businesses and small industrial companies, to the divisions of large companies, and sometimes even for the headquarters of multinationals. 'Commando' operations in decision-making situations, at the heart of international groups, the setting up of several management charters, developing and deploying visions, and the process of alignment (creating coherence), management actions with these visions such as recruitment, annual appraisal, and so on, the elaboration of the coaching chart, the supervision and support of numerous team-building operations, all this has given my Transformance practice intense life and activity. It has been rather like the life of an aircraft carrier, where consultants ceaselessly land and take off, some just passing through, others creating their own work space and structure.

I have also had the opportunity to participate in different professional bodies such as the APM (Association for Progress in Management of the MEDEF), the Baltimore Club run by the talented Philippe Le Roux, director of the organisation 'Key People'.[5] Especially since 1993, I have been privileged to participate in the birth and development of the Club EVH 'Entreprise Vivante par et pour des Hommes Vivants' (Living Enterprise of and for the living) presided over and led by Bertrand Martin. Today this club involves about 50 senior managers who come together for two days every three months to undertake a fundamental reflection together.

I have held numerous individual support sessions in the form of coaching combined most often with team building, or again sessions for consultants asking for personal coaching through supervisory sessions.

I must also mention my part in co-leading several seminars a year with Father Minguet of the team from the 'Business Centre' of Ganagobie Monastery ever since its creation in 1992. It was there in fact that I took part in the quarterly reunions with a team of senior leaders deeply involved in this research, both existentially and spiritually.

Furthermore two books have been published, one with Bertrand Martin[6] in 1996 and one with Alain Godard[7] in 1998. Writing these two books and working with the testimonies of these two leaders represented for me a very stimulating partnership, and one that most definitely contributed to giving credibility to this still ill-defined profession that had not at that point found its clear reference points in companies or in the eyes of the public.

Moreover, the many conferences, interventions in colleges or companies, the training of consultants, the supervision of numerous situations, the meeting with authors whom I consider to be leaders in their field,[8] all of these have contributed to enriching my thought process and my practice.

Finally, the launch in 2000 of an educational group of coaching teachers, (the 'EEF', in French 'Enseignants En Formation') and the second level 'Master CT IC' (Coaching and Team building within Collective Intelligence), have given these activities of Transformance, a dimension worthy of the label, 'The School of Coaching'.

This pioneering work and crossing of deserts has curiously and quite unexpectedly led to a positioning at the very heart of the company's nervous system and genetic code. It is at the centre of the internal and relational dynamic, not only of the principal players in the company but in reality potentially everyone. In fact, I believe that coaching is going to become accessible to all in the business world.

When I look back at those 10 years, so full of events, meetings, actions, developments, as I have sketched out, it seems to me that the essential is to be found in the following:

■ The conviction that out of all the above what is at stake is 'transformation'. Much more than putting in place actions for change, techniques and training, and so on, it is a question of creating conditions in which the questioners are aware that the changes they wish to bring about around them pass through a transmutation of their own identity, their role, their position, through the change in their representation, through cultural change and permanent self-questioning. 'The caterpillar becomes a butterfly' unceasingly, and each decision involves a personal interrogation.

- What appears to be necessary is that the coach must create conditions for growth in the form of a development of autonomy and of responsibility through self-organised behaviour in those who are being trained for this profession. I have tried to mobilise within the people I have supported this dual attention that Collins and Porras[9] discuss, namely 'preserving the essential while stimulating progress'. While being well aware of my human frailty, I do believe that I have tried to meet this challenge in my own life and for the coaches whom I train.

Coaching, Team Building, Organisation Development[10] and Work on Shared Visions

Collective Intelligence represents an essential concept that must bring into synergy its constituent elements (see Figure 1). These are coaching, its combinations with team building, with Organisation Development and what we can call 'work on the vision'. Further, Collective Intelligence now seems to be an approach to be seen as upstream and to be permanently activated, in comparison with the different actions offered by firms that focus on management and organisational consulting (see Figure 2).

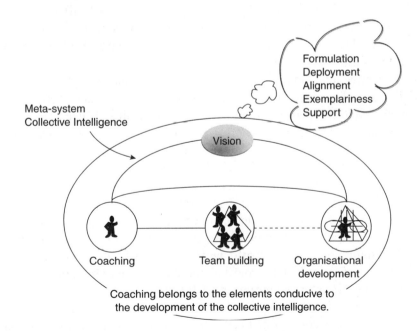

Figure I   How the constituent parts of Collective Intelligence are linked

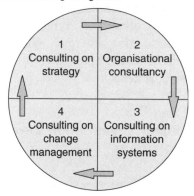

Collective intelligence must:
• be upstream of strategy;
• traverse the four levels and transform the other consulting categories.

Figure 2   Positioning the Collective Intelligence

Up until now, we have seen consulting firms deal, more or less in this order, with first the strategy, then the organisation, the information systems and finally, change management. It seems to me that now, Collective Intelligence operates as both a preliminary and a parallel influence at the heart of these dynamics. Without this, the company is unable to root itself in the deep layers of its life. **Our work often begins just where the procedures and organisational systems cannot reach**.

In this now unavoidable complexity management cannot continue to function in today's conditions with yesterday's tools which were chiefly mechanical and trapped in the logic of linear causality. It becomes necessary therefore for the players to bring to completion their previous models of representation and behaviour, without destroying them, and switch to the new models based on complexity, on the circular and recursive causality in which each player is simultaneously cause and effect: 'the whole is indeed in each player' even if 'each player is in the whole'.

Organisations, both network and matrix based, combined with hierarchical management, represent a complexity such that **a control-based and hierarchical management proves insufficient**. The linear logic is in contradiction with the relational needs in the midst of complexity: **meaning and processes are of prime importance compared with the contents**.

The need for a management in which meaning is shared, obliges the players to rethink their concept of Leadership. The boss must learn to become again a participant in the group and the only true leader, as Warren Bennis says, must learn to become a 'leader of leaders'. In the era of knowledge, the boss is the one who must always show that he has listened before making a judgement. Remember Peter Drucker's phrase: 'You cannot manage knowledge workers.' Globalisation, new technologies, the permanent cross-cultural mix in business and in society, all this compels management to become the managers of 'interfaces'. They no longer only play the role of mediator. **Their own personality is constantly brought into question and tested in their capacity to share in the meaning, to change anguish into confidence and the complexities and contradictions into coherent positions and actions**.

The organisation can no longer be satisfied with the logic of objectives and planning. It must live, at the same time, an approach that focuses on a permanent state of construction and of co-development with (and between) players. In this way, the much talked about vision and strategy now become the subject of permanent reconfiguration operated by the players, with the concern for each player to integrate into it both 'the global' and 'the local'.

At the heart of this complexity lies coaching. Coaching encompasses or represents the vital thread of teamwork, of Organisation Development and of the constant reconfiguration of visions. Thus coaching becomes a major ingredient of Collective Intelligence.

The Present and the Future

Three simple ideas: the need for teamwork, the integration of new technologies and the holomorphic dimension of management.

First, the Need for Teamwork

The leader is no longer the one who works on his own, comes up with ideas and then communicates them to others. He is at all times obliged to co-construct solutions with others. Thus, he has imposed upon him a new relationship with himself, and others, and a new way of collective production. The determining factor is his capacity to generate teamwork, in which each member feels included, listened to, accountable as a unique and interdependent 'contributor' at the same time unique and interdependent. This is much more than 'teamwork' and the mastering of new techniques. It is a question of **identity transformation**, a new way of **representing roles and status**, and **a new positioning**.

Project management is an example of this transformation since it assumes an endlessly renewable capacity to construct and deconstruct, to learn and to know how to unlearn, to know how to build strong relationships that are condemned to end once a project is completed. **The player in a state of permanent movement is forced to find within himself elements of stability and references, as sole guarantees of coherence**.

The New Technologies

New technologies force us to find the right place for the virtual compared with the present and vice versa. Management at a distance now operates as much in the dimension of globalisation as from shared time and spread out companies. How is it possible to conduct this management at a distance within structures that are paradoxically 'local'? Telephone conferencing can increasingly replace face-to-face meetings, video conferencing replaces the intercontinental trip and communication between members of a team becomes asynchronous thanks to e-mails and answering machines. The new technologies create the paradoxical conditions for continuous work.

The Holomorphic[11] Dimension and Management

Managing a small team often includes dimensions of complexity sometimes as great as those of a large organisation and the mastering of relationships by the players becomes of prime importance. Until now, competence in this area was the fruit of experience and talent. Henceforth, it proves to be a competence that is basically of the same order as, for example, the traditional professions of finance or engineering. The capacity of the person in charge to position himself, to manage his identity and stress, to optimise his interfaces with the teams around him, becomes a central competence in his management. This is the capacity modelled by coaching (coaching of which he is both a beneficiary and the provider).

So, managerial development and its individual and collective dimension, forces the manager, whatever his level in the hierarchy, to **think through and constantly review his identity**. The manager owes it to himself to stay in development if he wants to be a 'developer of talents' in others. His leadership obliges him not only to manage relationships, both individual and collective, but also to manage the paradox of education: 'how to help others to sort matters out by themselves', and what is more, to work interdependently. As of now, the manager's identity and his own personal potential and his limitations show the measure of the potential and limitations of the organisation in his charge.[12] Mastering technical skills and managing complex processes can only be done if he is capable of co-constructing with others a collective meaning. This implies a permanent ability to see things and 'clean one's spectacles', to be simultaneously focused on himself and open to his environment, and to build meaning.

Thereby, the organisation and its managerial space can also become the place where managerial identity is built and, through it, the place for the development of persons.

Half humorously, I invite players who feel concerned to enter this paradoxical movement of commitment and non-commitment: to mobilise themselves for action, knowing that they must permanently remain in a withdrawn 'meta' position and thus become reflective players, and, why not, tongue in cheek, embark on transformance.

The essential at the heart of the important

The Viewpoint of This Book

In 1989, I published a package[1] called *Managers as Carriers of Meaning*. It consists of four 90-minute cassettes and a 100-page booklet that summarises a course of some 20 days spread over a year, given by consultants. Subsequently, this book was prepared on and off over a period of a little more than a year as a means of formalising my approach and my thoughts on my profession of consultant and trainer of consultants.

It is perhaps useful at the beginning to indicate my point of view for the reader's benefit.

For some 20 years I have found myself at a convergence: my profession as a company consultant (and trainer of consultants), therapist (and instructor) and a third pathway, that of seeker of 'meaning', having always known that what lies at the heart of the real is one's spiritual life.

The problem has been how to reconcile these worlds and discuss them without appearing incongruous in a book that focuses on business practices.

Olivier Lecerf, former chairman of the Lafarge-Coppée group, recalls in his remarkable book[2] on the profession of director, his actions when heading his group and the importance he attached to defining the general directions and the standards of conduct within the group, known at Lafarge as 'Action principles'. He reminds us that these principles of action only deal with the collective behaviour of individuals as members of an organisation. They do not interfere with matters of individual conscience. He also says: 'people's activities operate at three levels, the "game", the "important" and the "essential". The realm of the game, in my case sport and horse-racing ... the important domain (politics, economy and business) and the essential domain, the person, his destiny, his life and death. The latter is the domain of

God for those who are believers. Of course, the domains of the game, the important and the essential do not have closed borders and may overlap, but for me there is a crucial distinction ... I have become convinced that successful managers are those who are known or perceived to be relating in their actions to a system of values, even though the latter is not declared. ...'

It seems necessary to recall at what point the essential (in the sense of a person's growth and spirituality) conditions the important (the added value that business must generate). If we speak of the economy and the organisation, how can we not concern ourselves with a minimum of trust and hope necessary for the survival and growth of organisations? Bertrand Martin, a company director I met recently, reported a conversation with Olivier Lecerf: 'What counts is not creating barriers between the important and the essential. It is important now to experience the essential at the very heart of the important.'

I support this view. Like Olivier Lecerf, I take care not to mix the realms, and am anxious that the business does not burden individual consciences so far as the essential is concerned. At the same time, I believe that is primordial for organisations and managers to be receptive to, and allow the growth of, values and meaning.

Therefore, I take the risk of setting the operational approaches presented in this book in this perspective and consider them inoperative if they are not rooted in meaning.

After finishing my studies in 1965, followed by an MBA course at the University of Chicago Graduate Business School, I spent some six to eight years gaining personal and professional experience in different fields. I produced advertising and industrial films, studied acting, managed a financial product sales team, discovered and became a keen practitioner of yoga, which put me in contact with Indian mystics and Benedictine monks. I reached the point of spending about two years at the Abbaye de Fleury at Saint-Benoît-sur-Loire (near Orléans, France). It was not until 1973 that I discovered the writings of Carl Rogers, Transactional Analysis and the humanist psychology movement. I began to earn my living as a teacher and consultant in practices specialising in training and Organisation Development (OD). This resulted in my occasional involvement in managing important sites for national or multinational firms with employees sometimes numbering several hundreds.

In parallel, I underwent the experience of therapy and training in Transactional Analysis (TA). I became co-founder of the French Institute of Transactional Analysis (IFAT) in 1975, then its president. I was subsequently elected (from 1982–84) president of the European Association of Transactional Analysis (EATA), which at the time already consisted of more than 1000 practitioners from 11 different countries, and member of the American board of trustees of the International Transactional Analysis Association (ITAA). I completed my training in TA, became an instructor; I also took a Ph.D in psychology in the United Kingdom. In addition, I trained in the different techniques of humanist psychology (bioenergy, Gestalt, warm pool work) and played an active part in promoting in France and the business world the approaches to personal and professional development brought through TA.

The implementation of training or OD that I carried out in firms (such as Moulinex, Esso, Kodak, Rank Xerox and Thomson – now Thales, to mention a few) led me to help individuals and teams in situations where the problem encountered was well beyond the technical content of training, or the processes of change that they needed. It was always a problem of participation in the institutional process and of change that these firms experienced. Behind this, I always found an insatiable thirst for finding and instilling meaning to their professional life. In more recent years, I have also had occasion to support directors and their teams and internal consultant teams, and have thus developed with them both a synthesis and my own models. In new areas, I have had to produce my own maps.

During these years I have very often felt myself to be divided and torn between these three polarities of the world of business, the world of personal development and therapy and the world of spiritual development. My experience in these three worlds has often led me to keep them very compartmentalised. The meaning of my own life, both for me and for those I support, has up until now been to contribute to the resolution of contradictions, to turn dead ends into bridges, and enable each of these three worlds find its meaning in partnership with the other two. I have therefore sought to unify the human being who is in the organisation and the organisation that is in the human being. I now know that one can have a place in a company, or in the world of work in the broad sense, and contribute to the human and spiritual development of those advancing with us. I believe that this approach is always difficult, ambiguous and fragile. It is not original and is in line with the great spiritual traditions that I have encountered: that of Karma Yoga (or 'service' yoga) in India, or more specifically for me, the great Benedictine tradition which, for 15 centuries, has been able to integrate institutionally prayer with work (*ora et labora* is their motto) and thus show the way to man's unification, something that is especially necessary in the Western world. It is the monk's vocation (monk derives from the Greek *monos*, alone) to help man find his identity in the image and resemblance to the One God (the Hebrew Adonai Echad). Any attempt to live this ideal through what might be called a kind of 'interiorised monasticism' implies removing many contradictions, managing intense complexity and clarifying the specificity and complementarity of each of these approaches.

This book aims at sharing a few maps of these territories and thus at bridging them together. I believe that each individual in his work can be 'responsible', that is, capable of answering why (am I doing this)? Even if we are only carrying out the humble task of breaking stones or digging holes, we are able to distinguish the cathedral that is mysteriously growing with us, thanks also to our contribution.

I currently spend more than a half of my time in support of managers and management teams. With associates and the team of Transformance, we develop the consulting firm I founded. I also organise long-term training (covering one or two years) of consultants in coaching and team building. I have discontinued my therapist activities and courses since 1996 and now operate quite selectively as a therapist and generally only the view to orienting or introducing people to therapy. Since 1986 I have remained in close contact with the Benedictine abbey that is established at Ganagobie to the north of Manosque, where I contributed to the establishment of the research unit of the Business Centre of the Ganagobie monastery. I have since conducted every year several sessions with the reverend Dom Hugues Minguet; these involve people who come to further their personal or professional development through a spiritual approach, or sessions for the clergy or managers of congregations.

This book focuses more on the world of labour, business or institutions. I had not written since the beginning of the 1980s (when I produced three books on Transactional Analysis), and for a long time I had wanted to share the models that I have developed in my teaching. I published them first in audiocassette form; it was now time to confirm this in writing.

I have come to discover in myself an identity as a guide who helps the business people open up to themselves, to change, and to the radical cultural transformations that have become absolutely necessary in current management. I contribute to making them see to what extent the transformation required by these necessary cultural changes implies both an opening up of one's own frame of reference and answers to unavoidable questions, such as meaning, development of autonomy, access to meta-communication, growth, management of change, conflict resolution and so on. In fact, when one wants to manage change, carry out training or introduce new management tools, one is always forced to follow processes that allow individuals, teams and the organisational system to take ownership of these elements and learn how to manage the development of their autonomy. The educational process cannot take place with a minimum of 'support'

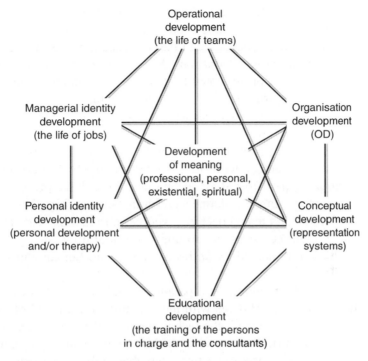

Figure 0.1   Components of integrative management

and intervention, hence my adoption of the terms coaching (support for the individual) and team building (support for teams).

In trying to describe what I do in my profession, the skills that are required, the dynamics, culture and experience that I employ, I can find no better expression than 'integrative management'. As shown Figure 0.1, this book aims to give an account of the different approaches that articulate in the fashion of a cut diamond.

It is necessary for each facet of a diamond to be correctly cut for its true brilliance to appear. The task for 'integrative management' is to recognise and try to master the relevance of each approach, then co-ordinate them and arrange them systematically, all against the shimmering flashes of meaning that spring forth from each facet.

I sometimes act like an obstetrician when I work with a manager and his team. I am not the one producing the baby, but my intervention is sometimes just useful, sometimes crucial. Relating to my profession, I also see the image of the oysterman who has to master the subtle and forceful art of opening oysters. For me, there is the advantage in this marvellous profession that through its wound, each oyster becomes the carrier of a pearl.

As a coach, I am also often the person to witness others scoring the goals, and to experience the joy of seeing champions develop and teams form and grow. For a long time I believed that I had the vocation to be a stage director, then an actor, a master of illusions. But, in my profession as business coach, and therapist or professional trainer (for consultants or therapists), I have the deeply inspiring feeling of doing something more than art, and of contributing in a modest but real way to co-creating human beings. For me there is no finer profession.

This book will cover many elements relating to training, communication and management, together with different techniques for supervision and helping relations. Apart from these techniques, through the presentation of a set of concepts, the aim is to define a preliminary, necessary cultural envelope for individual and team coaching. Another aim is to provide an introduction to a practice. It is an attempt at integrating an operational professionalism, illuminated by an investigation into human and spiritual development.

Part I sets out the requirements, paradoxes and definitions of coaching and team building. Part II deals with the constitutive elements of the cultural envelope, without which the techniques would run the risk of being mere gimmicks. Part III discusses the coach's 'control panel' that represents the common trunk for coaching actions, whether with the individual or the team. Part IV is devoted specifically to individual coaching, with Part V covering the models suitable for team building. A final short sixth Part on 'the fourteen focal points in the coach's work' presents a synthesis of this still emerging profession as I see it.

This book may be read from cover to cover; it may also be read by diving into individual chapters. I would warn readers though that only a systemic understanding of the complete contents will allow the different concepts to be integrated. These concepts are all closely interdependent and, at one extreme, a reader could begin at any chapter and link that chapter to any other. As Edgar Morin has expressed it so well: 'the whole is in the part even if the part is in the whole'. Some of my clients, company directors, often tell me that, while they have immediately understood the techniques and concepts presented, it has sometimes taken them months to assess the implications, and draw the conclusions both for their jobs and for the representation of their identity. I hope that this book will be a companion for you in your process of growth and cultural change, and that it enables you to find more meaning and unity in all aspects of your life. This implies changes and grieving and a constant reconversion of one's identity. François Varillon[3] summarises this in his humorous remark: 'the butterfly is not a fat caterpillar'.

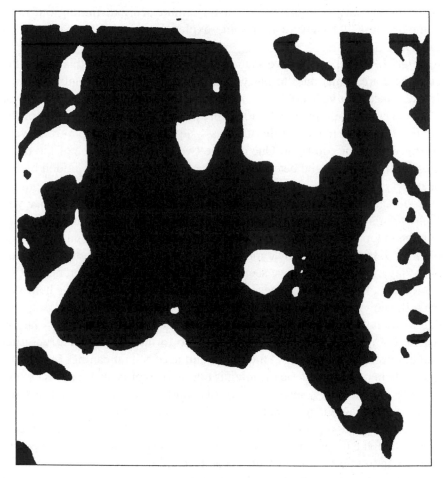

Figure 0.2

Access to Meaning: An Exercise Illustrating the Progression in This Book

Here is an exercise that I often present at the beginning of a seminar on management or on communication, and especially when I am working on the subject of the 'vision' (in particular the vision shared by a management team). It is an aerial photograph taken in the Cordillera Range of the Andes. I shall give the name later.

Stage 1: Look at Figure 0.2 closely, and without turning to the following pages, I invite you to discover its meaning and say what you see.

After looking at the figure for at least a minute without finding out what it means, turn the page to find some explanations. Will you accept this exercise?

Stage 2: Perhaps you have made sense of Figure 0.2. If this is not the case, here are some clues to put you on the right path. The figure shows a bearded face of a very noble and majestic man, which could be the face of Christ. The photographers who took this picture called it the 'Christ of the Andes'. One can make out this face as a highly contrasted photo, lit very strongly from the top right. One can see two eyes, the outline of the nose, the mouth hidden in the beard and the shape of the face also hidden by the beard.

Look again at Figure 0.2, now that you have these indications. Once you see 'Christ's' image, look at Figure 0.3. If you still do not see the image, do not spend too much time poring over it (it is not very important).

Stage 3: Let us assume that you have not yet clearly interpreted the image as at stage 1. Either you have seen it or you have not. Later, you notice that something clicks and this image appears clearly or not at all. To help you we will show you, in Figure 0.3, the image of stage 1 with added graphics that artificially highlight the features of this face. In psychologists' jargon Figure 0.3 represents the Gestalt, that is the form, our mental structuring that allows us to comprehend the image and access its meaning. In fact, we may note in passing that the meaning is not in the words, as Françoise Dolto reminds us, but it lies between the words and beyond the words. The same applies in management. Understanding how a team functions or the strategic vision for a company lies beyond the graphics or the material elements that go to make up organisations; it is found in the mental picture that everyone has individually and in their capacity to achieve a Gestalt, or a communicable and shareable form. Management can do little more than present this Gestalt objectively, but it can also create the conditions for people to develop this Gestalt for themselves, by presenting information and symbolic elements, and generate the relational process that encourages open minds, trust, communication and verbal expression. This causes people to advance beyond the Gestalt by accepting it and thus gain access to the meaning. Thanks to the 'symbolic' (the Gestalt presented), everyone's 'imagination' becomes structured, can access the meaning and therefore 'see the reality'.

At stage 3, when you look at Figure 0.3, you make the definite step towards seeing, in stage 1, the image of Christ; in other words, you access the meaning. Look now at stage 4, and then go back to stage 1.

Stage 4: Have a look at Figure 0.3.

Figure 0.3

Stage 5: If you are at stage 5, there are two possibilities:

■ Either you have not seen Christ's image, which is not a problem; you will be able to look at it again and it will become clear to you. I have often presented the example at seminars and have seen that sometimes people take two or three days before they see it clearly.

■ Or you have seen Christ's image. In this case we can together note several factors:

1. Access to the meaning probably occurs through a sudden click and through using the right hemisphere of the brain, the 'synthetic' side. It occurs as a kind of revelation usually accompanied by an exclamation 'Ah, Ah!', as pronounced by the famous psychotherapist Fritz Perls, or like Archimedes with his 'Eureka'.

2. This access to meaning corresponds to a qualitative leap in perception, which causes a profound moment of pleasure.

3. At that moment, one is aware of two things. Before, one was looking, but not seeing. So, one can look, but not see. Once we have seen, we cannot imagine the image without its meaning. Thus, conversely,

we can no longer look without seeing Christ's image, and it is very difficult to look at the image through the eyes of someone who has not yet seen the image.

This is very similar to the situation within a team, where some members have the strategic vision while others do not yet possess it. The former are literally 'enlivened' and 'inhabited' by the meaning, while the latter feel frustrated and empty and sometimes even guilty or rebellious compared with their colleagues.

This book will be concerned, in almost every concept and part, with a process for which the preceding example acts as a metaphor. Gaining a full understanding of each of the models to be presented implies an intellectual effort identical to what we have just experienced. There will be moments when the map of the territory does not make sense; then, at a given moment, the Gestalt will 'set' (like mayonnaise). For some concepts and processes, this may involve several months of coming and going between theoretical reasoning and practical experience in the field.

My final wish is for readers to obtain satisfaction from the book and to find in their professional lives as much meaning and joy as I have had in writing it.

We are speaking of the joy of a revelation, in contemplating the mystery of man and his development, particularly in the professional world. But, as François Varillon says, a mystery is not something that one does not understand, but something that one understands one will never finish understanding.

PART I

Definitions of Coaching and Team Building

At the heart of the manager, a champion;
At the heart of the champion, a prince;
At the heart of the prince, a 'new man'.
At the heart of the 'new man', the 'Divine Spirit'.

Summary

Coaching can be defined as informed guidance of a manager or of a team in the context of their professional lives.

The key is to have the eye of a trainer for a champion or a winning team.

Team building is the coaching of a team. Implementing team building involves a combination of three ingredients: Daily Operations, a Regulation period and situations of Training (the ORT model, Figure 2.2).

As with a team, the champion manager needs support because he is confronted with the following three paradoxes:

■ When he needs something, he thinks he must sort out the situation by himself.

- Those who want to help him, those closest to him, are too involved to be sufficiently objective.

- The manager (like the team) becomes the least competent with those with whom he has problems.

The champion or team needs someone neutral and competent in order to

- Listen to them;

- Advise them;

- Help them find their own solutions.

Coaching and team building will make it possible to deal with and integrate the different levels:

- Personal Identity Development (PID);

- Managerial Identity Development (MID);

- Relational Identity Development (RID);

- Team Identity Development (TID);

- Cultural Identity Development (CID).

For more effectiveness, the ideal is to combine coaching with team building. This allows integrated development that may, through performance and profit, enable people develop their talents, their personal and spiritual unity and also give greater meaning to their work and their lives. In this way, coaching and team building contribute to making managers 'carriers of meaning'.

CHAPTER I

The Manager's Paradoxes

The person responsible for a business or an institution has undeniable needs. Often at risk of being trapped by paradoxes, he finds it difficult to handle these needs. Let us examine these various paradoxes.

The First Paradox

It is at the moment when the manager has the greatest need for help that he finds himself most alone.

In fact, the more a manager has grown, the more he feels obliged to continue handling matters alone. The fact that he holds the institutional position he does is generally because he possesses one or more distinctive qualities in comparison with others. His will power, talent, effort and fortune (in both senses of the word) are all involved.

But apart from the conditional qualities that this position demands, the manager may assume different functional levels such as a more global function that adds a new managerial dimension. For example, he may also take on the position of 'social representative', or entrepreneur or even that of transferring from director of a subsidiary to a corporate post. In these different examples, this new position represents a quantum leap so far as his identity is concerned. The person who becomes manager has, at a specific given moment, made the decision to adopt this role and assume this identity.

The dynamic underlying this decision represents an act of independence in comparison with other professional relationships and possibly a new intraphysical positioning, especially in comparison with the introjected parental figures. In other words, this decision induces and assumes grieving, in particular because the manager becomes the person 'most responsible' for the function or organisational entity that he is in charge of, whether this be a project for which he becomes the boss, a department for which he is made manager or even a business for which he is appointed social representative. As a result, this act is by definition an action that isolates him.

The manager is therefore often in danger of believing that if he has reached the top, it is because he was alone, and that he has arrived at that point alone. The dynamic of this thinking of assuming this managerial identity therefore contains the danger of believing that solitude is the only route for such achievement.

There are but few who succeed in escaping this paradox of solitude as a constituent for success. This is because reaching the top is only the first stage; the real problem is in staying there! How can one resist succumbing to the 'impostor complex'?[1]

Whereas in the world of sport, it is well known that to remain at the top, an athlete needs support, the same does not yet apply to the world of business even though the 'game' that the manager plays never ends.

Nowadays, no tennis champion or a successful football team can exist without a trainer. The fact that these people need a trainer is regarded as obvious and an indicator of their status. Unfortunately, for a manager the situation is quite different; in calling upon the services of a coach he risks this being interpreted as a sign of professional shortcoming, lack of autonomy, even weakness.

The manager will therefore tend to deny his need at the very moment that it is most urgent. However, such an investment is especially important. There needs to be someone who listens to him, advises him, helps him develop his own solution, clears out the dead wood, gives him his 'permissions' (that is the encouragement to say 'yes' on those occasions when calculated risks must be taken) and who helps him provide himself with 'protections' (warnings and encouragement to say 'no' to behaviour that would be dangerous).

The Second Paradox

The manager fantasises about others as they fantasise about him. There is the danger that he will remain a prisoner of this fantasy world.

The status provided by his new function, which is accompanied by a title and a number of attributes of power, is for him and for others an identity envelope that relates partly to a reality and partly to a dimension of fantasy. The objective reality part that I call the 'me skin' (a term borrowed from Didier Anzieux, cf. the chapter on the 15 parameters, OKness, p. 183) corresponds to his status, his salary level, the budgets for which he is in charge, the number of people he manages, the physical organisation of his office, and so on. The fantastical dimension corresponds to what goes on in his imagination in relation to the representation that he has of his function and identity and in relation to that of his associates, his imagination being more or less strengthened by what might have been said about him in the media and his professional milieu. At a deeper level, his position as manager locates him in his relationship with his ideal of the 'self'. Does he allow himself to remain a human being with limitations, or is he a prisoner of his narcissism or of subconscious demands emanating from his 'superego'? As for his contacts within or outside of the business, they can obviously fantasise about him to the extent that they can project and transfer on to him largely subconscious and unrealistic expectations. Because he is the boss, he is expected to know everything and to have an answer to every problem. This fantasised dimension does however form part of reality; the manager, having developed some ontological security, will no doubt feel able to accept his limitations, even to the point of often saying that 'he does not know' when faced with a situation or fully expressing his doubts. Moreover, he must be very attentive to the fact that his colleagues are not always willing to be witness to his doubts and limitations. He will therefore need, on one hand, to 'get off his high horse' on which he may have placed himself or on which others might have placed him, and on the other hand be careful with regard to the fantasies of others that might risk being destabilised.

The Third Paradox

Those who would most want to assist the manager, those near to him (wife, husband, friends), often do not know enough about the manager's job and environment, or are too influenced by their close ties to be sufficiently objective.

This is why a surgeon does not operate on a member of his family or barrister does not defend his brother before a tribunal, because he risks using impaired judgement. Similarly, the spouse of a manager is often frustrated and in rivalry with the workload of the other. The result will be a lack of necessary objectivity. Sometimes the level of frustration and suffering concerning the manager's job may be such that, although concerned, the partner is too judgmental and biased to be a useful adviser.

The Fourth Paradox

The manager and those who are most concerned by the problem become the people least able to resolve the relational problems for which they are responsible.

Somewhat like the father who has a crisis relationship with his adolescent son, the manager is the person least competent to handle the problem, his colleagues not wanting to hear any more about it, and he himself being stuck in his relationship with them. The manager and his colleagues are therefore sometimes trapped in 'closed loops' or 'vicious circles' where everyone feels paralysed by the other's behaviour. He justifies his own blocking behaviour by the blocking he identifies in the other person. By isolating themselves and no longer being able to communicate, the two parties cannot 'comprehend' one another. It is therefore necessary to call upon a third party, a neutral mediator, who can re-establish communication.

The developmental needs of a manager are, by nature, virtually unlimited. It is however important for the manager to recognise at least some of his needs, experiment and take the calculated risk of an initiative of coaching and team building, and measure the 'return' on his investment.

He also needs to know that coaching and team building exists, that he wants it and gives himself 'permission' to participate in it. Experience has often shown that it is a long way from recognition of a need to asking for it. We can however give some instances where this need is particularly apparent.

First in coaching; taking a new position, negotiating with a company or a new owner, outplacement situations, a public presentation, consideration of one's objectives, preparation for a complex and difficult decision, managing stress, one's time, one's motivations and so on.

In team building: clarifying a team's mission, its interface with clients, launching new products, a reorganisation, integrating new arrivals into the team, managing conflict, the cultural change required through a reorganisation, mobilisation of teams in order to carry out a business project, management of relationships between teams, preparing for a merger and so on.

Let us now examine a few definitions.

CHAPTER 2

Definitions

What is Coaching?

Coaching is 'help, guidance and a co-construction' that is offered to a person (or a team) through timely intervention, or more often long-term support.

This assistance and co-construction are part and parcel of a situation that is professional, and/or managerial and/or organisational.

Their aim is to create conditions for the person (or the team) allowing him to find and build his own solutions.

They establish prompt or, in the short term, sought-after resolution, with a view to a development that is both lasting and global.

Assistance and Co-construction

Coaching is part of the paradoxical process of assistance and co-construction, close to the basic educational process: 'helping a person to manage by himself'.

It is help to the extent that, without the support offered by coaching, the person would have difficulty in finding his own solution. This process is complex in that the solution emerges through the intersubjective relationship that exists between the person and his coach. The coach believes that in the end the solution must be the one in which his client takes full possession. Therefore, the more the development is borne by the client, the more likely he is to take possession of the solution. Consequently, the coach must give preference to the reference framework of the person coached (by adopting the formula: 'the power is in the client'). Nonetheless, the solution will still be developed through the mystery, subtlety and intersubjective skill of the coach.

Situation That is Professional and/or Managerial and/or Organisational

Coaching, as compared with other approaches relating to assistance (such as therapy, counselling, advice, training, etc.) is situated on these three levels (the level of importance) while taking into account the other personal levels (psychic, existential, etc.) that also make up the entirety and mystery of the person (the essential level) without intervening directly.

Finding One's Own Solutions

It is from this intersubjective alchemy between the coached person (or team) and his coach that his (or the team's) solutions emerge. This does not imply that the coach is not interventionist in both the process and the content. Depending on the degree of development and the set of parameters that allow him to optimise his position (see chapter on the 15 parameters), he must maximise the energetic and relational system that makes up the relationship in which he takes the leading role. His stakes are the development of the autonomy and freedom of his client, together with the capacity to take on responsibility. Coaching therefore contributes to an education of freedom, in order to facilitate beyond that access to responsibility.

From the Point of View of Lasting and Global Development

While the aim of coaching is to find concrete solutions in time and space, such solutions that may often be symptomatic and ascribed to the short term must not be damaging in the long term. Therefore, making the professional choice of using negotiation with the help of a third party about positioning within the organisation may resolve the situation in the short term. It is for the coach to ensure that solutions found today do not represent problems for tomorrow (which we refer to as lasting development), and that solutions for the individual or the team do not create difficulties in the environment that might cause damage to the general well-being and to the system to which the coached individual or team belong, since this might cause an upset in the long run.

This support resembles that of a 'trainer' working with a champion or highly skilled team.

When applied to an individual or to a team, coaching is often referred to as team building in the case of a group within a company. The approach adopted in coaching is that shared by the manager or consultant who considers the person, or the accompanying team, from the viewpoint of his current performance but even more so from that of his unrealised potential.

This approach embraces a philosophy, an attitude, behaviours, skills and procedures.

The Philosophy

The philosophy takes the view that managerial development lies more in liberating a person's potential energy than in motivating him externally. It holds the belief that people are 'OK' at the core of their ambiguity, that is, they are capable of participating in their own development and managing their change, and that it is possible to share with them knowledge that will help them develop.

It aims to build the development by planning it in advance, rather than responding promptly to moments of crisis.

It is a philosophy that resembles oriental or alternative medicine that aims to strengthen health and help a person get better rather than simply treating an illness or symptom.

To use a sports analogy, it aims to help people in good health become athletes rather than endure physical re-education after body trauma.

From this viewpoint, everyone has something to gain from having a coach and considering his professional development as an investment and not as a cost.

Attitude

For the consultant/coach or the director of a company, attitude consists in seeing the manager, or his supporting team, as subject of growth rather than as objects of production (see Figure 2.1).

The manager is locked in a relentless ambiguity. While he holds a position that must be relatively interchangeable and therefore neutral, he nevertheless remains a potentially evolving human being. In this framework, with his motivation being strongly conditioned by the respect shown to him, he also needs:

▪ To be understood and respected;

▪ To be supported and provided with the means that he requires;

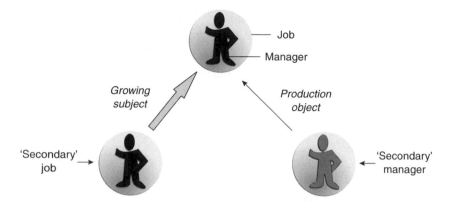

Figure 2.1   Managerial ambiguity

- To see himself as the object of the trust to which he aspires;
- To be in a position to give of his best;
- To have access to the meaning of his action;
- To feel that he belongs to a group and to be able to be fulfilled...

These are all determining elements for the champion and his team.

Behaviours and Skills

Working as a coach, whether as consultant or manager, is something that can be done without any specific training. Everyone does it without realising it. But, professionalism in this field can make all the difference between a blocked situation and one of true development. A manager who often spends 10 to 15 years becoming a specialist in a technique at best receives only a few weeks of management training, and even less training in communication and human relations.

How can the conditions for maximum motivation be created, how can one learn to attract the best managers, how can they be retained, how can one reach the point of offering career paths that allow them to develop and therefore remain within the company's management?

The necessary behaviours and skills are those of the world of 'human resources', that is, according to the Taylorian and human relations schools, behaviours and skills that regard the human factor and the management of human resources, as strategic factors in the business.

The managers and directors of a company will only implement the firm's strategy constructively if they have the feeling that they have contributed to the development and establishment of this strategy.

For the firm, it is also a matter of creating, through real attentiveness and mastery of communication, conditions in which the peoples' skills will truly be taken into account and welcomed. This presumes that the mangers possess specific skills such that only those who have professionally worked on their perceptiveness can really undertake the task. These will often be sales force co-ordinators, managers who really worked on communication, people with a gift for handling relationships and/or those individuals who have brought themselves into question in the face of principles or questions such as those studied by humanist psychology:

- Serious attention to motivation;

- Validation of others and of oneself;

- Skill in resolving conflicts;

- Taking emotions into account;

- Subtlety and complexity in managing human parameters and change.

It is also a matter of applying the philosophy, attitude and skills of what is referred to as the organisational development (OD) approach. The aim of OD is that, after a process of education, the firm becomes autonomous in the resolution of its problems and all its members, at all levels, and at all interfaces, tend towards becoming catalysts for change.

Procedures

There are four different ways of coaching a person or a team.

1. Using an external consultant
   Disadvantage: cost.
   Advantages: Competency, which often at the beginning the firm lacks, but especially neutrality, in regard to the institutional, hierarchical and systemic stakes.

2. Using an internal consultant
   The disadvantage lies in his relative non-neutrality, because he belongs to the institution. The advantages are a lower cost and experience within the firm.

3. The boss takes on the role of a coach
    The disadvantages result from the limitations of the ambiguity that his
    hierarchical role includes with the stakes it involves. The advantage is
    that he is very close to the situation and can implement concrete action.

4. Other managers in the firm can play the role of the coach, working
    with colleagues from other divisions or departments, or with their own
    colleagues or even with the chief executive.

From all of these possibilities, we need to remember two things:

■ Every director of a firm gains from establishing a coaching procedure
  with his colleagues that is not restricted to an annual appraisal interview,
  but which provides for at least four interviews per year (over and above
  the relations necessary for operational life and his routines and style
  of management and delegation); one for appraisal, one for setting
  objectives, and at least two, spaced at three monthly intervals, to re-
  examine during the year the objectives and the requirements of the
  individual;

■ Every managerial team gains from having, among its options for managing change, development and crises of interpersonal relationships,
  coaching procedures that can be provided by an external consultant. It is
  an option that, having once been tried, it is difficult to imagine being
  without.

What is Team Building?

We refer to 'team building' as the work done by a coach with a team. In the
American sense, it refers more particularly to a localised event where
co-workers spend two or three days at a location outside the firm engaged
in a bonding activity designed to make the team think about itself and how
it operates.

The fashion has also emerged for outdoor courses that are sometimes spectacular, involving activities such as bungee jumping or white water rafting.

Such changes of location may be very beneficial, provided that, aside
from the stimulation of the event, conditions are created for true communication between the members of the group, and care is taken to ensure that
the link is maintained between the experience of the event and real life back
in the firm.

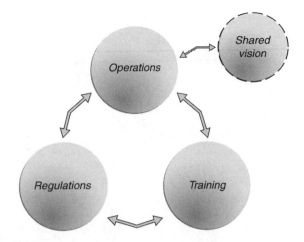

Figure 2.2 The ORT model (Operations, Regulations, Training)

Our interpretation of team building aims to encompass the different approaches but focuses more on the support of the team:

- In its daily operational life;

- At those times of adjustment that it needs;

- The educational process necessary for its increase in competence, in the knowledge that, as we shall show later, profitable cohesion (Figure 2.2) will only be achieved through a process that integrates these three aspects.

This approach to team building includes all the aspects of coaching that we have already discussed, and at the same time proves, of course, to be more complex (see Chapters 23 and 24 of Part V).

Coaching and Team Building Combined

Figure 2.3 shows that the manager who finds himself at the centre of all his varied identity envelopes must be able in order to develop, to benefit from the integrated development of each of its specific layers.

Note: by Personal Identity Development (PID) we mean on the one hand therapeutic work, and on the other personal development work.

It is not possible to tackle therapeutic work in the firm. By its very nature, it is considered by many to be the domain of the unconscious, the emotions, the body and parental figures. Such work often assumes a regression and a preliminary analysis of the scenario.

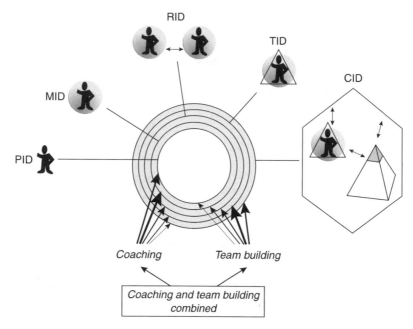

Figure 2.3 Combined coaching and team building

Furthermore, most of the time it is not the province of the manager or the firm to broach this subject. Moreover, they generally do not have the required means or protection. If the manager does not himself pay for this type of service, his view of it risks misinterpretation through a connection distorted by money. As we shall see later, it is often at this level that the major blocks occur. Although it involves an area that is too sensitive to be tackled by the managers of a firm, it will be convenient to invite them to acquire a minimum of knowledge on this subject, in order to be able to recognise the stakes and unknown difficulties that underlie personal and professional motivations (see Figure 2.4).

By personal development we are alluding to the taking into account of attitudes and behaviour, that is, the beliefs or the view that person has in regard to himself or to others (life positions) on one hand, and on the other hand the way in which he manages his relations with others, through his behaviour. These competencies will include:

- His capacity to listen (this cannot be overemphasised);

- His way of conducting an interview;

- His capacity for managing his emotions and his change.

Therapy	Personal development
• Regression	• Here and now
• Past	• Attitudes and beliefs
• Infancy	• Behaviour
• Father, mother	• Competencies:
• Work on the emotions	– listening;
• Scenarios	– communication;
• The unconscious	– change.
May not be tackled in the company	May be tackled in the company
But the manager gains from having a minimum of education in this field.	The place for awareness and indispensable intensive training.

Figure 2.4 Personal Identity Development (PID)

Identity envelopes   Stress management

Stages of development   Motivation

Time management   Decision-making

Figure 2.5 Managerial Identity Development (MID)

By Managerial Identity Development (MID), we mean a certain number of constituent elements for the identity of the manager (see Figure 2.5). This open-ended list includes:

- *Management of his own stress and change.* This domain is becoming better known, but it is decisive for the manager required to take on important responsibilities. These elements are indispensable if he wants to master his workload, his trips and visits, the constant adjustments caused by the changes that he must bear and constantly master, the multiple, double constraints that constitute his life. We develop this topic in the management of chaos (Part II, Chapter 7).

■ *His motivation.* Here we place all the aspects and contradictions that he must accept, including his personal aspirations, his managerial ambition, his role as leader and his most profound aspirations.

■ *Decision-making.* A manager is someone who must make decisions, in the absence of an abundance of time, the competencies and information that he would like to have. But he has to decide and continually take action. How can he develop his decision-making?

■ *Time management.* The manager must constantly re-evaluate his managerial objectives to stay in line with the firm's and his own personal objectives, adjusting the different rhythms that affect him. The assumption is that he has the very specific skill to integrate thoughts and concrete tools to manage his most valuable possession, his time.

■ *Stages of development.* Here we are referring to the aspects of his career plan that include the stages and training resources. We shall examine more specifically in other chapters the three stages of the professional manager and possessor of a trade, 'the manager' and 'the leader'.

■ *Last, the identity envelopes.* These can be likened to a set of Russian dolls (Part IV, Chapter 19). It is necessary to verify the coherence between the energies at their different levels.

The foremost aim of coaching is to specifically support the manager as he relates to his managerial identity.

By Relational Identity Development (RID) we mean the manager's capacity for communication and meta-communication, to be discussed later; this is his ability for adapting to different personalities and leading a team.

Given that the director of a firm spends at least 70 per cent of his time in human contact (on the telephone, in interviews or at meetings), his relational identity is a major factor in his development and that of the team for which he is responsible (Figure 2.6).

Many people operate at an overly emotional level, surrounding themselves with colleagues who reassure and validate them. Others, for narcissistic

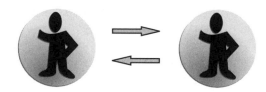

Figure 2.6 Relational Identity Development (RID)

reasons, choose colleagues similar to themselves, thus considerably restricting the richness of their team. Still others are simply unable to operate with certain personality types.

The more a manager is able to understand different personalities, identify their specific needs and operate with a team of complementary people whose differences he appreciates, the more he is in a position to accumulate the various skills that he needs.

Team Identity Development (TID) is a specific application area of team building that sets out to pinpoint what stage of development the team has reached and, in particular, what stage it needs to attain. We shall present several models of this. This identity consists of a number of parameters that we shall explore by using the Berne organisation theory model as well as those of other management theorists (Figure 2.7).

Cultural Identity Development (CID) involves integrating three constituent levels of this identity and relationships between these levels (Figure 2.8).

■ The relationship of the team to its institutional structure (1);

■ The relationship of the structure to the environment (2);

■ The relationship of the team to the environment (3).

Figure 2.7   Team Identity Development (TID)

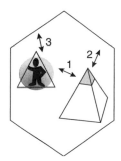

Figure 2.8   Cultural Identity Development (CID)

We enter the domain of 'complexity management', so dear to Edgar Morin, in which 'the whole is in the part' but 'the part remains in the whole'. In fact, a management team will contribute to the structure of the institution for which it is responsible, while being conditioned by this institution and by the environment with which it interacts.

In Figure 2.3 we see that coaching applies most to MID, although it is not without relevance to PID, RID and TID, and sometimes even CID (particularly if the client is a CEO or a member of the executive board).

Team building mostly applies to TID, although it clearly affects the four other levels shown in the figure.

The coaching and team-building approach is optimised when the two are combined. At his first face-to-face meeting with a manager, the coach analyses the situation with the manager's participation, along with his problems, needs and request for help, then outlines with him the terms of a potential contract. Then (ideally) he meets the manager's team, individually and/or collectively, going through the same questions and producing a feasibility document. A contract is then produced, again with the manager, taking into account the different aspects of the relationships between the coach, manager, team and institution, considered to be the priority.

Before, during and after each meeting with his team, the coach, together with the manager, will adjust and exchange perceptions of the work to be done, either as a shared task or separately.

We should also note that these two tasks mutually add to their potential if they are combined. The manager may find support and strengthened assistance from his team thanks to the mediation of his coach, who separates him from the management of relational problems and from management of the process and of the team. In his dealings with a colleague prepared through coaching, the manager benefits from greater attention, more patience and a more controlled stress level owing to the many levels of identity that he would find more difficult to make use of if he were alone.

CHAPTER 3

Conclusion

As we have seen from Figure 0.1, in the management of the considerable complexity caused by the exercise of his responsibilities, it is in the interests of a manager to have his decisions and operating methods validated by a person skilled in the five levels set out in the figure.

The director of an important company said recently: "I should like to ask a psychologist to help me to see my way more clearly through my subconscious motivations, and avoid mistakes in my decisions and behaviour, but there is the danger that he will not understand the stakes and the strategic and institutional implications. From another point of view, I should like to approach a consultant who understands strategic problems, but I fear that he would not fully appreciate the personal stakes that are involved in all of this. It seems that your role of coach allows you to cover these different areas that are indeed all decisive."

If we consider the development that a manager requires, we can regard the work of coaching and team building as one of the valuable approaches for the development and the deep unity of the person in his search for coherence between his personal life and his professional life, while regarding it fundamentally from the viewpoint of his spiritual coherence.

By 'spiritual' we include the different elements that give a meaning to life, and more particularly the existential values around which existence is organised, the spiritual values that control our relations with the cosmos, with all other people and ultimately with God if the person is a believer, and the confessional values that are the specific expression of one's individual faith.

The work of coaching aims at seeing the manager as a 'champion', with the eye of a therapist looking at this same manager considered as a person. That is, an eye that sees the Prince within the Toad, to use Eric Berne's metaphor (in our pathology where we live as 'bad-being' like the toads that we have become, under the harmful influence of a bad twist of fate foisted upon us by our parents, and when we are locked into our own scenarios. The therapist must play the role of the good fairy that allows us to become the Prince again when in reality we have never stopped being him).

This view can itself be coherent with that of a spiritual supporter on the person, who is regenerated by divine grace, as the supporter identifies the 'new man' in the 'old man' (to use Christian terminology).

In Figure 3.1 we have placed spirituality near the bottom of a funnel, because if we make profit and managerial performance the unavoidable aim, it only takes on any meaning if the ultimate aim is the development of the person. In addition, a person can only achieve his own aim through existential, spiritual and confessional values.

This work of developing champions is ambiguous by nature: it can be put to the exclusive service of narcissism, individual or collective egoism.

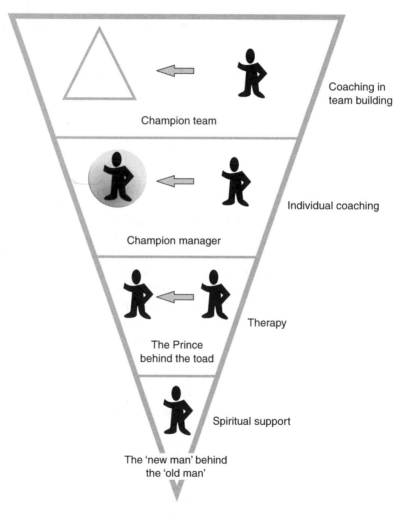

Figure 3.1   Coherence and integration of development

I believe though that this ambiguity can be accepted or left behind if it is put to the service of the future of humanity and of values that represent a kind of transcendence. For without a minimum of transcendence, there is no solidarity, and without a minimum of solidarity there remain only human constructions that collapse like houses of cards, and there is therefore no permanence in collective work. In the long run, a successful team can only be a united team.

In this sense, the spiritual aim of the person who takes the development route of increasing wealth and developing talents is not a reserved domain outside the business sphere but is part and parcel of his daily activity through the growth in the meaning of his work, which permits the manager to become a true carrier of meaning, a person who leads for meaning.

PART II

The Minimum Cultural Envelope

Coaching is in a sense the change agent's prose. Everyone does it without realising it; everyone engages in communication, process management, development, growth, change, meaning. Should we not be trained for all that?

CHAPTER 4

The Necessary Basis for Any Shared Culture

Summary

Most of the time, the implementation of management tools is inadequate for their effective operation. Tools such as quality circles, appraisal interviews, training courses or company projects must be integrated into the operational framework and must be coherent with a management system (total quality, participative management and so on). But that is not enough. The tools and management systems in turn, in order to function properly, must be implemented by managers who share a minimum cultural envelope (MCE). This MCE is made up of objectives, values, cultural benchmarks, experience and shared skills. This MCE also applies to the following key management themes:

- meta-communication;
- development of autonomy;
- development of meaning;
- development of growth;
- change;
- acknowledgement of organisational cultures.

First, the Tools

Generally, when a company makes a request of outside consultants, it is asking for tools, such as the setting up of an appraisal system, a business plan, training courses, quality circles or annual team projects.

This request reflects a real need. However, when the consultant comes to analyse the situation on the spot, he finds that these tools are insufficient in themselves, since the situation is always more complex than that described. Most of the time, the problems are not simple, the needs are many and various and the explicit request is generally off the mark from the latent request.

Nevertheless, even if the request suits the need, what often happens, even if the person who made the diagnosis is competent, is that the simple fact of implementing the tool means it must be integrated into the other management tools of the company if it is to be effective. For example, training given must be consistent with the company project, quality circles, appraisal interviews and so on.

Tools, Yes, but Provided they Integrate with the Systems

Tools alone are not sufficient. To be integrated, they must be conceived within a functional management system. For example, implementation of an appraisal system may involve analysis of:

- the values and objectives of the company;
- the recruitment system and the manager's ability to be consistent in his selection of people recruited;
- the objectives of the teams;
- the way in which managers support their colleagues;
- the overall company goals.

Unless all of these are addressed, the new tools will be useless, filed away and forgotten.

It is therefore necessary for the manager to take a global view and introduce such systems as total quality and participative management.

However, our experience shows that this is still not enough.

The Minimum Cultural Envelope

It is supremely important to verify that the company managers share the same vision of the ultimate aims of their work. That is, they are mutually in agreement on a minimum of common elements namely:

- values;
- objectives;

- shared experience;

- a personal, comparable and understandable career path;

- skills;

- common models and languages;

- a receptiveness to change.

This is what we refer to as the minimum cultural envelope (Figure 4.1).

It is also necessary for the partners in the company to have a shared understanding; common objectives are insufficient. In his book 'The Z Theory', Ouchi tells the story of a Japanese bank in California. He interviewed the American vice-presidents, all of whom said that they were enthusiastic about working in the bank, under this particular Japanese president. Their only complaint about him was that 'He does not set us clear objectives!' When interviewed in turn, the Japanese president declared

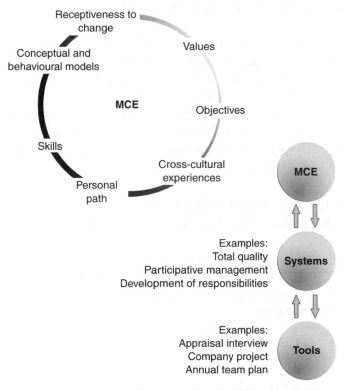

Figure 4.1 The minimum cultural envelope (MCE)

himself to be very satisfied to have such dynamic American vice-presidents. His only complaint was 'They don't understand what an objective is'.

Ouchi analyses the story thus. The American vice-presidents belong to an individualistic culture in which the objectives are highly quantitative and defined in a restricted time span. The Japanese president is in a systemic culture in which the life of the group is primordial, the objectives are more qualitative than quantitative, the culture is multi-temporal, and it is more important to react consistently to events and with a speed adapted to the circumstances, rather than strive at all costs to achieve quantitative objectives that have no meaning in the face of unforeseen events. It is absurd to want to maintain quantitative objectives that are rendered meaningless by an oil crisis, the fall of the yen or a change in the market.

It is in fact more important for a management team to share the parameters that we have just described as belonging to a minimum cultural envelope and therefore to have a parallel vision and dynamic, while taking into account the complexity of the changing environment.

MCE Must be Consistent with the Tools

It is not enough to have the tools or a MCE. It is not enough to have raised the level of debate to take account of complexity. It is also necessary, after adjusting the MCE, to return to these constituent elements and establish the implementation of the operational tools; this occurs through the consistency of the tools of management. For example, the introduction of an appraisal system allows all the values and objectives and the MCE of the firm to be evaluated. After this analysis, it is necessary to re-specify what is required from the appraisal interviews.

The Coach's MCE Must be Consistent with the MCE of the Company or Individual Client (Figure 4.2)

In our first contacts with our clients, time must be spent verifying that we understand one another. For, once again, the implementation of management tools, coaching and team building calls into question the entire complexity of the firm.

One Step at a Time

This adjustment of the MCEs of the firm and the external consultant occurs progressively and sometimes in fits and starts.

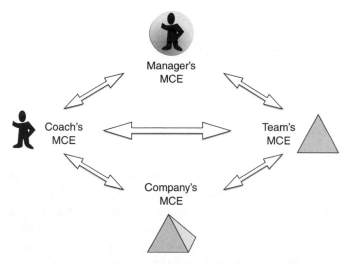

Figure 4.2   Agreement between the MCEs

For this reason, in his relationship with his individual client, with the team and with the firm, the coach takes care to advance in short steps so that each step does not endanger the participants. In this manner, they are able to make adjustments that guarantee the successful outcome of the operation.

The Strategy of Paradoxical Introduction

A client wishing to implement coaching and team building needs to present this activity to his team with the help of his consultant, in terms of a paradoxical strategy. In other words, while strongly desiring this action, he must also verify that his MCE is thoroughly compatible with that of the coach and vice versa, and with that of his team. Furthermore, the more he wants to take this action, the more he must leave a generous margin of freedom to manoeuvre to his team. This is necessary to avoid any rejection of the action and the consultant by the team.

For his part, the consultant must be careful not to presume any *a priori* solutions, and show by the quality of his attentiveness that he is sensitive to the team's specific problems. The more important the required changes appear to him, the more he must adopt a low profile, while still demonstrating his own ability and understanding of the problem. This will create the conditions for an 'alliance for change' between the members of the team, the manager and himself.

Agreeing on the Facts

This taking into account of the MCE by all the parties involved presupposes an agreement on certain facts:

- *Meta-communication*. The members of the team must not only learn to communicate better but also to regulate and adopt a position that may be described as 'meta' in relation to their way of communicating, that is, to communicate about their communication.

- *Autonomy*. The development of the performance and the competency of people cannot be done without the establishment of delegation systems. For this to be effective, it is necessary for the partners in the alliance to have common models for the development of autonomy. This involves a complex process that moves through specific stages, periods of regret and division, dependence and interdependence.

- *Meaning*. Motivation and the problems of meaning presuppose that the persons thought about the ultimate aims of the firm, and know how to experience and implement any consensus with a view to a shared vision.

- *Growth*. Personal, managerial and organisational growth involves a series of successive transformations and periods of regret, the progress of which is often not linear, but rather cyclical and complex.

- *Change*. In a team or an organisation, change is necessarily systemic. That is, the partners in the alliance for change must appreciate the extraordinary capacity of the system to maintain its homeostatic state ('the more it changes, the more it remains the same'), and therefore prepare themselves for a profound and much more difficult change than the apparent functional changes.

- *Complexity*. Entry into a new way of thinking about complexity. I refer the reader to Dominique Genelot's remarkable book on the subject.

- Finally, the MCE must take account of the simple typologies of organisational and managerial customs at the level of the individuals – the managerial stages of development.

We shall further examine each of these points in the following seven chapters.

In order to communicate, it is necessary to learn to meta-communicate.
In order to play music together, we need to first discuss the rudiments of music.

CHAPTER 5

Communication and Meta-communication

Summary

By meta-communication we mean communicating about the way in which we communicate. Each of us has our own cultural reference points (professional, language, country, etc.). These are generally subconscious and permanent elements. Our concept of reality is very strongly conditioned by this culture, and we continually have to distance ourselves from it in order to communicate with another person. This is taking the 'meta' stance.

This concept is illustrated by a few simple exercises. If the coach or the manager of a team wants the strategic vision to be shared, he must learn to invest heavily and permanently in meta-communication for his approach to succeed.

Boring's Image

Look closely at Figure 5.1. How old would you guess this woman is?

You have no doubt guessed her age. Do you think it could be something else? Might there perhaps be two women of a radically different age in this drawing? To check, examine the drawing again. Can you not see two faces? If not, look at Figure 5.2.

You now see three images; the original (Figure 5.1) above and the two different images of Figure 5.2.

On the left we have the profile view of a young woman aged between 20 and 30; on the right an old woman of 60 to 90.

Now that you have distinguished the two different faces, you may be able to see them in the first ambiguous drawing, known as Boring's image.

Whenever I introduce this classic exercise in communication courses, I proceed in two stages (I stress this because I believe it is a basic reference

Figure 5.1   Boring's image

Figure 5.2   Two Boring images

exercise). First, after dividing those on the course into two groups, I show first the drawing of the young woman, and then the drawing of the old woman. I ask both groups to debate their perceptions, and then I show the original drawing. Both groups only see in the original the image that they were first shown, namely the separated-out drawing. The dual perception inevitably provokes discussion among the participants. Some stick to their position and the tension mounts, some accuse each other of insincerity and outbursts follow: 'I don't believe it!' 'I can't see the other woman!'

Despite the discussion and the reciprocal descriptions of their image, some take refuge in their incomprehension to the point of provoking an insight, that is, a moment of revelation beyond all logic, thus indicating that the person has caused his intuitive and analogical right side brain to operate and not the analytical left side.

Thus the perception that we have of the total image is a perception that may be described as 'structured as a whole'. It is what psychologists call a gestalt. It is all embracing and exclusive; it structures our imagination, determines our perception and excludes others. In fact, when we look at the image, we see either the old woman or the young woman.

At the beginning, when we see one gestalt rather than another, it is only possible to see the second gestalt by rejecting the first. This involves a short period of grief and change, a period of uncertainty and emptiness, an attitude of active expectancy and a sudden, uncontrollable moment of insight. Each of these stages may be difficult to experience but is a *sine qua non* condition for attaining the meaning. In fact, if this route is not followed, the image or the new image is not seen and access to the meaning is blocked.

We should note that successful perception is always accompanied by a sensation of pleasure, or openly expressed joy. They remind one of Archimedes' 'eureka' or the 'ah! ah!' of Fritz Perls (founder of Gestalt therapy). It is important to see that access to meaning becomes a source of pleasure and motivation, of revitalisation of energy, whereas non-perception of the image and therefore of meaning, is experienced as something sad and frustrating, even mortifying.

In the process of communication between two persons, in order for the one to understand the other, each must abandon his own gestalt and believe in the sincerity and coherence of the other.

When the partial elements of each whole have been perceived and translated into the total gestalt, the two gestalts will then be comprehensible to both individuals. Most frequently, this is only possible because one individual has clearly perceived the two gestalts and plays the role of translator or cross-cultural commentator.

He can then say: 'What you see in the face of the young woman (total gestalt) and you call an ear (partial gestalt) is an eye (partial gestalt) is the image of the old woman (total gestalt). What you see as a nose (partial gestalt) in the image of the old woman (total gestalt) is a chin (partial gestalt) in the image of the young woman (total gestalt).' 'Complicated isn't it?'

This exercise, used in the communication part of many of my seminars (on negotiating and management styles), shows company managers the importance of a shared vision (projects, objectives) and fundamental difficulties that must be overcome in order to achieve a shared vision. Often, there is instead a compromise; the opposing parties agree that the woman is 50, which is a ridiculous, demotivating outcome that satisfies no one.

In general semantics, we must continually recall something that cannot be overstated: the map is not the same thing as the ground. The fact remains that we continue to identify and combine the following:

- the real;

- reality (what our senses are able to perceive of what is real), our perceptions (the way in which our imagination can represent and organise this neuro-sensory information in an all-embracing and exclusive way);

- the different methods and levels of abstraction and communication of these perceptions (referred to as the 'symbolic').

We must therefore regularly stand back from our perceptions, in a way similar to remaining objective when reading a given newspaper's report of an event. This presupposes a degree of asceticism, that is itself only a preliminary compared with the even greater asceticism required for the reception of another person's perceptions.

The 'Meta' Position

In the following two illustrations, we show the fundamental ambiguity to be taken into account in communication and meta-communication (how to communicate the ways in which we communicate successfully or unsuccessfully). This is something that has to be constantly reconquered, like a ridge from which one continually slips back (see Figures 5.3 and 5.4).

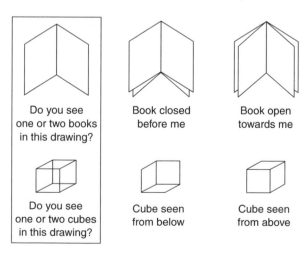

Figure 5.3 The 'meta' position

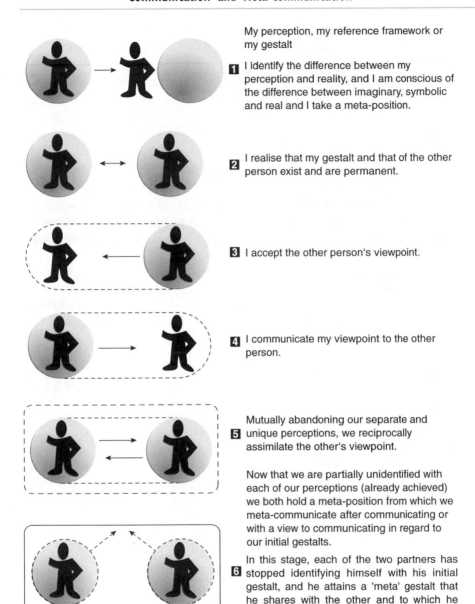

My perception, my reference framework or my gestalt

1 I identify the difference between my perception and reality, and I am conscious of the difference between imaginary, symbolic and real and I take a meta-position.

2 I realise that my gestalt and that of the other person exist and are permanent.

3 I accept the other person's viewpoint.

4 I communicate my viewpoint to the other person.

5 Mutually abandoning our separate and unique perceptions, we reciprocally assimilate the other's viewpoint.

Now that we are partially unidentified with each of our perceptions (already achieved) we both hold a meta-position from which we meta-communicate after communicating or with a view to communicating in regard to our initial gestalts.

6 In this stage, each of the two partners has stopped identifying himself with his initial gestalt, and he attains a 'meta' gestalt that he shares with the other and to which he would not have had access without passing through this six-stage process.

In this figure, the new common gestalt is represented by the solid arrow and the previous gestalts by the two dashed circles.

Figure 5.4 The six stages of meta-communication

Stage 1: I randomly project on to the left-hand frame one of the two images on the right, and I identify one of the two images on the right with the image on the left.

Stage 2: Standing back or responding to another perception, I realise that there is another possible interpretation. This is an insight, something that most often occurs as a result of a communication with another person.

Stage 3: Alternatively, I perceive in the left frame the two images, realising that they are mutually exclusive.

Stage 4: I adopt a meta-position with regard to my initial perception and in relation to what conditions the communication between two people.

For both the coach and the company manager, this training to achieve a meta-position is an abstraction superior to all training in communication. Within a company, this training is most frequently done in the following way:

- training for appraisal interviews;

- various approaches from the human relations department (time management, communication, group dynamics, conducting meetings, etc.);

- sales training;

- course on management styles, etc.

Alternatively, training for meta-communication is done through specific techniques, such as neuro-linguistic programming (NLP), transactional analysis (TA), systemic analysis (SA), and so on.

No matter what kind of specific training the person has had, training in the meta-position implies a higher achievement, attaining a level that few managers, to the best of our knowledge, have been able to reach, as it corresponds to a true asceticism.

What general semantics develop in particular, are this distancing from the real and the taking into account of the systems of representation.

The resolution of conflicts, the adjustments of representation systems and the clarification of the reference frameworks of each individual, all lead the manager to position himself constantly in this viewpoint of meta-communication.

Those managers who have had occasion to undergo a major cross-cultural experience, such as living in a culture totally foreign to their own, are especially well prepared for this concept of meta-communication. For someone who has worked with the Japanese or in Arab countries, the cultural shock is such that it leaves an indelible mark. I recall my own experience in the United States during the first months that I attended the

Chicago Business School, at a time when I did not yet know much English and where I felt closer to the Europeans whose language I spoke badly (Germans, Italians) than to the Americans whose language I understood.

Our representation system only allows us to draw 'maps' that are always distanced from the complexity of the real territory they are supposed to represent. We also have to become comfortable, in this meta-position, with managing and changing the 'real' using maps that are always inadequate by nature, and which for this reason contain a paradoxical dimension, as illustrated in Figure 5.5.

Note that, as the figure reveals, the paradox exists only in our heads and not in reality. It is easy to copy this drawing on to a sheet of paper, but it is almost impossible to describe it in a few words or to imagine it in one's mind. Just try.

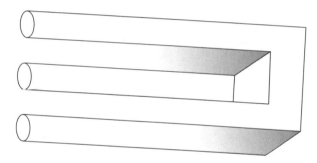

Figure 5.5   A paradoxical drawing

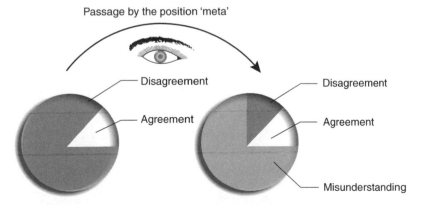

Figure 5.6   Meta-communication and conflict resolution
(based on a model by Raphaël Benayoun)

If we transfer these different experiences illustrated in these examples to the corporate world and the mobilisation of a team on a given project, we can better appreciate the enormous task of communication and meta-communication required to ensure that a strategic vision is shared.

The operational team thus finds its best field for expression when it establishes a consensus on complex realities, and when team members from different cultures agree.

In the resolution of conflict, as we see from Figure 5.6, somewhat in the style of Boring, the belief, not specified by the protagonists, is that they are in an agree/disagree situation, in which the disagreement is clearly stronger. By working through the communication and meta-communication the protagonists are able to arrive at a situation similar to the one on the right side, where the bulk of the disagreement has been transformed into an explained misunderstanding.

CHAPTER 6

Autonomy

Autonomy is not independence.

Summary

The development of autonomy is a concept that concerns both groups and institutions as well as economic, social and political entities (nations, etc.). Autonomy is never an acquired state, but a complex and ambiguous process that is continually evolving. This process includes breakdowns and other unavoidable stages, which must not be confused with access to independence. Each stage comprises positive aspects and possible deviations. It is important to identify the needs and constraints of each stage.

This process follows a cycle of (six) degrees:

- Degree 0: Dependence of the 'doormat';

- Degree 1: Counter-dependence of the 'hedgehog';

- Degree 2: Independence of the 'naughty child';

- Degree 3: 'Unison' interdependence;

- Degree 4: The paradoxical and ambiguous position of the manager;

- Degree 5: A meta-level of a different nature: the level of meaning. Access to meaning transcends the cyclical development process and greatly assists its implementation.

It is indispensable to master the process for the development of autonomy if one wants, in a corporate structure, to master the problems of delegation. There will always be the question of a 'relational system' management consisting of a manager or a coach, a champion (client or subordinate) and of their relationship. The needs of the champion can be in danger of being in conflict with those of the manager/coach.

The theme of autonomy is the heart of every coaching and team-building action. In fact, there is always the question of the development of autonomy of the individual, team, company or of a larger entity, such as a social or professional group, economic entity or even nation. This theme thus involves everyone, but is nonetheless a misunderstood concept. People tend to identify autonomy with independence, and to consider an autonomous person to be someone who can manage by himself. This is of course true, but when we speak of the development of autonomy as a coach or company manager responsible for such development, we quickly see that there is a much more complex process to be managed.

Some Preliminary Thoughts

Autonomy is not a state that is acquired once and for all. It is:

- An ongoing, never completed growth process.

- This process includes successive stages, none of which can be omitted.

- The passage from one stage to the next presupposes transformations: each transformation involves going through processes of grief, a true 'death' followed by a 'resurrection'.

- Each stage comprises a positive aspect (OK+) and a negative aspect (OK−).

- Each stage presupposes specific needs and constraints that are important to identify and address.

- Autonomy is not a reality in itself; it always grows within the context of a relationship, and is consequently by nature a systemic phenomenon that can only be handled as such. For example, an adolescent can only assume his independence according to the margin of freedom to manoeuvre allowed by his parents.

Autonomy is always experienced in a situation of ambiguity and paradox:

- In ambiguity because, within the same relationship, one can be dependent on one level, counter-dependent on another, independent on a third and interdependent on a fourth. For example, a woman may depend on her husband financially, complain about the fact that he does not allow her to develop, manage by herself while he is out of the country and not make a decision concerning their children without a full consultation with him.

- In paradox because sometimes this autonomy may evolve towards interdependence. That is, experiencing at the same time the fact of managing by oneself while maintaining a certain relationship and contact with the other person.

- Finally, the most paradoxical aspect of autonomy is where the person who increases his autonomy ('living by his own rules') reaches a conception of autonomy that becomes a true heteronomy ('living by integrating an external law').

Physical example. It is through taking ownership of an external law like the law of gravity that I am progressively able to free myself to develop my skiing in order to manage by myself ('be autonomous') on skis.

Spiritual example. By making the law of the love of God my own, and by embracing the constraints to which I submit myself, I become, through this very commitment, paradoxically more free to love.

Marital example. It is through commitment to a faithful marital relationship that, paradoxically, I shall feel more free.

Existential example. By accepting my inevitable death, I shall be able to live a full life, here and now.

To gain a better understanding of the four degrees of autonomy, we need to use two concepts from Transactional Analysis: the concepts of the Ego States* and the concept of symbiosis.*

The Ego States

According to Transactional Analysis, everyone is made of three Ego States: Parent, Adult and Child (see Figure 6.1).

In each of these Ego States are recorded the systems of thought and feeling linked to specific behaviours.

- In the Parent, we have introjected the imprints of people external to us. Obviously, these are most frequently the parental figures and elements of the family cluster.

- In the Child we have recorded our own past experiences.

- In the Adult, we recognise the experiences that have contributed to our state as an adult, these being distinct from the child that we have been and from the introjected parental figures.

* See Glossary.

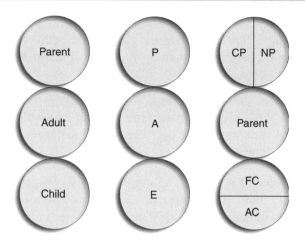

Figure 6.1   The Ego States

Functionally, the Parent Ego State is split between a Normative or Critical Parent (CP) who defines the norms of the person, and a Nurturing Parent (NP) who grants permissions. The Adult functions separately from the Parent and the Child.

For his part the Child is split functionally between the Submissive or Rebellious Adapted Child (AC), who on the one hand, reacts to the external by conforming or rebelling in relation to the parental values and the Free Child (FC) who lives spontaneously, being free in relation to his own parental figures and introjections or those of his environment.

Symbiosis

Symbiosis describes a relationship between two persons in which they function as one. The one provides the Parent and the Adult, the other the Child, and each excludes the other Ego States (see Figure 6.2).

According to the work of Nola-Katherine Symor on the 'cycle of dependence' (Symor, Actualités en AT. AAT vol. 7, 27 July 1983), autonomy appears to us as necessarily following a cycle of four stages, each corresponding to a degree of autonomy (see Figure 6.3).

It is interesting to note that one cannot pass directly from dependence to interdependence; it is necessary to pass through counter-dependence and independence.

We shall now examine the characteristics of each stage.

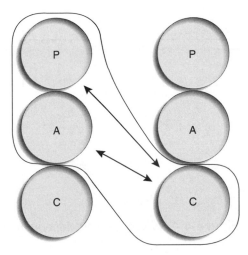

Figure 6.2 Symbiosis

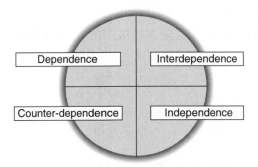

Figure 6.3 Four stages of autonomy

Dependence: Zero Degree of Autonomy

Comments on Figure 6.4. In its positive form, this stage is where the person identifies with the relationship to the other person and is in no respect autonomous. Within a company, it is where the person knows about his job or profession, but cannot yet make decisions (his Parent is not yet formed) and does not yet have sufficient information (his Adult is not yet formed).

It is the normal starting stage. If it has to last longer than necessary, it becomes negative for the person and the relationship, generating a 'yes-man'; hence the derisive name of 'doormat' for this stage.

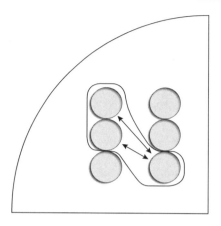

Figure 6.4 Zero degree: dependence

- *what characterises the person*: symbiosis, appropriate submission or inappropriate submission (yes-man);

- *keywords*: 'we', 'us', 'one' rather than 'I';

- *identity*: the Me of the person is identified in the relationship, it is defined by a membership; the Me, the I, is not distinct from the figure of authority;

- *life position*:* − +;

- *generic term*: the doormat;

- games:* submissive victim, model child.

Counter-dependence: First Degree of Autonomy

Commentary. In this stage, the positive aspect resides in the fact that the person identifies with a process of separation and struggles both against the other person and against the real external world to find his identity. His Adult and his Parent being only partly formed, he needs to distinguish himself from the Adult and Parent that have formed him. He therefore needs to say no and oppose in order to know what he wants and who he is, and to begin to experience the real.

The negative aspect lies in the fact that he locks himself into this opposition like a rebellious teenager, does not take responsibility for his life and his decisions, remains in an accusatory position vis-à-vis the other,

* See Glossary.

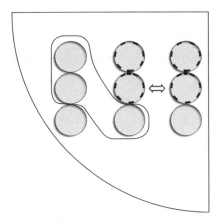

Figure 6.5 First degree: counter-dependence

and plays the game of 'without you', expressed in a company context as: 'Oh, if only my boss wasn't there, if only there were no clients, the other department ... then perhaps we could get something done.' The problem therefore lies in the fact that the person makes the other responsible for his own passivity and tends to accuse and to rebel. This is why we have termed him the 'hedgehog' (see Figure 6.5).

- *what characterises the person*: still in symbiosis, but ambivalent;

- *keywords*: 'no';

- *identity*: still ill-defined, an expression of ambivalence revealed by rebellion and accusation; the beginnings of 'I';

- *life position*: − −;

- *generic term*: hedgehog;

- *games*: being fed up, without you, rebellious victim or persecutor.

Independence: Second Degree of Autonomy

Commentary. The person takes on the form of a Parent and an Adult by himself through experiencing the real. He is no longer conditioned by those who formed him, but through his relationship with others, with whom he has entered into a new relationship.

In a company structure, it is the stage of the person who no longer requires anything from his boss and who functions independently, as a

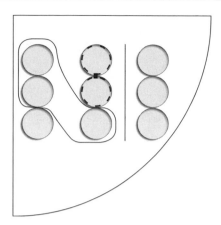

Figure 6.6   Second degree: Independence

profit centre, the only acknowledged constraint being his client (internal or external).

The negative aspect lies in the fact that, having acquired a taste for his independence, the person tends to focus on himself and on his own rules, seeing as the centre of the world. At the psychological level, it tends to become bound up in narcissism, and at the company level there is the danger that he will not want to be held accountable. Hence our name the 'naughty child' stage (see Figure 6.6).

- *what characterises the person*: emergence from symbiosis is experienced as a separation;

- *keywords*: 'me', 'by myself';

- *identity*: the Me of the person is being formed; the person feels able to take care of himself; narcissistic phase;

- *life position*: $+ -$;

- *generic term*: naughty child;

- *games*: individualistic.

Interdependence: Third Degree of Autonomy

Commentary. The positive part of in this stage comes from the fact that, having become a complete person with his three Ego States, the person is in a position on the one hand to manage by himself, and on the other hand to

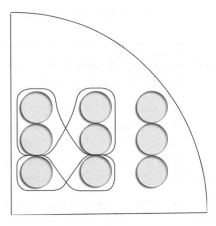

Figure 6.7 Third degree: interdependence

experience apparently symbiotic situations without identifying with the symbiotic relationship. He may submit to authority or himself take care of another person (even the person who previously held authority over him) without losing his identity.

The symbiosis is therefore functional, not structural. Moreover, the symbioses may be inverted. In fact, the person has the choice between a functional symbiotic relationship and a relationship of pure and simple independence.

The negative aspect of this relationship is minimal, but important to note. A person who remained at this stage of interdependence without moving beyond it would run the risk of only being able to function when left to his own devices, or with people at the same stage of development. It is therefore desirable for the person to achieve the fourth stage of autonomy in which he will become capable of symbiotically taking care of those who have not yet pursued his path(see Figure 6.7).

- *what characterises the person*: change in the nature of the relationship and in his relationship to the Ego;

- *keywords*: 'yes … if', of someone in authority who may say 'no' and lay down limits;

- *identity*: the Ego is no longer defined by external relational forms but by an internal choice of his identity;

- *life position*: + +;

- *generic term*: unison.

We can give a light-hearted example of the four stages in the case of a married couple:

- Degree 0: the couple sleep in the same bed and can imagine no other solution because it would be 'a negation of their love'.

- Degree 1: one of the pair, disturbed by the other's snoring, is woken up, then becomes annoyed and angry. Through the conflict and guilt that he/she overcomes, the one either wakes the other or goes to sleep in another bed (counter-dependence), only to return to the bed the following morning, sad and guilty, in order to be forgiven.

- Degree 2: they decide to sleep in separate rooms and not to quarrel about the subject (independence).

- Degree 3: still retaining a separate bedroom in case of need, when one snores or the other does not want to run the risk of a disturbed night, they can sleep in the same bed to make love or simply for the pleasure of being together, each exercising free choice depending on the current situation in which they are living (interdependence).

The first four degrees of autonomy correspond to the four stages (see Figure 6.8).

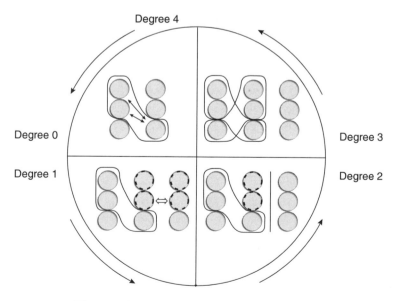

Figure 6.8   From degree 0 to degree 4

The first degree is reached when the person crosses the path that separates dependence from counter-dependence.

The second degree is reached when the person crosses the path that separates counter-dependence from independence.

The third degree is when he moves from independence to interdependence.

The fourth degree is when he moves from interdependence to dependence, but at another level.

The Fourth Degree of Autonomy

In the fourth degree we illustrate, through the dynamic of a spiral, a stage in which the person experiences a relationship in which he is dependent in a symbiosis A–B taking the position of the Child, the relationship of symbiosis B–C having the position of the Parent and of the Adult vis-à-vis a subordinate, and position D in which he is independent (see Figure 6.9).

This is the most frequent and ambiguous situation, where the person finds himself in an institutionally systemic situation within the company, where he is always subordinate to someone else (to a certain extent the chairman, himself, depends on his board of directors, public authorities or his electors). At the same time the hierarchical superior to someone who does not enjoy his level of development, while still remaining in multiple relationship with collaterals.

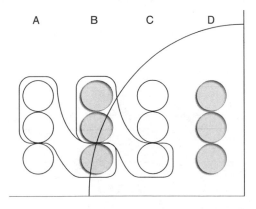

Figure 6.9   The fourth degree of autonomy

The Passage from One Stage to Another

Each act of passage includes a process of grieving that, according to the model of Elisabeth Kübler-Ross, includes five stages that are experienced in succession, but sometimes with steps backwards and forwards, and sometimes with overlaps. These stages are: denial, anger, bargaining, sadness and acceptance (see Figure 6.10).

Example. An independent person has to join a new group in his company, because he is being reintegrated with a team after being in charge of a special mission.

At first (denial) he will tend to behave as before like a naughty child, and operate according to his own rhythm without concern for the rest of the team.

Once called to order by his boss, he may become angry (anger) and annoyed by useless meetings. He then agrees to take part in certain meetings (bargaining) on condition that the agenda is modified along with the method of conducting these meetings. He then becomes resigned (sadness) to taking part in these meetings, still believing (and often justly) that he is wasting his time while regretting his previous autonomy. Finally, he comes to accept (acceptance) this constraint, noting that everyone has to follow the same rule and that this is a necessary condition for the creation of a synergy within the team.

It should be noted that an understanding of this process proves very useful in the management in any situation of individual or collective change.

Experience has shown that in cases of industrial reorganisation, job transfer, outplacement, merger and so on, in one way or another and to varying degrees, these five stages are unavoidable, and that it is preferable to anticipate and deal with them rather than ignore them and then be obliged to endure them.

These stages of grieving are specific for each degree.

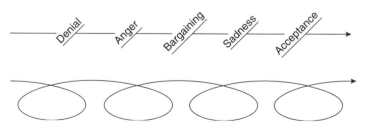

Figure 6.10 Stages of grieving according to Elisabeth Kübler-Ross

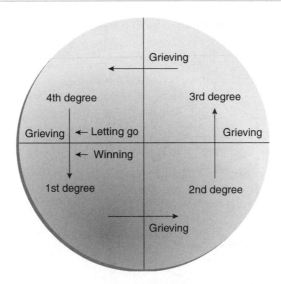

Figure 6.11 Passage from one stage to the next

At the first degree, the person abandons (Figure 6.11) the comfort of being in charge; he gains permission to say no and to assert himself.

At the second degree, he loses the possibility of passing the blame completely on to others; he attains a clearer self that is stronger and more responsible.

In the third degree, he must give up living at his own pace and gains the richness of a synergy.

In the fourth degree, he loses the fact of being among equals; he gains the possibility of managing the relationship with another person, whatever that person's level of autonomy.

The Fifth Degree of Autonomy: Access to Meaning

The preceding four degrees represent a logical sequence in a spiral development that may be prolonged indefinitely. However, it seemed to us that a category of a different nature would allow greater freedom and autonomy for the person, independently of the preceding stages. This would be the degree of meaning (see Figure 6.12).

It effectively appeared to us that a person could be in a situation of dependence or independence, while simultaneously being freer and more autonomous because his situation was charged with meaning for him.

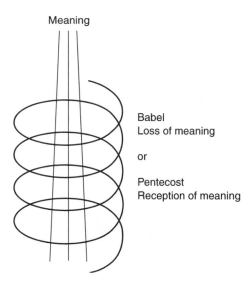

Meaning

Babel
Loss of meaning

or

Pentecost
Reception of meaning

Figure 6.12   The column of meaning. The core of
the development of autonomy

He could therefore not identify himself with this relational situation, but, finding a more profound meaning to his life, take a transcending view of his life.

For example, take the case in which a mother has to endure interrupted sleep in order to perform the 'ordinary task of looking after her baby'. She can find existential meaning in this relationship because this relationship forms the basis of her existential aspirations; she can also tolerate the constraints of this situation much more lightly. Contrast the autonomous single person who might not tolerate being woken by an unexpected telephone call.

We shall return later to this concept of meaning and its complexity. We shall simply note that according to François Varillon's formulations (see Bibliography), the term 'meaning' has at least three accepted usages:

- Meaning as direction (the way we speak of the direction of a street), which translates into 'objective' in corporate terms.

- Meaning as significance (as in the meaning of a sentence), which corresponds to value in corporate terms.

- Meaning as experience (the way we speak of a meaningful situation) which affects our conscience as a whole and our system of representation and which, in a company, corresponds to motivation.

We can see this meaning at three levels: personal, managerial and company.

1. Personal

I am referring to the existential, spiritual and confessional aspects of meaning. These are distinct, but often linked realities.

Existential. I am alluding to the values that make up my life. These are most frequently the values that appear when confronting the conundrum of death, and that prove that my life will have been worth living. Either I shall be able to define how I wish to live from now until my death, so that in terms of objectives, values and experiences my life seems to me to have been fulfilling, or, on reflection, values emerge such that I would rather die than see them scorned, these being freedom, patriotism, truth and respect for humanity.

Spiritual. I understand the meaning of the life defined by my spiritual anthropology, and which bases my existence on an identity that surpasses my own person, and corresponds to belonging to a human community. The latter transcends my own existence or a religion considered to be the equal of other religions; belief in God, in a hereafter beyond the grave and material consciousness; belief in a possible communion with others through art or history, within humanist spirituality.

Confessional. I understand the meaning of the life as defined by the content of a personal faith shared with others, that beyond a spirituality tolerant of other spiritualities, affirms a difference and an indivisible specificity – the faith of a Jew, Christian, Muslim or Hindu. These cannot be absorbed one into the other even though they accept each other by recognising a certain community of values that allows them to share a certain degree of communion. In an earlier work I have spoken of the fifth, sixth and seventh levels of autonomy by referring to these three aspects of personal meaning.

2. Managerial

At the managerial level it is a question of the meaning that the person may find in his job in terms of his objectives, values and the experiences that his job will allow him to implement. It might involve one or more of the nine levels of meaning (see following chapter) and also that which, when I retire, will have given meaning to my professional life.

3. At the company level, the meaning of the company is made up of the objectives, values and experiences offered to its employees.

This is what we have referred to as the Minimum Cultural Envelope (MCE). In most cases, the 'company plan' aims to be the concrete and shared representation of it.

One of the fundamental aspects of the development of motivation in a company is allowing the existence of an optimum consistency between these three levels of meaning (personal, managerial and company). We are careful to say optimum in order to avoid any identification with the company that would turn this into an idolatrous, sectarian or fascist organisation. We mean optimum in the sense that if the managers want to attract the best people, they must allow their members of staff to feel that their company is a place where they can grow and a place where that growth is consistent with that of the company.

The managers are the carriers of meaning to the extent that they allow individuals and groups in the company to find room in the company plan for their own values and objectives. If we imagine this project as a constellation of stars, each individual or team must find at least one of his stars in the company constellation. On one hand, we can refer to the metaphor of the tower of Babel or the loss of meaning, for an organisation in which a development spiral for individuals is offered, but in which they would lose their souls, and the individuals (and in due course the company) would experience a loss of meaning.

On the other hand, we can take the metaphor of the Pentecost, evoking the biblical situation where people are different and do not speak the same language, but they understand one another because they receive the same spirit and transcend their differences through participation in the same MCE (see Figure 6.12).

On one end of the scale, there is Babel where all speak the same language but end up no longer understanding one another, divided by their anthropocentric objectives and not accepting the same meaning, since they are not in a state of shared reception of a common meaning. At the other end, there is the phenomenon of the Pentecostal type of rallying for a human community in which each person accepts the differences of the other because they are filled with the same receptiveness to meaning.

It is this positive attitude to meaning that, in our opinion, distinguishes the leader from the manager. For us, the leader is a person who incarnates this meaning to such an extent that, no matter what his hierarchical status is or what his specific skills are, he enables others to:

- belong to the organisation;

- feel motivated by the meaning that they have derived;

- contribute to strengthening coherence through their support for the meaning. They pass from acceptance of the meaning to the desire to promote it for themselves and for others.

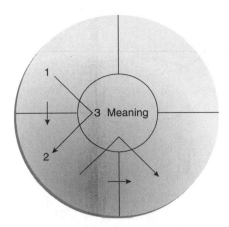

Figure 6.13   Change, grieving and meaning

It is through this that a manager can be a leader and a carrier of meaning independently of specific position in the hierarchy.

In the grieving process referred to earlier, the passage through the five stages corresponding to each of the levels of autonomy is greatly facilitated by the concept of meaning, as shown in Figure 6.13.

Because passage from 1 to 2 has been transcended by the 'meta' position provided by the meaning, any meaningful change allows the five stages to be traversed more economically.

First, the passage via meaning provides values and objectives that compensate for the frustration linked to the phenomenon of grieving, and fear of the unknown that always accompanies the next stage. From the point of view of the caterpillar, transformation into a butterfly is a catastrophe.

Second, the manager may be a true catalyst for change to the extent that he correctly gives meaning to this change. He points out the cause of it (the 'why'), the aim (the 'for what') and the significance of it. Just as in mountain climbing one needs two safe holds in order to find a third new hold, the person undergoing change situated at 1 needs hold 3 that the meaning provides in order to attain hold 2 and then release hold 1.

Now that we have seen the five degrees of autonomy, we shall study how to experience the different stages in the process of the development of autonomy, and the implementation of effective delegation:

- first for the champion;

- then for the coach, whose particular task is to manage the relationship (see Figure 6.14).

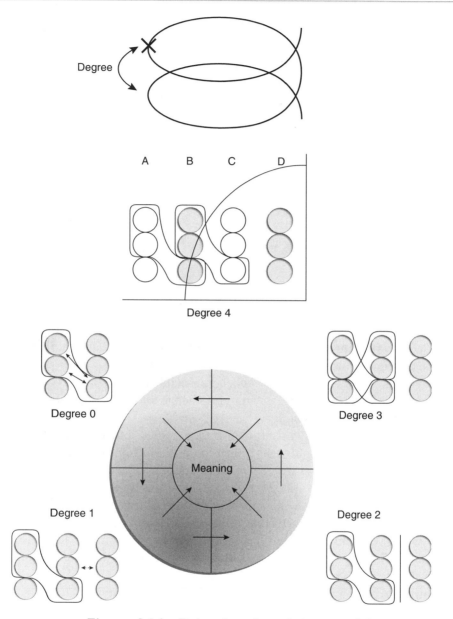

Figure 6.14 Delegation, the culmination of the
development of autonomy

To be successfully encouraged, each degree of autonomy requires an appropriate management style, proper consideration of its own needs and a specific problem to be handled.

In order to be able to deal with the champion's situation, the coach must have dealt with his own management style, his own needs and his own problem.

The chief–subordinate relationship is systemic, it is not a question of a linear relationship, and one of the partners may not isolate one of the poles. Each element of the system is interactive with the others; hence the complexity of the relationship.

Autonomy level 4, the 'let us manage' level, arises from the complexity of the preceding stages. The person who has reached this stage must also manage his own internal complexity, being simultaneously chief, subordinate and an independent person.

The systemic relation coach–champion, or chief–subordinate, operates at a multitude of levels and meanings, all of which are interactive (as we shall see later, there are always at least eight or nine levels of meaning).

From the champion's viewpoint:

- Degree 0: the base position is that of submissive adaptation (+ or −). He needs protection and permission from the Parent and the coach and he needs information (from the Adult). There is the danger of becoming a yes-man (doormat).

- Degree 1: the initial position is that of someone who asserts himself through his opposition to initiatives that he is frightened to take. His position is therefore ambivalent; it is partly submissive and at the same time rebellious (hence the description hedgehog).

- Degree 2: the initial position is derived from separation and refusal of the relationship; the champion needs his own space, his rhythm and to find his own identity. The problem is the lack of communication from someone who is only concerned about himself (hence the 'naughty child').

- Degree 3: the initial position is that of an exchange, which has once again become possible, but on new grounds. The champion is independent and can thus take care of the chief. The champion needs to be recognised in his Parent and his Adult; he is effective in delegation (hence 'unison').

- Degree 4: the initial position is that of someone caught in crossfire who must have the qualities of these four degrees and the capacity to integrate and mobilise each of the four preceding degrees. He needs to be comfortable in each of the positions of the preceding degrees both as champion and as coach (hence the description 'let's manage').

From the coach's viewpoint:

- Degree 0: it is essential for him to have a strong Nurturing Parent, who is encouraging and permissive and a firm Normative Parent, as well as a clearly defined Adult. This is not likely for the newly promoted chief.

- Degree 1: in addition to the qualities of degree 0, he must be protective when confronted with ambivalent behaviour, manage in dual control and above all control his frustration when faced with passive or reactive aggression from the champion or subordinate.

- Degree 2: the initial position is one in which the coach must allow his champion the maximum amount of room and therefore come to terms with the frustration of non-communication. Hence the importance of clearly negotiating objectives.

- Degree 3: the initial position is that of someone who becomes an alter ego and needs to be recognised as such. The coach will have to recognise with sincerity the Parent and the Adult of the other, to the point of agreeing to place himself in his Child in regard to him.

For the first, second and third degrees, the coach must above all have carried out the grief for the Parent position that he had in symbiosis, as well as in his role of Adult 'who knows everything'. This presupposes that the coach possesses an ontological security and a high degree of 'OKness' (that is, the ability to remain OK).

- Degree 4: with regard to a champion in the fourth level, the coach must show understanding when confronting the complexity of this position, flexibility and firmness in the face of the different needs of each stage (usually dealt with inadequately) and above all an 'OKness' when confronted with the frustration, ambiguity and paradoxicality of these situations of continual double constraint.

It is not sufficient to focus on one of the polarities of coach or subordinate; it is essential that both, but especially the coach, perceive the complexity of the degrees undertaken. It is useful to pass from intraphysical or behavioural growth to systemic growth. An example can be found in the development of the relationship between father and son; it is no longer a question of looking to the therapy of the child or the father, but to the family system. Management of the relationship is therefore in line with the systemic view.

CHAPTER 7

Meaning

Meaning is the light that illuminates our consciousness.

Summary

The concept of meaning can only be perceived by accepting the mystery of individual consciousness. This concept is made up of a variety of objectives, values and experiences that resound in an individual's consciousness.

Sharing this meaning lies at the heart of the difficult and ambiguous role of managers who must mobilise teams with a minimum consensus and a 'shared vision'.

For the individual to resolve his contradictions, he must establish the coherency of the meaning of his life, and that of his professional and organisational life. Finding meaning in his personal and professional life supposes that he sets up protections (being able to say no to certain things) and permissions (being able to say yes to others).

The manager's principal task is to manage the complexity of the nine levels of meaning that all operational actions include. Every action of production or operational life implies a psychological dimension (subconscious or conscious), which affects the definition of functions, the whole of organisational life, the situation within an environment, the choice in regard to transcendental values (social, productional, spiritual), a certain concept of the identity of the person and a way of controlling power.

Finally, the manager is always partly immersed in 'chaos'. He therefore needs to develop a number of qualities, including managing uncertainty, imperfection, his own ambivalence, paradox, frustration and his capacity for change.

The only way to outstrip this asceticism is by endowing his action with meaning. By embracing this meaning, he will be able to transform the experience of chaos into a sentiment of 'co-creation' with others and, if he is a believer, of co-creation with God.

Can't you see that I am not simply shaping a stone? I am building a cathedral.

In the previous chapter, we gave a definition of the concept of meaning and spoke about personal meaning (existential, spiritual and confessional), as well as managerial and entrepreneurial. We tried to show to what extent this is central to the themes of leadership, autonomy development and change.

In this chapter we hope to describe some aspects of the problem of meaning that need to be understood in order to manage its complexity and achieve a consensus for mobilising management staff around a shared strategic vision.

The Concept of Meaning Occurs Necessarily Through Human Perception

Commentary on Figure 7.1. At first glance, you see black shapes against a white background. You also probably do not see the complete image to which these shapes belong. Study the figure more closely to discover the overall image. If you find it, turn to the next (facing) page to check. If you do not find it, do not look too soon, but take note of the following:

- consider what you are 'looking at' and what you do not 'see', and experience the frustration of this.

- the situation in which you find yourself is similar to that of a team member who does not perceive the vision presented to him by the team leader who does possess this vision.

- I imagine that you have already experienced this type of situation and I suggest that you imagine the two symmetrical frustrations: that of the manager or team member who 'sees' and cannot understand why the

Figure 7.1

Figure 7.2

Figure 7.3

other does not, and that of the team member who does not 'see' and who does not have access to the meaning. So long as neither one nor the other have shared this vision, somewhat similarly to the case of the Boring image, whatever the comments or compromises made, they cannot replace the quality of the relationship and co-operation achieved through rallying around a shared vision. You are experiencing the 'drama' experienced by most members of operational teams or members of a company who most of the time have only fragmentary perceptions of this vision.

Figures 7.2 and 7.3 reveal the complete integration of these fragments to produce the overall image (the vision). Compare this with the earlier Figure 7.1.

When you examine Figure 7.1 again, you are able to re-establish the meaning contained in the original shapes. You can see that its meaning lies within these fragments. This small exercise is a simple but significant illustration of the process that we all have to go through to attain the meaning of our action or our life. In all cases we have to construct a personal coherence from the fragments that make up our life, and when a collective activity is involved this task is all the more complicated because it has to be carried out through interaction with others, and all the more so because each individual has only one indivisible angle of vision in relation to the global vision.

This situation is like the story of the ten blind men who come into contact with an elephant. Each knows that it is an elephant in its totality, but if each describes it according to his sense of touch, one will say it is a snake (the trunk), another a tree (a leg), another a wall (the body), and so on.

The Concept of 'Existential Meaning'

What gives meaning to my life?

From Figure 7.4 we see that the action that I put forward here and now in my existence, in my professional or personal life, may find its meaning not in itself but through the fact that it is a carrier in terms of directional significance or experience. In other words, through the way in which this action will resonate in my consciousness. Consciously or subconsciously, I will give it meaning through wilful use of my conscience.

Remember the parable in Peter Drucker's story from the 1960s (I remember reading it in an American newspaper at the Chicago Business School in 1965 and have never forgotten it):

> I met a man digging a hole beside the road and asked him: What are you doing there?
> He replied: As you can see, I'm digging a hole.
> I continued on my way and met another man digging another hole.
> What are you doing there?
> As you can see, I'm building a cathedral.

However, the meaning that I give to my action, here and now, is not simply an answer to the question 'what' or 'how'. As a human being, I have to appeal to a major constituent of my consciousness, which is my memory, and therefore reply to the question 'why'. One of the basic aspects of therapeutic work is precisely to re-establish the link between my actions and the dimension of actualisation that they represent in relation to a

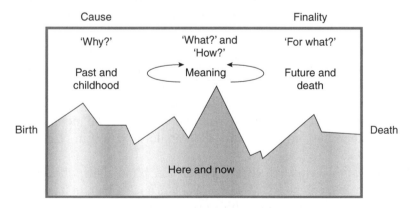

Figure 7.4 Map of existential life

wounded consciousness in which the subconscious and the processes of repression and distortion of memory have actually blurred the access to meaning. In as much as I am unable to reply to the question 'why', a large proportion of my actions have strictly speaking no meaning, because they are stirred by a subconscious and the links that enclose this wounded consciousness. Since Freud, our culture has been marked in this respect by psychoanalysis.

Perhaps of even greater importance, for attainment of meaning, are consideration of the question 'for what' and the ultimate aim of my actions.

This is the main answer that I have to the unavoidable problem posed by my death. This reply could be considered the cornerstone of my values.

We use the expression 'existential refocusing' to describe the reading of the meaning of our action that I can give after replying to the four questions: 'what', 'how', 'why' and 'for what'.

We note in passing that the question of the meaning will bring me from the causal world (the question 'why'), that belongs to science, to the world of purposes (the question 'for what') that belongs to beliefs, faith and religion.

Meaning and Coherence (What is it That Makes Me Run?)

One of the most important aspects of time management arises from the previous discussion and the establishment of values and existential objectives. Then follows confrontation with professional values and objectives or those of the organisation. By finding the means and making choices we can better harmonise them and progress from a divided and dystonic self to a unified and syntonic self. That is, a self in which one's energies are no longer scattered and divided but converge in the absence of internal contradictions (see Figure 7.5).

Reorganisation or Life Conversion

From our experience in therapeutic work and in our coaching work we have observed that this task of life reorganisation stimulated through meaning most frequently involves elements of reparation and work for construction or reconstruction on five levels of reality as shown in Figure 7.6. In practice, it is necessary to focus on one of these levels, but we recall again that this work is not linear in a strict sense, and to be coherent one should always integrate the four other aspects.

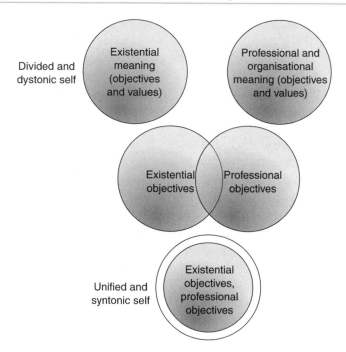

Figure 7.5   Meaning and coherence

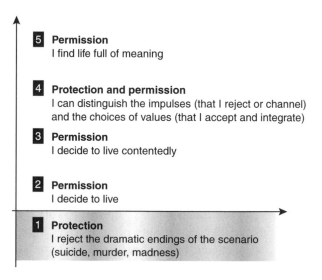

Figure 7.6   Stages in the reorganisation or conversion of life

Definition of the scenarios. Our history is broadly reprogrammed by our defence system. In fact, it is as though a 'map for life' decided in childhood through our parents' influence, or by subsequently experienced traumas, makes us live our lives like a film preview, as though the scenario was already largely written.

To make a scenario evolve, it is effective to:

- help the person being coached to become aware of his scenario by having him analyse his beliefs and the way in which he perceives them.

- direct him towards a new decision (a rethink) of another scenario.

The three Drama Scenario Endings (DSEs). Sometimes we 'choose' one or more of the following three DSEs at the heart of our scenario:

- murder,

- suicide,

- madness (or a terminal illness).

How can the rethinking be provoked and the DSEs counteracted? First, it must be discerned whether the person:

- is in real danger, having already embarked on the DSEs, or indeed might embark on such a course.

- If there is no such danger, whether there is a strong commitment to fantasy present, most often partially subconscious, and linked with more or less archaic decisions in which, even if the person does not take action, he retains his psychosomatic energy blockages.

The task is therefore to identify the real dangers and the fantasy life in order to encourage the person to convert the energy (fixed and blocked) directed to DSEs towards life. A good way to proceed is to transform this energy by way of an integrated approach (conscious and subconscious, cognitive, emotional, physical and spiritual) into energy for life.

The Nine Levels of Meaning

First, the example of the cathedral builder. We refer to Figure 7.7 that sets out the nine levels of meaning and the action of the man digging a hole or shaping a stone:

- At level 3^1 (social or operational), one can indeed say that he shapes a stone.

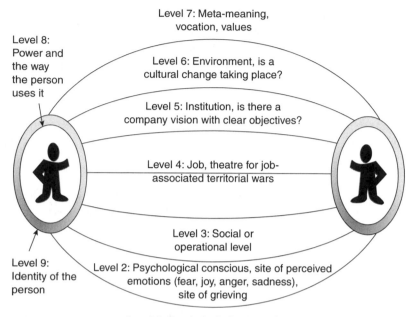

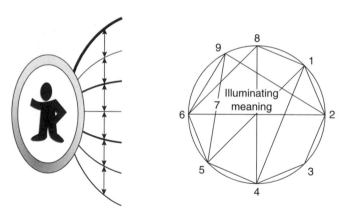

Figure 7.7 The nine levels of meaning

- At level 2 (psychological conscious), he works quickly because he wants to appear the best of the team of stonecutters, or, he works slowly because he is rebelling against his boss's orders.

- At level 1 (psychological unconscious), without knowing it, by seeking recognition from his boss, he is trying desperately or unconsciously to obtain the recognition that his father did not show him (according to the American therapist Bob Goulding, this is the case of 90 per cent of Western males).

- At level 4 (as foreman at his job level), he is valuing his job in comparison with the other jobs in his company (for example, production compared with sales, and vice versa).

- At level 5 (the institution), he implements the company project, fulfils his employment contract and thus earns his living.

- At level 6 (in relation to the environment), he is perhaps campaigning as union representative or perhaps is in the process of introducing a new technology. It is this that chiefly imbues his work with meaning.

- At level 7 (meta-meaning level), he builds a cathedral. As the third diagram of Figure 6.12 shows, this level lies at the heart of all other levels of meaning.

- At level 8 (power), he exerts influence on others at all the preceding levels, and it is possibly through this beneficial or baleful influence that he finds the meaning of his action.

- At level 9 (identity), he builds his self and fulfils himself as an individual.

As the third diagram of Figure 7.7 shows, these nine levels of meaning are experienced by the person at the same time. However, his consciousness is focused, from time to time, on one particular level. Furthermore, depending on the situation and his stage of development, one or another of the levels will attract more attention.

We have developed this model that has proved very useful in our coaching work, both in an individual context and for team building, because we have observed from our experience in therapy that explicit discussion could never be isolated and distilled, and always carried with it a latent meaning that was partly unconscious and multidimensional. For example, at a meeting focusing on an operational problem such as the launch of a new product, all of these levels of meaning will come into play for the members of the team involved.

I propose two thoughts to clarify understanding of this model.

1. *From the laws of communication in Transactional Analysis (TA).* The concept of the dual base in TA distinguishes two levels of meaning: the 'social' (explicit and apparent) level and the psychological, latent and hidden level, such as in the following situation of Adult to Adult. A says

to B: 'Do you know what time it is now?' and B replies Adult to Adult: 'It is 10.15'. At the latent and unsaid level, A frowns and points with his right index finger, showing by the tone of his voice and his angry air that he is clearly in the Parent and B responding by blushing and speaking somewhat fearfully revealing that he is in the Child and feels guilty. The communication law in TA indicates that the latent or psychological meaning of the dual base transaction is much more significant than the explicit or 'social' meaning.

My experience in companies has also shown me that in the management of an interview, meeting or seminar organised on an 'official' topic, what is explicitly and clearly set out in an agenda causes the participants to speak clearly at quite another level of meaning and in a more or less explicit manner. Repetition of this type of situation led me to distinguish these nine levels of meaning and to identify that the majority of meetings go off course or are paralysed by stakes that are well beyond that of the level 3 operational level. In addition, since these other levels of meaning are often confused, latent or inexplicit, they generate much frustration and power games among the players, resulting in a very ineffective running of such meetings.

2. The levels 8 of power and 9 of identity are of another order and represent poles that merit close attention.

(a) Most frequently, power problems are linked to problems of identity for which they compensate.

Moreover, in a negative way, these power phenomena of generated counter-powers in the participants, which results in levels 8 and 9 feeding on each other and hiding behind the seven preceding levels and may, because they are hidden, create a suffocating atmosphere.

In positive terms, if the people are clear about their identity and use the power that they possess, the players will be able to bring their identities and energies to bear in the resolution of the stakes and problems located on the seven other levels. In this way, the atmosphere will be stimulated.

(b) In the context of coaching, the coach and the different managers of these meetings (directors or operational managers) will benefit from paying close attention to the identity stakes of the players present (level 9). Therefore, a permanent policy aimed at creating a climate of trust, and allowing the OKness and ontological security of the players to be built and re-established will be a protective and resolutive means of handling the situation as a whole. Judicious use in TA of recognition signs combined with the approach of William Schutz[2] (inclusion, control, openness) is quite practical. We recall that work on inclusion allows the players to recognise each other as important and to develop their sense of belonging. Work on control allows the players to be clear about their own view of their skills and to put in perspective the stakes of power, decision, rules of the game and their contribution to production. Third, work on openness strengthens the players' capacity to be close to themselves, to their real feelings, and, in their relationships with others, to feel sympathetic and therefore dare to express their fears and needs and raise topics of annoyance with confidence.

It therefore appears very important to us for the managers of the team and for the coach to be as attentive to the process as they are to the content of the order of the day. This reveals the levels of meaning that cause blockages and where investment must be made in it in order to advance the cohesion of the team and its production. We note with amusement that, paradoxically, the fact of being largely ignorant about the profession of the participants at a meeting often allows the coach to play out fully his role of team facilitator and, being completely detached from any understanding of the content, to have the power to perceive the psychological, functional or institutional elements at play in the discussion.

For an operational manager, training in meta-communication will allow him to conduct much more effective meetings, because training at the meta level allows him to focus on that level of meaning where the energy of his team is blocked, like a photographer focusing his camera on a subject.

It is vain for you to rise up early, to sit up late, to eat the bread of sorrows: for so he giveth his beloved sleep. Psalms 127.

To be OK in Chaos Management

The managerial situation henceforth must face up to external reality, the most immediate aspect of which is uncertainty (Figure 7.8). It emerges that a manager's functioning is conditioned by his way of managing his relationship to perfection, both his own and that of others.

Figure 7.8 Uncertainty

Fear and guilt are the feelings that one is obliged to confront in the management of chaos since nothing turns out as planned. From that standpoint, there are two possible attitudes:

- one adopts a defensive position and spends one's time protecting oneself against criticism, self-justifying and avoiding taking any risk for fear of making a mistake;

- one gives oneself the right to make a mistake and escape from the fail–succeed dichotomy and move into a situation of trial and adjustment. Our position is to invite each manager to consider that, while he is not looking to make mistakes, at least 20 per cent of his actions are 'calculated risks'. If he does not do this, he will only do those things that he knows he can do perfectly and are likely to lead to his becoming locked into a routine. He will then turn into a diplodocus condemned within a world of constant change. Acceptance of uncertainty and a degree of imperfection are the gateway in the management of chaos. The manager must learn to be comfortable with ambiguity, ambivalence, paradox, frustration and the capacity for change, all of which are the constituent and unavoidable elements of chaos management (see Figure 7.9).

1. By ambiguity, we mean the continual presence of different levels of reality and meaning that we have discussed earlier.

For example, if the manager has to conduct a meeting, it is perhaps more important for the meeting to be longer than foreseen. It should not conclude

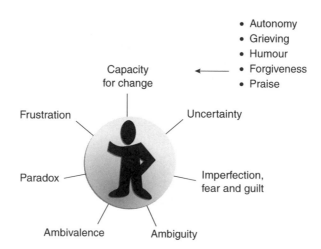

Figure 7.9   Constituent elements of chaos management

with an operational decision if it has brought about the unblocking of a psychological conflict between two people who were impeding the team's progress, or if it succeeds in resolving a power problem or integrating a member of the team who had felt himself excluded.

We shall examine this later but in greater detail, but it is the manager's lot to be constantly dealing with the ambiguity between content and process. It is not a question of two contradictory realities but of two polarities between which managerial reality is constantly placed.

2. By ambivalence, we mean the basic contradiction that every manager must resolve, namely desiring one thing and its opposite.

He wants to be considered 'the boss' but at the same time he wants his subordinates to be able to function when he is not there. He wants his team to come up with ideas without him but at the same time he is unhappy that his ideas are not immediately accepted. He wants his colleagues to take the initiative with internal or outside clients but he is unhappy that his clients deal with someone other than himself.

3. By paradox, we are referring to the manager wishing to move in a particular direction, but then having to express his desire with prudence in order not to provoke a situation of rejection or blocking on the part of his colleagues.

In his book on chaos management, Peters lists some 18 paradoxes that have to be dealt with in the management of change. Here are three:

- The more importance attached to the quality of a product, the more one must distance oneself from it in order to face up to the necessary technological change.

- The more intense the change imposed by the exercise of his profession, the greater the need to find strong areas of stability, such as, for example, confidence in the team to which one belongs and security of employment.

- The most important paradox to be managed is: if I want to retain some control of the situation, I basically must abandon controlling people.

4. By frustration, we mean that the manager demonstrates his true capacity for chaos management to the extent that he is capable of bearing the inevitable frustrations arising from the gap between the real and the desired situations.

5. By capacity for change, we refer to a number of qualities that the manager must possess, such as autonomy, already discussed, the capacity for grieving, a sense of humour that allows dramatic situations to be defused

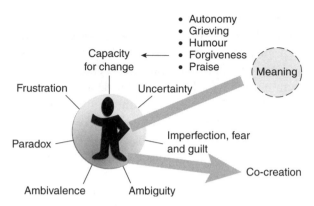

Figure 7.10   Being OK within chaos

and testifies to a position of meta-communication and an attitude of for-
giveness, both towards others and towards oneself.

From a spiritual point of view (not easily found in a company), it is possible, apart from forgiving others, oneself and God, to reach a state of
'praise' where one's individual will and limitations are in line with the historical reading of a mysterious sense of meaning. The latter escapes us.
Through the grace of the Divine, everything may come together and work
towards the ultimate good of those who dedicate themselves completely to
it. Ignatian spirituality is eloquent on the subject: 'Act as though everything
depends on us, and at the same time pray and praise as though everything
depends on God.'

All these elements are aspects of the chaos and disorder in which the
manager generally develops. He can only come to terms with this chaos by
reframing it within a meaning, for which he becomes the carrier through his
vision. This organisational and individual meaning is made up of the values
and objectives that drive him, as we have already seen in the chapters on
autonomy and of the levels of meaning within a profoundly existential and
spiritual background that is ever present even if it is repressed or simply not
yet identified.

The manager, the carrier of meaning both for himself and for those that
he manages can be OK and see his actions move on from the absurdity of
chaos to a future of creation, or rather co-creation, with others and with
what lies at the heart of his spirituality (God being alive within him and in
communion with humanity, if he is a believer) (see Figure 7.10).

CHAPTER 8

Growth

Summary

The growth of the organisation occurs within the economic world, the realm of wealth creation. It is a complex world conditioned by geopolitics, society and technology.

At first sight, it seems that its ultimate aim is only profit. Although profit is an element, it cannot be dissociated from the added value of technological capitalisation and above all the development of human beings. The creation of wealth is not an end in itself, but is located within the other two planes of growth, namely the development of people and the development of meaning.

It is the aim of the manager and his coach to establish a coherence for these three planes of growth.

The external map for the creation of wealth, most frequently the only one to provide the values for an institutional project, is ambiguous and not in itself sufficient (see Figure 8.1a).

- It is ambiguous because it may, by itself, be dehumanising if it favours the organisation over the individual.

- It may be ambiguous in relation to itself because the production of assets or wealth is only of value depending on its ultimate use and not of itself. The best technology may turn out to be contrary to man's interests (nuclear, scientific, etc.).

Economic growth can be dehumanising and result in the exploitation of people (the North–South question). It may take four aspects, one of which (degeneration) is fundamentally negative.

Degeneration

This is often the fate of overworked managers, who are victims of stress, external pressures to succeed or their own internal psychological stakes that

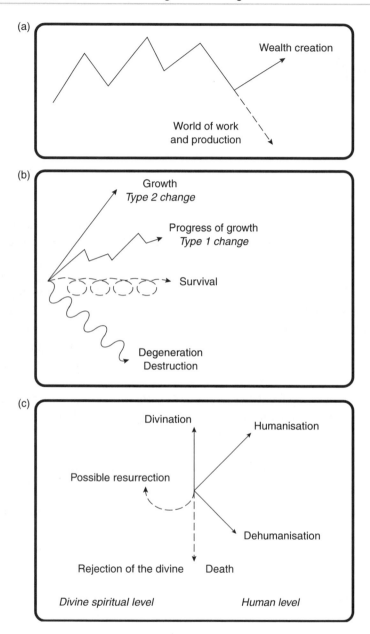

Figure 8.1 Different planes of growth

lead to heart attacks, addictive dependency (tranquillisers, alcohol, tobacco, bad eating habits) or to commitment to work as if it were a drug (workaholics).

One aspect of coaching is to help managers free themselves from such attitudes and learn to manage their own stress and time in order to avoid such pitfalls.

Survival

People are enclosed in a plan for life that is largely subconscious, having been pre-programmed throughout their lives by their educators, thus preventing them from making the best choices. In Transactional Analysis (TA), this is called 'life scenarios'.

Progress

This reflected in the so-called systemic 'type 1' change. These people are very active and apparently change their behaviour, although the fundamental choices in life (beliefs, basic protections, somatisations, emotions, memories, etc.) have not been altered. The person only changes externally but the underlying structure remains the same. It is simply progress.

Change

This is reflected in the 'type 2' systemic change. The person has basically brought his types of degeneracy under control, has refocused his life, has grieved and made choices, has found a meaning to his life and realigned his life in line with those very values that give his life its meaning.

At the heart of this person, hidden and mysterious, lies the plane of existential, spiritual and confessional meaning.

For convenience, Figure 8.1 presents the situation from the Christian point of view. We should also recall the other spiritual routes:

- humanist (agnostic, atheist, open-minded and syncretist);
- pagan (non-Judaeo-Christian);
- esoteric (holding knowledge to be the means by which man fulfils himself);
- monistic and ascetic (like the main Eastern movements);
- biblical (Jewish, Islamic, Christian, directed towards saintliness, that is, accepting the grace of God, the creator who deifies what man has humanised, and as a consequence his work that becomes a co-creation).

Since the different spiritual pathways are present consciously or unconsciously at the heart of everyone's ultimate aims, the economic construction of the organisation can only remove its fundamental ambiguity by placing itself in a strong position in relation to this plane (see Figure 8.2).

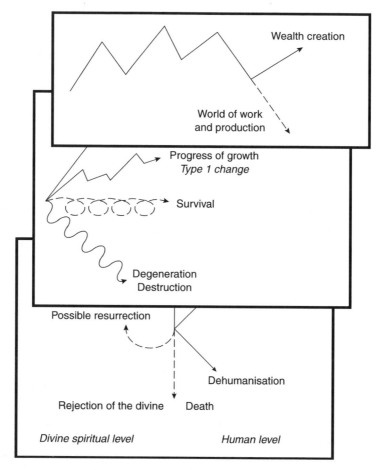

Figure 8.2   Relationship between the three planes of growth

In conclusion, it seems to me that the manager can only be a carrier of meaning to the extent that he integrates these three planes, namely wealth creation, psychological development and development of meaning.

CHAPTER 9

Change

It is a long way from perception to hearing, from hearing to understanding, from understanding to interiorising, from interiorising to conviction, from conviction to commitment, from commitment to conversion.

Summary

Throughout the course of this book, we have already shared thoughts on change. For the work of coaching and team building to achieve its aims, it is necessary to understand that most of the time change is rarely linear but systemic; it is also complex and cyclical, and includes griefs and breakdowns as well as an element of paradox.

We have already referred to several essential aspects of the management of change for an individual or for a team. The concepts of breakdown and grieving that we have seen in the development of autonomy, and the generally non-linear, but rather systemic, circular and cyclical process that change involves.

We shall examine four concepts that relate to change.

Type 1 and Type 2 Changes

By type 1, we refer to progress or functional change, that is, the modification of one or more elements within the system that it remains unchanged. For example, an alcoholic stops drinking through a voluntary attitude. But his psychological structure remains the same; he has become a dried-out alcoholic. The family sees its schizophrenic member become 'cured', but the family has not changed. The symptom is only temporarily suppressed.

By type 2, we refer to change, possibly modest but radical, that involves the implementation of a change in the system itself in its structure and in the interactions of its elements. It presupposes a new representation of reality.

In this case, the alcoholic has not only stopped drinking, but also abandoned and rearranged his beliefs, his parental programmes, decisions taken in the past and baggage wished on by his parents, and so on. The family has analysed its defence mechanisms based around the scapegoat who revealed the symptom. It has accepted its relational problems and has changed its myths and beliefs.

Roles of Speaking and Listening: The Need to Develop and Integrate

The actions of coaching and team building, as we have seen, offer the means for protection, permission and power in the management of changes.

The key aspect of the process lies in the possibility offered to those, both individuals and teams, who must experience the change, the stress and the frustration that result from it, to have the space, time and a place to speak about it. When supported and accompanied, they can then express all or part of their resistance to the change, whether conscious or unconscious, because they have the means for:

- an explanation;

- a repairing;

- a development, especially in the grieving processes;

- an implementation;

- a co-operation;

- a development of identity;
all being necessary for true change.

Institutional managers who are locked into mechanical and linear thought, in a hierarchical or numbers dominated culture, can only understand and manage effectively the change made necessary by network structures, and the fundamental paradoxes within them, when they have acquired in one way or another these indispensable cultural referents which this book sets out to explain.

The Scenario System According to Erskine and Zalcman[1]

Each element of the system, if it is altered, may alter the whole, represented by a series of gears. However, a single element that resists being altered

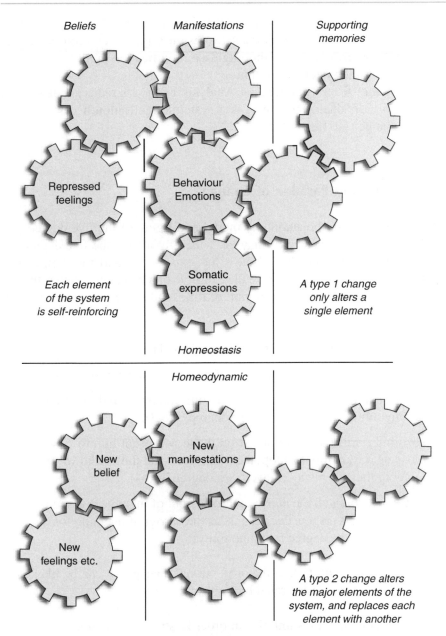

Figure 9.1 Systemic change (based on the scenario system
of Erskine and Zalcman)

may, on its own, paralyse progress of the whole gear train. So, in order to escape homeostasis, it is important to design a type 2 cultural change to implement progressively and thoroughly a modification of all the elements that make up the system and culture.

This model from Transactional Analysis (TA), a simple synthesis that applies to individuals and teams, is a systemic realisation necessary for a type 2 change (see Figure 9.1).

Complexity and Paradox of Change

If we refer back to the autonomy model and figure of the five degrees, an action of change, whatever it may be, generally affects the five degrees of autonomy at the same time. Hence the complexity and the paradoxical dimension of this change. To take the example of a manager who has to conduct a meeting in a very short period of time, and sometimes even simultaneously, he must:

- affirm his presence (move from degree 0 to 1);

- stop clashing with the participants of meetings (move from degree 1 to 2);

- experience the frustration of abandoning his own rhythm and adjust to the rhythm of others (move from degree 2 to 3);

- absorb the frustration coming from those who want him to be directive, those who want him to adopt their approach and those who would prefer to act in their own way (move from degree 3 to 4);

- as well as doing all the above, not lose sight of the objectives and values for which he is responsible, that is, as the carrier of meaning for his team (focusing on the degree 5 of autonomy).

This is the difficult task of the professional manager. It can be likened to a muscular action, as illustrated by Figure 9.2.

1. He must contract his muscles in order to strengthen them;

2. He must at the same time release his hold (by breaking contact);

3. He must allow his muscles to stretch as though he needed to stretch (by listening to others and adapting to them);

4. He must relax despite the considerable tension that is apparent;

1: Contracting muscle
2: Release hold
3: Stretch
4: Relax
5: Accepting the pain of a slight
   defocusing of oneself in return for
   transcendental meaning

Figure 9.2 Degrees of autonomy and a muscular metaphor

5. He must accept the physical suffering and stress of a situation where he is buffeted and is not in complete control (but in which he finds meaning).

CHAPTER 10

Consensus

You will see that you will be in complete agreement with my definition of consensus. (An anonymous CEO)

Summary

If we define consensus as 'agreement between the parties', we can identify three types of consensus:

- symbiotic consensus, characterised by a narrow hierarchical relationship;
- partial consensus or compromise;
- shared consensus.

Each of these three types has advantages and disadvantages.
    It is important for the managers, potentially in their conception of their identity and their power, to be in a position to implement the form of consensus appropriate to the situation and people involved.

Consensus 1 – Symbiosis or Imposition

Type 1 symbiotic consensus (see Figure 10.1), the outcome of a directive style of management, implies two States of Self (Parent and Adult) in one person, and only one State of Self in the other (Child and a very small amount of Adult), the other States of Self being excluded from the relationship.
    There are mainly two vectors present:

- *Parent* ◄► *Child*: 'do what I say' or 'I don't understand the meaning but I obey' (Child's response).
- *Adult* ◄► *Child*: 'this is how you...' or 'I don't understand but I will conform to the model you suggest' (Child's response).

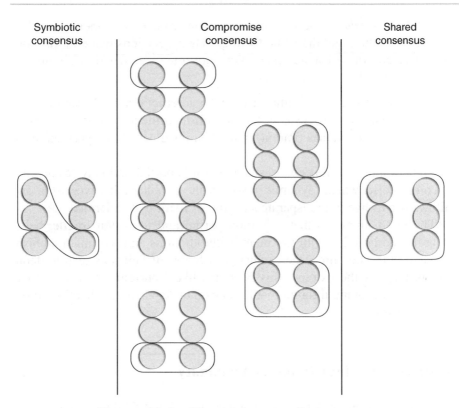

Figure 10.1   The three types of consensus

The advantage of this consensus is that it allows for rapid decision-making (convenient in a crisis) particularly between people of different cultural levels, skills and responsibilities.

The disadvantages are: little discussion, no consultation, no creative use of the three States of Self and above all, finally, if it is management's exclusive method that predominates, a dependence and infantalisation of the subordinates.

Consensus 2 – Partial Exclusion or Compromise

Consensus 2 can take varied forms:

- *Parent* ◀ ▶ *Parent*: The individuals agree on the values but they ignore the Adult (reality) and their real feelings (Child).

▪ *Adult* ◄ ► *Adult*: The individuals reason from real elements but they exclude values and their true feelings. Their decisions made in this consensus do not withstand crises. They are often sabotaged or simply not implemented.

▪ *Child* ◄ ► *Child*: The enthusiasts make an emotionally-driven decision (Child) but this consensus does not withstand the test of objective reality (Adult) and values (Parent). One then imagines all the permutations.

The advantage of this consensus is that it is partial and may result from a compromise whose dynamic resolves the problem. It saves time and allows one to live with disparate staff too difficult to standardise.

The disadvantage is that it is only partial and too often fragile, being volatile and branded with too many contradictions and too much ambivalence. At the same time, the exclusion of States of Self may lead to dehumanisation. At the extreme this becomes like Courteline or even worse, Kafka, after moving through totalitarianism or legalistic applications close to the absurd.

Consensus 3 – Integration or Unanimity

Consensus 3 (Parent Adult Child ◄ ► Parent Adult Child) belongs to the multicellular cultures or the so-called network culture. It is what is found in quality circles, creativity groups or the most successful teams. It is what mobilises all aspects of those concerned.

Decisions made therefore have a better chance of being rapidly implemented. It is what surprises us Westerners most about the Japanese. They spend a long time reaching a decision. But once it is taken, it is implemented very quickly and with no obstacles, hence the rapid global response and increased profitability. It is also the most attractive consensus for the persons involved and the most suitable to ensure their growth in the long run. For the managers, it is the most preferable one to go for, both psychologically and operationally. Failing this, the managers run the risk of being marginalised by new generations and people who, having experienced this consensus, cannot go back. Furthermore, he who can do the most can also do the least.

However, its disadvantage lies in the fact that it requires similar levels of competence, culture and responsibility in the partners and in every case very long periods of consultation or inter-reaction. It is costly, long, difficult to implement and is therefore clearly not the best solution in an emergency, or where there is too great an inequality between the partners.

In the work of coaching and team building, three points should be observed:

1. Aim to make the team members, in the long run, capable of integrative consensus suited to the culture of the network.

2. Depending on the development of the people and the situation (situational management), accept to adopt one of the three forms of consensus as being the most appropriate.

3. Be ready to manage and overcome the contradictions felt by those who, because they have not yet completed the educational process, see the combination of observations 1 and 2 as a 'manipulation', with remarks such as: 'What do you mean? We are told to express ourselves, participate, etc., and then we suddenly find arbitrary decisions thrust upon us! How do you expect us to believe you?'

CHAPTER 11

Company Cultures[1]

Summary

In every organisation, we find, with varying degrees of development, the following three types of culture:

- Taylorian;
- matrix;
- networking or multicellular.

The perception of these three cultures and their consequences in the managerial function are often misunderstood, leading to great confusion.

Managers have much to gain from identifying them, managing them in an integrated way and preparing and training themselves for the radical changes that they imply in the individual development of managerial identities (DMI).

Types of Company[2]

Every organisation in fact includes more or less the components as shown in Figure 11.1, at one and the same time and to varying degrees which causes the manager to experience ambiguities and paradoxes that are often very difficult to accept. These paradoxes presuppose a cultural maturity that is rarely completely developed.

Sometimes this situation becomes unbearable because of the associated confusion, because the manager does not always posses the means or the competence to understand these contradictions. He thus suffers from second-degree frustration. Apart from the frustration of the situation, he has the frustration of not being able to talk about it and conceptualise it clearly.

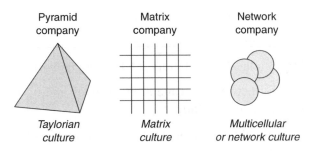

Figure 11.1 Three company cultures

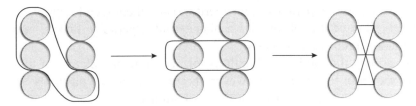

Figure 11.2 Management style

In every reasonably developed company, we therefore find three types of organisation and cultures that flow from them:

- the pyramid company with a Taylorian culture;
- the company organised as a matrix;
- the network company, with the resulting multicellular culture.

As Figure 11.2 shows, for these cultures there are the corresponding types of relationship and consensus that we have already examined. There are three major consequences to be drawn from this situation.

Associated Management Styles

The appropriate management style for each of these cultures is:

- symbiotic for the Taylorian company;
- variable in the matrix culture;
- interactive in the networking company where it operates much more in relationships characterised by personal intuition.

The method control and the actual managerial experience that result from them depend:

- on a unique hierarchical and arbitrary relationship in the Taylorian culture;

- on the ambiguity between two hierarchical lines and on conformity to procedures in the matrix culture;

- on the multiplicity of interpersonal relationships in the networked culture (see Figure 11.3).

Most of the time in a complex organisation, the person understands the three managerial experiences by superimposing them (see Figure 7.8) and the definition of the job implies a managerial experience that is as paradoxical as Figure 11.4 suggests.

Describing the job is as difficult as forming a mental picture of the diagram shown in Figure 11.5. However, the manager must constantly accept the ambiguities and paradoxes of these situations.

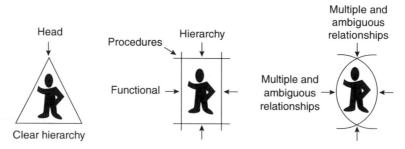

Figure 11.3   Actual managerial experience belonging to each culture

Figure 11.4   Actual experience: Complexity and paradox

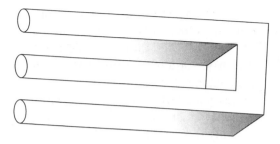

Figure 11.5   Paradoxical drawing, a metaphor
for a 'clear' description of the job

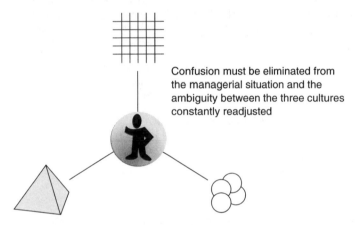

Confusion must be eliminated from
the managerial situation and the
ambiguity between the three cultures
constantly readjusted

Figure 11.6   Equilibrium and tensions between the three cultures

The manager must accept the tension between the three poles represented by the Taylorian job description (defined by the arbitrary power of a boss), the matrix job description (defined by procedures and standardisation) and the network job description (defined by the persons themselves in an entre-preneurial spirit and by interpersonal regulations). Each of these three poles brings an indispensable richness to the company. If it locks itself into one of these, it runs the risk of failing:

■ in the Taylorian case through the lack of individual autonomy;

■ in the matrix case through progressive inadequacy of procedures and people failing to assume their responsibilities;

■ in the network case through disorganisation and general mayhem (see Figure 11.6).

It is important for the managers to develop as complete people capable of interdependence and therefore to accept delegation and apply it to others. For this they must not be locked into a symbiotic style of management, but in the longer term strive for a management style defined so far as possible by interpersonal contracts (see Figure 11.7).

These three consensuses are OK in regard to the situation of the persons and the culture. The third is that which requires a more significant development of cultural identity (see Figure 11.8).

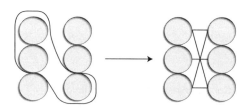

The management style evolves towards the network model. Managers who are not able to handle this style are condemned to be excluded, otherwise their company will not survive; or they remain within the limits that their own personality imposes on the development of their team

Figure 11.7   Necessary evolution of management styles

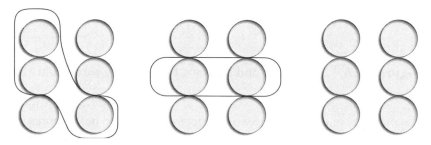

Figure 11.8   Permanent cohabitation of the three consensuses.
The manager experiences these three poles concurrently.
They must be maintained or the company may fail.

PART III

The Coach's Performance Indicators

In this part we shall present a number of concepts and models that may be used equally well in individual coaching or team-building situations. They thus represent the central theme common to both approaches.

CHAPTER 12

Development of Integrated Identities

In Part I, Chapter 2 we described the content of each identity level. We will not be reviewing it again (see Figure 2.3). Here we simply recall that these five aspects, basic understandings or identity levels are inseparable from one another. When the coach listens to a manager, it is not just someone in his office; it involves a complete systemic and interactive entity that has to be taken into account. It is a person who is:

- in a relationship with his job,

- in a relationship with his team(s), for every manager belongs to several teams. This team is itself conditioned by

- its relationship to the company, taking into account all the intermediate levels (services, departments, divisions, subsidiaries). Again, the company itself is

- in a relationship with its environment,

- its sector of activity, and so on.

The coach must constantly monitor what is significant in each of these reality levels and how to focus on one aspect or another.

CHAPTER 13

A Model for Action

It is a long road from understanding a need to expressing a clear request.

Summary

It is not enough to intervene (strike it with a hammer); it is indispensable, as a preliminary, and permanently throughout the period of coaching, to manage the parameters of the coach–champion client relationship (knowing *where* to strike it with a hammer).

Before intervening, at least four elements must be clarified:

- a definition of the real;
- identification of the problem;
- identification of needs;
- clarification of the request;
- drawing up a minimum contract.

If this procedure is not carried out at the start, the coach's position risks being 'off target'.

Before any intervention, the coach owes it to himself to verify a number of preliminaries. For a better understanding of the attitude required, we quote Eric Berne's anecdote from his introduction to his book on organisations.[1]

It runs as follows. A plumber called to repair a boiler arrives with his tools. After checking over the pipework and the machine, he takes a hammer from his toolbox strikes the boiler at a particular spot and, as though by magic, the boiler starts up. Amazed, the customer exclaims:

'Well done, how did you manage that? What a marvellous result! What do I owe you?'
The plumber replies: '100 dollars.'

The customer replies, shocked: '100 dollars for hitting it with a hammer?'
'Yes', answers the plumber.
'I need an invoice for this', says the customer.
'No problem, here it is.' The plumber writes out the invoice. On line one he puts: 'Knowing where to strike with the hammer comes to $99'; followed by: 'Hammer blow $1. Total $100.'

This story is a good illustration of the importance of initial and continual thought that needs to be given in any intervention.

It involves the following:

- management of the complexity of integrated identities, as noted in the previous chapter;

- taking into account a certain number of parameters that will condition the approach to the resolution of the problem;

- everything that goes into creating the relationship between the problem and the person or team that deals with it;

- the relationship with the coach.

We shall see in the following chapter that we can regroup these parameters into a set of 15 categories. In the current chapter we look at a shortcut in four or five elements about which the coach has much to gain from being clear, whether implicitly or explicitly, before intervening (the hammer blow).

Few people in their professional life, where they have constantly to manage a relationship (telephone, individual interview or conducting a meeting, when they are consulted about an action to be decided upon), hold this process consciously and clearly in their minds. For consultants, it is especially damaging to plunge too quickly into replies and suggestions for action.

Paradoxically, when a relatively short interview is involved, it is sometimes even more necessary to give time to forethought rather than plunge in blindly. It may even prove appropriate in a 20-minute interview to spend 10 or 15 minutes on the preliminary questions, as indicated in Figure 13.1, before coming to the option, and the hammer blow. As we shall see later, the process between the coach and the client is not strictly linear, but for the convenience of presentation, we first adopt a sequential approach.

Identification of the Real

It is essential to obtain replies to the simple questions listed in Figure 13.1. The more confused the situation for the client, the more difficult it is for

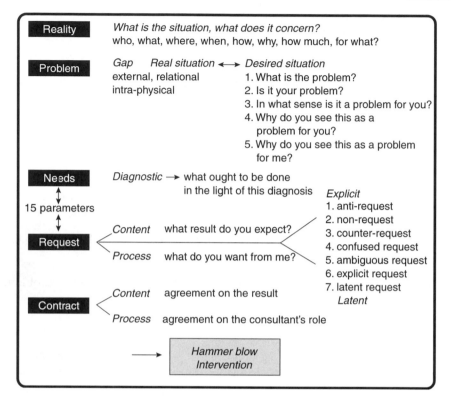

Figure 13.1   A model for action

him to concentrate on a clear description of the reality. He finds it difficult to offer concrete and indisputable facts, and at the same time, to talk at the required 'level of abstraction' (according to the general semantics). The client often has the tendency to lose himself in detail, to jump from one topic to another and make free associations. The coach's task is to pose sufficiently specific questions, and to adopt an attitude of flexible attention in which he combines the following elements:

- keeping silent;

- synchronising, that is, adapting to the client's behaviour (adjusting posture, breathing rhythm, eye contact, etc.);

- open or closed questions according to the circumstances;

- questions for clarification (what do you mean by ...?);

- recapitulation ('if I understand correctly, you said ...');

- sympathy with feelings (for example: 'when you talk about that, I can see that it is a subject dear to your heart').

Identification of the Problem

We find the five relevant questions outlined in Figure 13.1. This problem is defined as the gap between the desired situation and the real situation.

Distinguishing this gap comes after the stage of identifying the reality and represents a distinctly different stage from the preceding one.

It is also appropriate to identify through all this questioning whether the problem is an object external to the persons (an objective problem), a relational problem, or an intra-physical problem. That is to say, the connection between the relationship of the person with this problem, bearing in mind that all three may exist at the same time.

Needs, Diagnostic and Parameters

It is clear that the progressive identification of the reality and of the problem permit the coach to come quickly to a diagnosis and a formulation of hypotheses as to the needs of the person before him. The coach, in his head, can formulate diagnoses, identify needs and create intervention plans. Generally, it is preferable not to air this prematurely with the champion, either because of the stage of development reached, or because of the situation. It is often better to move on to the next stage.

Furthermore, the coach may already be tempted to suggest solutions or options. For this reason too it is important not to do this, but to move to the next stage.

Identification of the Request

As Figure 13.1 shows, the request is based on the following two pairs:

1. content/process
2. explicit/implicit or latent

Content/Process

Two questions, often wrongly combined, need to be asked:

- 'What do you expect to be the outcome of this interview?' (question on content);
- 'What do you expect from me?' (question on the process).

Explicit/Implicit or Latent

We note that the gap between what is explicit and what is latent is subject
to constant change, and that as soon as this pair no longer exists, it is quite
possible that a gap will appear at another level. The whole skill of the coach
lies in pinpointing the position of his interventions in the ambiguous space
between these two poles. Should he concentrate strictly on the explicit
request, or will he be able to bring forth the latent request that he perceives
intuitively?

We also note that the request may take on many shapes or forms:

- *The anti-request*: by this we mean a completely contradictory request.
  For example, it may be the request of:
  - someone who is forced to attend a course against his will;
  - someone who is ordered by his superior to approach a consultant and
    whose only wish is for the process to fail;
  - a manager who approaches a consultant with the more or less con-
    scious wish that his intervention or diagnosis will not be suitable,
    which will give him the advantage of proving that the consultant is no
    good, and give him the excuse of not feeling guilty for having not
    resolved the problem.

- *The non-request*: this is the position of the person who is 'not against'
  the request but has no real motivation. For example: 'I have approached
  you because it was suggested that I should do so, but I am not very convinced that it will do any good, because I am not sure that there really is
  a problem, but since I was told to see you, I have called you in ...'

- *The counter-request*: this form of problem is especially subtle and frustrating for the coach. He is faced with someone who is unable to state his
  request, because he has difficulty explaining himself. It therefore falls to
  the coach to put it into words for him.

  To each suggestion from the coach he responds with: 'no, it is not
  quite that, I think that ...'. The coach must understand that this process,
  however frustrating, is necessary for the champion, and is not directed
  against him. It is simply the champion's way of arriving at his own
  request, with the coach's help.

- *The confused request*: this is often the position of someone who is overcome by a problem and who is unable to put it into words, while in a
  psychological relationship with himself that is unclear.

■ *The ambivalent or paradoxical request*: this is a situation where the person wants one thing and its opposite. For example: 'Coach, help me to sort matters out by myself.'

■ *The explicit request*: in contrast to the latent request, the explicit request is often the first formulation put by the client to the coach, and it very often conceals other levels of request that can only emerge after a very specific description of the reality, after identification of the problem and consideration of the needs.

■ *The latent request*: this involves the preconscious or unconscious level of request (that will only emerge with time), a clarification of the three previous items (reality, problem, need) and an increasingly conscious position of the client in his relationship with himself and with the coach.

The Contract

Like the request, the contract should be formulated in the content/process connection, the content comprising an agreement on the result, and the process an agreement about the role of the consultant.

It is very important that the coach does not identify contract and request, and that once the request is clarified, he possesses sufficient 'ontological security' to refuse certain elements of the request:

■ either when the content is not within his competency or the time available to him;

■ or because the nature of the relationship that is requested of him appears 'dangerous' (for example, the role of Saviour). This 'ontological security' may be weakened if the consultant is a beginner, or if this is the first contact with the client and the client remains very confused or ambivalent, and the coach finds himself in the position of 'selling himself'.

The Hammer Blow, Intervention

It requires the five preceding points to be satisfied and clarified by the coach before the moment becomes ripe for intervention to be effective.

We have presented this procedure in a linear fashion. The reality of a coaching relationship presupposes that the coach is continually questioning himself about these five or six topics, and is considering them permanently.

For example, it would be quite normal for the coach to obtain the following after a two-minute discussion:

- a short and abstract description of the situation;
- an equally brief description of the problem;
- a formulation of the request;
- a contract.

After two minutes, the client would begin an account lasting 10 minutes describing the reality of the situation, followed by a discussion with the coach about the definition of the problem. There would then follow an exchange involving various kinds of interaction during which the client would be encouraged to rethink his view of the problem, work out his own solutions or accept the options put forward by the consultant (see Figure 13.2).

The process might be carried out several times, the first of which, lasting less than two minutes, could take the following form:

Client: 'I wanted us to meet, because since I have taken on this job I find that I have difficulties with several of my colleagues.'
Coach: 'Is that so?'
Client: 'The problem is that several of them are complaining that their status ought to be reassessed following our reorganisation ... .'
Coach: 'How much time do we have?'

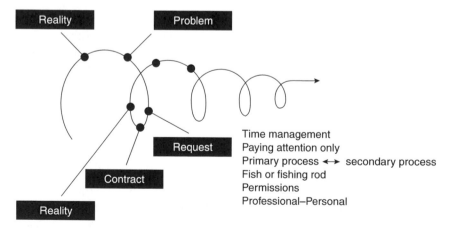

Figure 13.2   A model for action. Spiral of options suggested by the consultant.

Client: 'I thought we might have an hour and a half, but now I have been summoned to a meeting, so we only have thirty minutes.'

Coach: 'That's a bit short. What exactly are you wanting to obtain from this interview (process request) since thirty minutes on this topic seems to me rather a short time to resolve this problem today?'

Client: 'That's true, but if you could just hear what I have to say and give me a few ideas to think about, this would allow me to make some progress. If need be, we could meet again.'

Coach: 'Alright, you tell me something about it and I agree to give you some feedback and perhaps some options (establishing a contract). Could you tell me a bit more about your colleagues and what it is that is causing you problems?'

Here we see a short introduction to the interview that ensures that:

- both coach and client will not find themselves too surprised when the 30 minutes are up;

- the client will not be frustrated through having exaggerated expectations in relation to the conditions of their exchange;

- the coach will avoid being in a symbiotic relationship with the client, at the risk of embarking on a pernicious game of wanting to 'save' his client or wanting to 'prove' that he is competent, and providing a solution at all costs within this short period of time.

Some Additional Remarks

Time Management

Quite often the coach has to manage his time by 'playing the accordion', that is, he has to be trained to handle the same type of problem, in 10 minutes, 30 minutes or an hour, and so on, presupposing on his part great flexibility of thinking and a high level of concentration, particularly when the interviews are cut short or interrupted by unexpected telephone calls that the client is unable to refuse.

Paying Attention

Often just listening is enough. Sometimes the coach misjudges the client's ability to come up with his own solutions, and does not realise that one of the chief supports that he can bring to his client is to offer him, through his presence and through his time (for which the client is paying) a favourable opportunity and moment for productive thinking. Often, the mere active attention and presence of the coach allows the champion client to move from a primary process to a secondary process, that is, to allow his own latent solutions to emerge.

Options or Other Things

Apart from options or advice on courses of actions, the coach will gain much from recognising whether his client simply needs simple feedback, protection (mistakes to be avoided) and permissions (encouragement to take this or that initiative).

Fish or Fishing Rod

We shall see later how the coach has to manage the constant ambiguity of knowing whether he should provide his client with a fish or a fishing rod, while being aware that it is sometimes appropriate to offer a little of both.

Professional–Personal

The coach's intervention is always rooted in a level of complexity and ambiguity, between the integrated levels of identity already described, and with which he must be comfortable. His positive attitude is in itself a very important permission.

CHAPTER 14

The Fifteen Parameters

If it costs $100 for the hammer blow, $99 is for knowing where to strike.
(By Eric Berne)

Summary

The 'Model for Action' grid showed a way of combining the diagnosis (reality, problem, need), the request and the contract, before any intervention. This simple grid has the advantage of being extremely operational.

Experience with conducting thousands of interviews for coaching, meetings and the supervision of support professionals (consultants and therapists), has led me to consider at least fifteen parameters that represent as many lights on the coach's control panel. Only one of these needs to flash red for the coach to realise that he would be well advised to switch his intervention from the content of the current interview or meeting to the 'faltering' parameter.

Taking into account the different theoretical and conceptual elements and organising the parameters are the substance of the coach's strategy. Depending on how the situation evolves and on the most appropriate tactic, he can then optimise his interventions. What is most important is not the hammer blow itself, but knowing where and when to strike.

From the author's experience as a consultant, and even more as a supervisor and therapist, it emerged that the elements of the model-for-action grid were far from sufficient. In fact, it became apparent that the situation for the client in his relationship with the consultant took the form of a blind alley. The reason for this situation was that the consultant had not taken advance precautions with regard to a number of parameters.

In the author's view there are at least fifteen parameters, and as in the previous chapter, they can be viewed in the linear order in which we shall present them, while recalling that they are interactive and partially and mutually inclusive. They are like so many dials on the coach's dashboard, to borrow a driving metaphor. The coach drives his vehicle, he watches the road,

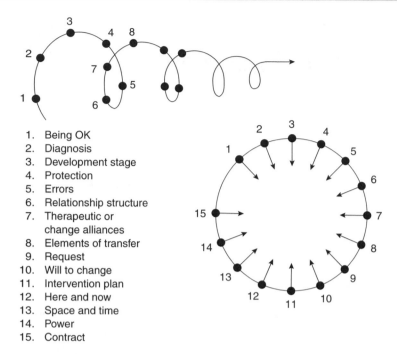

1. Being OK
2. Diagnosis
3. Development stage
4. Protection
5. Errors
6. Relationship structure
7. Therapeutic or change alliances
8. Elements of transfer
9. Request
10. Will to change
11. Intervention plan
12. Here and now
13. Space and time
14. Power
15. Contract

Figure 14.1   The fifteen parameters in time

but he also keeps an eye on the dashboard and the rear mirror. If he sees a red light he knows it is best to stop before he runs out of fuel or something else happens that might cause damage and interrupt the journey. Figures 14.1 and 14.2 show these fifteen parameters.

Being OK

This means accepting oneself, and others, accepting the situation, not as something that cannot be transformed, but as a series of meaningful elements to which one must adjust, that form part of current reality, and not tormenting oneself about how the situation could be different.

In fact it amounts to a whole philosophy of life:

- that is also rooted in a stoical attitude of handling one's frustration;

- that includes a mixture of acceptance, forgiving, humour, patience, capacity for grieving and handling emotions;

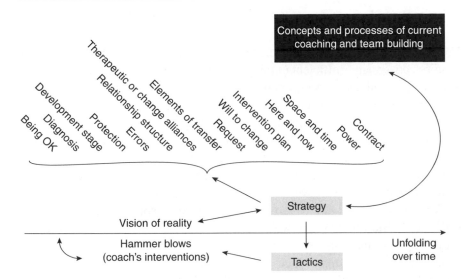

Figure 14.2 The fifteen parameters on the dashboard/control panel

- that also, as we have seen with chaos management, that is only bearable, beyond the attitude of stoicism, as long as we find a meaning in our lives, that of others and in the situation which appears to have been imposed on us.

Transactional analysts who consider 'OKness' to be a constitutive value of the therapeutic approach and a fundamental belief in the philosophy of change in people and structures, remain somewhat vague as to its significance. Do we say that man is good and adopt Rousseau's position? Do we regard work towards change as a readaptation and reinsertion of people into the political, social and economic system? The debate remains open. For us, transactionalists, it boils down to a few simple principles that are the keys to action. Being OK means being capable of change and contributing to that change:

Being OK is being capable of taking responsibility for one's earlier decisions, analysing them, repairing the damage and making new decisions. It means re-deciding about our lives, because we had earlier decided otherwise.

Being OK is believing that we can change our behaviour without necessarily having understood and analysed everything.

Being OK means considering that every situation, whether apparently positive or not, is an opportunity for growth.

Being OK is believing that simple language and a contractual relationship with those being assisted are possible and that both are factors leading towards autonomy and liberation for all.

Being OK, is First Being OK in Relation to Oneself

For the coach, as for the manager, this fact is by no means clear and it first requires possessing sufficient ontological security. It means knowing oneself sufficiently, and accepting oneself as such in order not to be destabilised at any given moment. It means regarding oneself as someone worthy of being fundamentally and unconditionally loved, despite our obvious limitations, despite the wrongs we may have done and the suffering we may have caused.

At the extreme, this means being ready to die having come to terms with the unavoidable paradox, namely that to be well grounded in the here and now presupposes that I have accepted the issue of death.

We could take this thought further and on to a spiritual perspective in order to define this OKness with regard to our relationship with God. We will simply remain at the human level and conclude the debate with the transactionalist position, which states that I am OK because I have within me sufficient strength for healing, growth and love to take ownership of my freedom and responsibility for my growth.

The consequences of this position on the professional plane are considerable, because they indicate that I am no longer dependent on my professional success in order to accept myself and come to terms with myself unconditionally.

This is being in a 'winning' position, according to Berne, that is, I know what I am doing if I 'lose'.

The fact of being OK also assumes that I take my professional competence in account, but I do not amalgamate the two individual and professional levels.

What is essential for me is to recognise myself as a Prince or a champion while accepting the negative part of myself (the 'frog' part), by acknowledging my own limitations, my ambiguity, my past and so on.

The Second Aspect of OKness Lies in the Fact of Being OK in Relation to Others

That is, I accept another person along with his unavoidable ambiguity, especially in the context of a professional relationship. I accept his specificity of age, sex, qualifications and identity. I cannot like everyone, but I must be capable of identifying the moment when I am not OK with someone to the point where the professional relationship with this person could run the risk of being compromised.

It is important to be OK with the organisations in which I intervene, and to identify the limitations and the type of clients whose values or identity are such that I would not truly be able to collaborate with them, rather like a barrister who could not defend just any cause.

To be OK in relation to others is also to be capable of saying no to a client without holding anything against him, to be able to face the failure of this or that action without feeling like a victim.

This also means having to experience grieving. The professional relationship that I have with my clients excludes certain confusions or a certain degree of intimacy, or when it comes to therapeutic work, if I intervene in a company. This implies clarifying one's relationship to power and money.

Being OK with Regard to Money

One very important aspect of the role of money is that it serves as a litmus test of reality. In the relationship (individual or institutional) between coach and client, exchanging money for the service provided by the coach allows analysis of whether the relationship is correct and healthy, or whether it is a symbiotic relationship that might give rise to the appearance of 'game playing', where the partners risk of entering the 'drama triangle'* that includes the roles of persecutor, saviour and victim. This is construed on the basis of the amount of the fee and from whether the time is invoiced or not.

The fee may be undervalued, implying that the coach is devaluing himself and therefore does not consider himself to be OK, either at the personal level (lack of ontological security) or at the professional level, that is, the coach has not found his managerial identity.

Once again, it is useful to recall the extent of this managerial identity (Figure 14.3), and this may be analysed along four axes:

1. *Internal recognition*: it may be that the person has not reached a stage where he recognises himself. He lacks confidence, feels inadequate or has insufficient objective information.

2. *External recognition*: the person has not received from the outside enough signs of recognition. He has no clients, no recognition from his colleagues and peers, he has had failures, his reputation is attacked in the press or there are rumours.

3. *The 'me-skin' (to borrow the term from Didier Anzieux again, 'Moi-Peau')*: this is the wrapper that goes to make up his identity, represented by his qualifications, his professional affiliation, the legal form of his

* See Glossary.

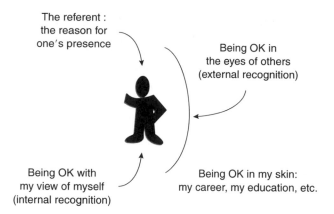

The referent :
the reason for
one's presence

Being OK in
the eyes of others
(external recognition)

Being OK with
my view of myself
(internal recognition)

Being OK in my skin:
my career, my education, etc.

Figure 14.3   The four components of identity

professional address, his letterhead, his legal registration details
(Chamber of Commerce, registration number as trainer, etc.).

4. *Referents*: the different elements that make up a 'transcendental' dimen-
    sion specific to a person: his beliefs, his representation of the world and
    his place in the world, his values, all of which usually revolves around
    real people or myths that give meaning to his life. These will be the
    introjected parental figures (stemming from his family group or his
    intellectual, philosophical, spiritual or religious development). These
    elements provide the person with a sense of order within the absolute
    in regard to the contingent dimension of his existence. The strength and
    stability of these referents are necessary in the face of the first three
    axes, which are often upset by events. Consequently, the loss of one's
    job, an illness or serious accident, the loss of someone close, and so on
    or any event causing high stress will affect the 'me-skin', shake one's
    image of oneself and often the recognition of others. The degree of
    strength and stability of these referents will provide the measure of his
    ontological security.

   This group of three axes must be balanced for the person to have sufficient
ontological security and to cease being plagued by his identity problems.

   Generally, the coach needs to control his invoicing by taking account of
numerous relational parameters with his client, since it is impossible to
write down all that needs to be done in a legal contract. Does a 15-minute
telephone call require an invoice? Probably not. Does a meal taken together,
equivalent to an hour's work, merit an invoice? That is more debatable. One
needs to take into account the different elements of the commercial

approach, the mutual services rendered, the degree of partnership involved, and so on. Finding the correct boundary on either side is not easy. In every case, money acts as a good analyst of the real extent of the client's request, and of the degree of maturity of what we shall examine next, namely what we call the 'alliance for change'.

A first error is the coach's tendency to under-invoice, putting him in the position of a 'saviour' who one day will become 'victim' and then 'persecutor'. In fact, by not asking a fair price, the coach is showing that either he does not believe that the client can pay, or he is giving him a 'gift', which is apparently a way of overvaluing himself in comparison with the client. At a deeper level this probably reveals a fear that the coach is more or less conscious of, namely the risk of losing his client if he were to ask for the market price.

A second error is to over-invoice or charge too high a fee. This may be a sign of narcissism on the coach's part that sooner or later will cost him dearly. Through this very fact, he generates a symbiosis leading to a victim position on the part of his client, resulting eventually in a build-up of resentment to be avenged through criticism or even rejection, with the client taking on the role of persecutor.

Grieving

We have already seen on several occasions (autonomy, growth, OK in chaos) that managing a professional relationship, including additional commercial dimensions, implies elements of grieving necessary to being OK. This applies in particular to the coaching relationship.

1. The complex, subtle, intimate and always ambiguous dimension implied by the job of coaching presupposes on the part of the coach a high awareness and a strong resistance against any temptation to allow the professional relationship to slip on to other planes, particularly a therapeutic relationship. Coaching is not therapeutic work in the sense that, as we have seen, it involves a difference between the development of the personal identity and the development of the managerial identity. This difference taken into account by the coach leads him to clearly recognise the limitations of his client, his own and those of the relationship. He must also avoid causing his client to regress, talk about his past and become too emotionally involved. The same applies in a group setting. However, the boundary here is not always easy to identify because it is the coach's role to help people become aware of certain

things, and especially to allow a latent request to emerge up to a point. The coach must always be prudent, in order not to turn coaching into a different relationship that is too intimate, too testing or too dependent for the client.

2. In his relationship with the client, owing to the element of transfer inherent in the job, the coach may be tempted to indulge in the fantasies of supreme power, to play a guru role or have access to all the aspects of power enjoyed by the client. He may be tempted to benefit from preferential treatment granted by the company, to betray confidences, and so on. It is therefore essential for the coach to be fully aware of such temptations and that he has assessed, either from past errors or through analysis, the inevitable consequences of a non-deontological attitude to the point of making an inviolable rule for himself on the matter.

He will only have resolved his problem when he has undergone his grieving for supreme power and the associated fantasies. This generally takes a very long time and it can never be said that one no longer needs to be vigilant.

The process involves cleaning one's 'windscreen' and sometimes even one's 'spectacles'. Sometimes we have to call the relationship into question and almost permanently check that we have both feet on the ground and are sufficiently stable to lend support to our client, who has every right to be destabilised; after all, he is paying for someone to offer him protection and permissions. Being OK therefore assumes that:

- we have gone far along the path of self-awareness, on both the personal and professional planes;

- we can maintain a permanent state of challenge, along with sufficient stability.

To conclude, after acquiring sufficient security in one's professional and personal identity, managing this parameter requires verifying whether the relationship with the client is not too affected by relational or emotional problems that could contaminate all efforts of coaching and team building.

The Diagnosis

This parameter would merit complete books on its own. We shall restrict ourselves to describing a few essentials.

1. To be able to establish a diagnosis, the coach needs to possess a framework of references built on the levels of identity development that we know (PID, MID, RID, TID). That is, he must have real experience of the business world, real experience of training, real experience of therapy at least at the personal level, through work on himself and a model well proven through experience that allows him to integrate all of these factors. For example, this might be an integrated knowledge of management theories such as those of Crozier, of organisational development (Bennis, Beckhard, Schein, Argyris) or Berne theory of organisations. The reference framework is in itself of little importance. What is important is for the person to be able to locate his coaching and team-building problem in his environment and to possess alternative maps to describe the territory in which he is to intervene.

2. Apart from being rational, the diagnosis must also be:

    - the result of intuition;

    - a strong ability to evaluate the unsaid;

    - free creativity;

    - a faculty for adapting intelligently to the situation;

    - the capacity for managing ambiguous processes; that is, being able to make instinctive diagnoses and being able to improvise.

3. It is not easy to be at the same time therapist, trainer, team leader, communication consultant, organisation consultant and strategic adviser. However, a coach must know the details of each of these professions and not appear wanting in any of them. He must embrace a complex reality, taking into account these different levels of practice, lest his diagnosis suffers.

Degree of Evolution

Here it is a question of gauging in the person, group or institution the level of cultural maturity, in other words, the experience and capacity to work at its best with its coach.

- Have the participants already had an experience of this type?

- Are they ready to be challenged?

- Have they any cross-cultural experiences, and so on?

In fact, it is another way of talking about the MCE and, more specifically, if we use the model for autonomy, a way of defining where the participants are located in the spiral.

- Have they integrated models for change, communication and the work involved in a shared vision?
- Do they have experience of working with a consultant?
- Can they conceive of the frustration that must be overcome in order to manage an organisational change, and so on?

Our coaching experience tells us that it often takes several months for the participants to begin to appreciate the sophistication that this work entails, as well as the investment in a partnership that alone can facilitate a true optimisation of the respective roles of clients and coach.

Protections

This is a key concept that might be compared to the erecting of scaffolding prior to the repair of a wall. There is no question of repairing the wall before conditions of security have been created to prevent any risk of the wall falling down. The situation could be likened to mountain climbing where it would be foolish not to be roped up.

Protection involves saying 'no', that is, taking precautions, giving information, putting rules of operation in place. In short, it is a complete device to ensure that action can take place with the certainty that it will not be harmful. It is interesting to make the link between permissions and protections: permission involves saying 'yes', protection involves saying 'no'. It is important not to say 'yes, go ahead and make changes' if there are not already in place a number of 'noes' that say 'don't do that, beware of this, you are not allowed to do that'.

Let us provide some examples. It would be dangerous during a training course to invite people to express themselves freely, to expose themselves in front of others, to make them talk about their personal difficulties (that is, permissions) if one has not first put in place a rule of confidentiality between:

- the participants;
- the participants and the trainer;
- the trainer and the directors of the company (that is, protections).

If that is not done, the supposed training course runs the risk of turning into an arena for evaluation and for open exercise of power that might first harm the participants, then the trainers and finally the organisation that commissioned the intervention.

Another example of protection in a team-building operation that we, as coach, systematically put in place, is that of a 'contract of confrontation' between the team leader and the coach. If there are difficulties, or deviant or harmful behaviour from the manager towards his team, this contract allows the coach to confront the manager, either in front of the group or in private. It stipulates that the manager undertakes to accept being challenged about his behaviour. This protection allows the client–coach relationship to establish a climate of partnership and parity that prevents symbiotic relationships and games.

Here is a short story. Hartman and Narboe, in an article on catastrophic injunctions (see Actualités AT 27) tell one of the versions of the tale of Sleeping Beauty. While spinning her wool with a poisoned distaff, Beauty pricks her finger and, realising that the poison has entered her blood, she sees herself in imminent danger of death. A beautiful fairy comes to her aid and plunges her into a deep sleep that magically stops the effect of the poison. Beauty thus lies on the ground, lost in sleep. A young man passing by sees her and falls in love with her. He cannot prevent himself from kissing her. This kiss, which awakens her, removes the protection of the magic sleep. Through his wish to waken the beauty and prove his love for her, prince charming, without knowing, causes her death.

At any moment, the coach in turn runs the risk of performing this same role, another incarnation of the sorcerer's apprentice. He must therefore assess the dangers at each step he invites his client to take; he must also see to it that he does not give them permissions to change, without having previously put in place the necessary protections.

Errors

In his book, 'Principles in Group Treatment', Eric Berne coins an important aphorism by saying: 'the amateur therapist is the one who knows what must be done. The professional therapist is the one who knows what must not be done.' I believe that it is not an exaggeration to say that one can gauge the maturity of a coach by the number of errors he identifies and warns about in the support that he gives to his client. The fact is that often, in his job as team manager or internal manager of change in an organisation, the client does not properly assess the complexity and the paradoxical dimension of the actions for which he is responsible.

For example, say the manager, believing that he is doing the right thing, decides to implement a tool while the conditions for its feasibility are not in place. Say, for example, he wants to launch a project when there is no assurance of a minimum of confidence or a minimum of cohesion within the management team. In such conditions, there is a risk of the project not appearing credible and boiling down to pompous declarations that are completely belied by the behaviour of those concerned. The result will be increased frustration among the members of the organisation.

Another example is a situation in which a director organises meetings that bring together several hundred management staff, thus in a pyramid-like structure with top-down communication, in order to deliver a message suggesting greater autonomy and more participation. The message received would certainly not be the one contained in his speech, but rather that of a double bind in which he has enclosed his audience, by delivering a speech that is at odds with the communication structure employed. We could give many other examples.

Structure of the Relationship

This is a complex parameter that conditions the entire content of the intervention. It includes what is referred to as the 'business contract', namely the agreement, usually written, about the fees and objectives and the frequency and form of the meetings. Apart from the legal contract, it is also very important for the coach and his client to find a way of arranging formal and informal meetings that enable the relationship to be structured with flexibility so that:

- the coach can remain on 'strategic watch' and operate as a true partner with his client;
- each can contact the other on the spur of the moment;
- the elements such as mail, invoicing, respective secretarial work, the nature of individual and collective meetings and relationships between the different systems of the company and the coach's firm, all operate confidently within open structures.

Therapeutic Alliance or Change

By therapeutic alliance we mean a sufficiently structured relationship between the client and his coach – as an extension of the preceding parameter.

This relationship assumes that both the client and the coach mutually commit themselves to a reciprocal trust and a capacity to sustain the relationship despite the inevitable frustrations. There will be numerous setbacks, inevitable misunderstandings and some disagreements; some confrontations initiated by the coach may be difficult for the client to bear, because they imply challenges and the recognition of mistakes. Equally, of course, the consultant too may make mistakes.

We would say that there is a 'therapeutic' or 'change' alliance if both of them, through the sufficient sharing of their MCE and the personal trust that they have in each other and in the objectives of their work, are able to overcome the frustrations they are bound to encounter.

As for the coach, who is primarily responsible for the establishment of the relationship and its structure, he must pay attention to the educative and progressive dimension of the process, to prevent the client from being victim of his resistance and prematurely breaking off the relationship and the work in progress.

Once the alliance is established, the partnership is in place and the client–coach exchanges can occur, not based on dependence or counter-dependence, but through interdependence.

Elements of Transfer

In his relationship with the coach, the client (individual, group or institution) will actualise what we call as the elements of transfer. He will invest in the coach or the relationship numerous unresolved elements from the past. The coach will be seen in his fantasy as:

- the bad father or mother if the transfer is negative;

- or, the ideal father or mother, or the Saviour, expected to bring magical solutions.

1. One of the first aspects of the transfer consists in projecting figures that the client has 'introjected' and that come from the past (parental figures, educators, bosses, society figures).

2. Another aspect of the transfer is the client's projection of his own image on to the coach. He imagines the coach as all good or all bad, or as a manipulator, as having designs for power, or all kinds of peculiarities that are only his alone, such as the head of a company, for example, who trusts nobody, and imagines that the coach does not trust him.

It is not our purpose to re-explain the Freudian concept of psycho-analysis, but simply to recall the extent to which it may be present. Furthermore, one of the chief capacities of the consultant must be the way he handles his counter-transfer, that is, all the affective reactions that are activated through the client's transfer towards him.

3. Finally, we must not forget the transfer from coach to client, that is, all the forms that he will project on to the client, coming from his own introjections or from his own unconscious perception of himself. Because the coach is someone who has to take into account the numer-ous identity levels of his client, it is essential for him to have worked on himself to the point of being able to analyse:

- the client's transfer;

- his counter-transfer;

- his transfer in relation to his client.

We are including in this section an element that belongs rather to the sys-temic approach and which comes under the heading of 'the whole is in the part'. In fact, the relationship that the client establishes with his coach is an excellent means for analysis of the entire relational system experienced by the client. So, in analysing all the aspects, dysfunctions, surprises and prob-lems that he encounters with his client, the coach is able to deduce many characteristics of the 'system' that is conditioning his client.

The Request

We have discussed this element in the previous chapter (see Figure 13.1).

The Will to Change

This involves two poles:

1. The client's will to change.

2. The coach's will to change.

1. The coach must gauge the extent of his client's will to change. This parameter appears quite simple and obvious but it is not, because at any moment the coach may forget to take it into account. It is so important

that, even if all the diagnostic elements have been thoroughly examined, particularly during an audit, and all the other parameters or lights on the coach's dashboards show green, should this one alone show red, the coach must immediately stop or at least suspend his intervention in order to:

- again verify his degree of OKness;

- control any frustration to the best of his ability;

- adapt to the degree of resistance demonstrated by his client.

The question to be answered is in the establishment of whether his client's three Ego States wish to change.

It may be that the Parent of his client believes that he should change, that his Adult knows very well how to change, but his Child does not want to change. If this is the case, the problem of change becomes intra-psychical for the client and the coach must concentrate on this internal conflict between the Child and the two other Ego States.

2. The other pole for the coach to take into account is the degree of intensity of his own will to effect change in his client.

Here again it is necessary to be constantly vigilant to ensure that his personal will to change is not greater than his client's.

Plan for Intervention

This refers to the methods and stages of the coach's intervention, after completing the diagnosis and identifying the needs. It is important for the coach to estimate the required duration in order to grade each of his actions in terms of time and importance. He must also provide for an alternative strategy, and then be ready for tactical positions.

The more he has prepared a global strategy with alternatives, the better his position to improvise at each stage with a clear grasp of the situation, showing creativity, without losing sight of the general orientation.

The Here and Now

By 'here and now' we mean all the various elements that emerge in the situation which were not foreseen in the 'agenda' for the meeting, but which must be handled as a priority. Failing this, the agenda would be completely upset, even distorted, and there would be insufficient energy to be focused where it was needed.

For example, say it was planned at a meeting or interview to deal with a relational problem, but the coach and the client are interrupted by a telephone call announcing bad news. The coach will know that he must allow sufficient time, even the remainder of the interview, to deal with the effect of this bad news on the client, if this appears appropriate.

Space and Time

Aside from the content and process of the interview, the coach needs to think of how to manage the relational space that will condition the climate of the interview or meeting. It is very important not to find oneself enclosed by the arrangement of furniture in a room and to see to it that people are positioned correctly and at a distance that respects the client's space, at the same time providing for an energetic relationship between the two persons. To sit to the client's left or right is not neutral. Similarly, if a table separates them, or if they use armchairs, some simple adjustment can make all the difference. Experienced therapists as well as skilled salespeople are well aware of this.

When it comes to a gathering in a meeting room, it is also very important for the coach (especially when he is not on his home ground) to feel free to rearrange the seating to reflect the type of meeting he wants.

So far as time is concerned, it goes without saying that a 10-minute interview is not handled in the same way as one that lasts for an hour or an hour and a half. It is disturbing to note, however, that a responsible client, who often identifies with his problem, tends in a 30-minute interview to embark on an account of his situation as though he has the whole day to talk about it.

- *First comment.* This parameter involves juggling with the model-for-action grid, and in terms of timescale, if it is short, forcing the client to deal very rapidly with his description of the reality, with defining the problem, clarifying his request and establishing a mini contract in order to then come back to the reality.

- *Second comment.* The shorter the time available, the more the coach has to resort to higher levels of abstraction and shift back and forth move from the microscopic view to the panoramic view of a helicopter.

- *Third comment.* With high-level decision makers, interview length often varies quite unexpectedly. The professional coach may frequently find himself restricted to 10 minutes when initially an hour or an hour and a half had been set aside. Other circumstances requiring the coach to adapt his approach are the client's delay, not through ill will, but owing to major constraints, such as an unexpected call from someone 3000 miles away. There are certain events such as these that force the coach to integrate this parameter into his relationship with his client on a continual basis.

Power

In our opinion, the parameter of power cannot be dissociated from that of identity, as we saw in the chapter on the nine levels of meaning. However, the coach does still need to keep it under permanent consideration, and in a way that prevents his ever having to threaten his client's power in their relationship, whether voluntarily or not. At the same time, he must guard against ever allowing himself to be trapped by his own power.

We should note that if the relationship polarises into a power game, it is an indication that other levels of meaning in the relationship have not been properly resolved:

- the two protagonists have not correctly adjusted their MCEs;
- the contract has not yet been clarified;
- psychological elements (fears, fantasies, projections, transfers) have not been analysed or even simply expressed;
- the identity elements of one of the protagonists have been threatened.

The coach's job cannot be done without the establishment of a high level of mutual trust. Because there is no power relationship between the protagonists, a high level of trust will allow the coach to exercise properly his 'powerful energy' (which does not belong to the domain of power), that is, by optimising the energy system made up of his client's energy together with his own, with a view to helping the client to achieve the objectives that he has set himself.

The coach can therefore be very directive and very interventionist. On the other hand, he may be silent, paying active attention, and practising judo-style interventions. What counts is that, in a climate of transparency and trust, he makes it possible for the champion, his client, to achieve his objectives without playing power games.

The Contract

By contract, we mean an agreement between two entities (individuals or teams) relating to objectives, means and process. In other words, the contract defines the results to be achieved and the respective roles of the protagonists.

In Transactional Analysis (TA), there are various types of contracts, such as 'business contract' or 'legal contract'. These generally define in writing the fees, conditions, objectives and operational methods.

A 'relational contract', which is a relatively informal contract, consists of all the stated and unstated details that will condition the relationship between the protagonists. Details such as the way that meetings will be conducted, timetables, how things are regulated, how they handle a conflict, how they share their time together (meals), their communication (telephone calls, seminars, meetings). This relational contract takes time to draft properly and necessitates important adjustments, since it is often the source of misunderstandings.

Then there is the 'secret contract' that designates the psychological and relational stakes of the two protagonists, these being partly pre-conscious, or even unconscious. For example, a manager may approach a consultant, unconsciously, not specifically because he is in search of a solution, but because he wants to obtain from him a permission and validation of a decision that he dare not take without feeling guilty. Another director of training (or human resources) may approach a reputable consultant, not for assistance through his skill and experience, but to prove to himself, sometimes to the detriment of the consultant, that he is now quite competent and able to handle things by himself. There are many such examples and the experienced consultant must be very vigilant to foil such games that may well be initiated owing to the number of secret contracts involved.

We should also remember that in all institutional life a contract is not simply bilateral; there is always at least a third party involved, namely the institution. As Fanita English originally defined it with her concept of the 'triangular contract', it is desirable for every contract for change to include this dimension. A contract cannot be valid if it does not define the reciprocal expectations shown at each pole of the triangle as in Figure 14.4. Since in most cases the reality of the system is more complex, the contract is frequently many-sided, as in Figure 14.5, with the coach working, say, with an internal trainer. In this case, the contract must take account of:

- the relationship between the trainer and those on the course;
- the relationship with the training management;

Figure 14.4 Coach's triangular contract
(based on Fanita English's model)

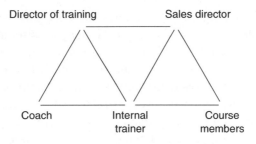

Figure 14.5 Multilateral institutional contract

▪ the relationship with the sales director who is expected to make an appearance in the salespeople's course.

In our experience as a transactionalist, a contract is a very precious tool, notably because it helps to limit confluent relationships and prevent games, as well as provide both client and coach with a sense of responsibility. It is important however to make sure that it is not cast in stone, but useful as a tool for clarification, reference and support in the work to be undertaken.

There often remains a strong temptation to become rigid at one point or another, to over-comply with the contract in such a way as to lose sight of the 'actual situation', as well as the usually systemic and complex dimension of the relationship and the problems to be dealt with. There is a danger that this may prevent a latent request from emerging and serve as an alibi for one or other of the protagonists' not dealing with the problems. We should not transform the means into the end.

CHAPTER 15

Intervention Zones

Summary

The concept of intervention zone allows the coach to avoid prematurely 'getting his hands dirty' with the client. He may thus focus on the client's problem or on the client himself, and consistently manage the ambiguity of his role, in particular by answering the question: 'Must I give a fish or a fishing rod?' In fact, the coach has a number of intervention zones available to him, reflecting different aspects of his relationship with the client, so that he can identify the 'hot potatoes' that his client may try to palm off on him, and thereby he can help his client avoid having such 'hot potatoes' palmed off on him by his colleagues.

The Eight Zones

The task of coaching in both an individual and a team relationship involves a complexity of a special kind. The champion has a problem to be dealt with, but it quickly becomes apparent that the support work does not simply or principally consist of dealing with this problem. Treating the problem is entirely conditioned by the relationship that the champion has vis-à-vis himself with regard to the problem, and by the relationship that the champion has vis-à-vis the problem. Based on this observation, the concept of intervention zones is developed step by step. From the coach's viewpoint, there are eight zones, as shown in Figure 15.1. The coach might very well include these features in his dashboard information, along with the 15 parameters already discussed. We shall first examine each of these zones.

Zone 1. The coach and his identity envelopes
For simplicity, we can speak of the personal identity envelope and the professional identity envelope. So, faced with a problem brought by the champion, the coach may find himself challenged in his personal

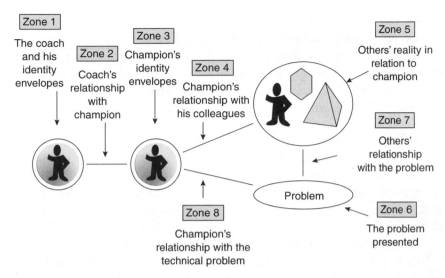

Figure 15.1 Zones of intervention

'scenario'* and find that he is emotionally upset or put on the defensive. There is the danger that he will react impulsively, in a conscious or unconscious way that would no longer be sufficiently objective to sustain a supportive relationship.

In his professional envelope, the coach may not have achieved a sufficient level of OKness, owing to the fact that his identity is called into question in the coaching context. Perhaps it is still early in his career and he is too dependent financially on his work as a coach to be objective, or he needs to prove his professional competence to his colleagues or to his client. The intervention that the coach may exert on himself may be likened to the role of someone who needs to clean his own spectacles or a driver who cleans his car windscreen.

Zone 2. The coach's relationship with the champion
Separately from the intra psychic elements concerning his champion, the coach has the particular responsibility of managing the relationship with his client. This must be sufficiently structured to prevent any merging, or on the other hand, any blurring of the relationship. He must avoid overwhelming his client with advice, and refrain from playing the role of an overprotective 'Jewish mother'; he must be equally careful to avoid being swamped by his client or by the scale of the problem presented to him. We shall later look closely at the concept of the 'hot potato'. In Transactional Analysis (TA),

---

* See Glossary.

we speak of the 'role' in the drama triangle of persecutor–saviour–victim, of games, of symbiosis, all referring to relational elements to be avoided.

To do this, this coach must return to the model-for-action grid and check the client's request against it, as well as the contract that was established. This aspect of the relationship also involves work to structure time, space and mutual frameworks of reference.

Zone 3. The champion's identity envelopes
The problem brought by the champion will have caused him to question different levels of his own identity. As we saw in Part III Chapter 12 (Integrated Identities), the manager must be regarded as a nested Russian doll, and the problem may destabilise him at the level of the personal identity envelope, even at his scenario level, as well as at other levels of his professional identity (PID, MID, RID, TID, CID). The coach has to take account of this complexity at his professional identity level and, at his personal identity level, he must prevent any slippage in the support relationship towards therapy (unless the contract specifically provides otherwise). He must also be receptive to how the problem echoes at the different levels of meaning, as the champion perceives them. Finally, the coach remembers that the problem reveals in the client a particular need that is specific to each identity level.

Coaching can be distinguished from 'therapeutic supervision' in the sense that on the one hand it must avoid slipping over into pure and simple therapy, while taking account of the client's existential dimension and his scenarios. On the other hand, the coach must integrate not only the elements of the professional envelope, but also the multiple levels that exist between the job and all dimensions of the institution.

Zone 4. The champion's relationship with his colleagues
In this zone, the coach shows or helps his champion to appreciate what is not healthy or appropriate in this relationship. As in zone 2, some readjustments are required. The champion may thus be led to break off his relationship with the other party (the colleague, team institution or environment) involved in the problem, or to limit the consequences of an institutional symbiosis, or to renegotiate a relational contract.

Zone 5. The reality of the party, or of the group, with which the champion is in a relationship
The coach can help his champion to diagnose better the problems of the people or teams to which he relates, so that they can better identify their own problems and choose ways of resolving them.

Zone 6. The problem presented
This is a zone that relates to a purely technical problem, outside of the preceding relational system. For example, the champion may lack technical information (marketing, legal, industrial, etc.) about a task to be done. Since he should be sufficiently competent, the coach should therefore provide the correct information or refer him to a specialist.

Zone 7. The relationship between the persons in contact with the champion and the problem
To take a simple example, the coach listens to a school manager (zone 3) or a teacher who has just contacted him about a pupil (zone 5) who has difficulty in passing or preparing for an examination (zone 6). Here the coach's intervention is to suggest an option to change the relationship (zone 7) between this pupil and his exam by helping him to distance himself from this problem, or by finding other options that remove the tension between this pupil and his exam.

Zone 8. The champion's relationship with the technical problem
The coach helps the champion to find options that give him more flexibility in his relationship with the problem. For example, he may find him someone to whom he can delegate the specific technical problem, or someone to provide him with the means to approach such technical problems from another angle.

Example of using the intervention zone grid
We shall now examine an example that suggests interventions in each of the eight zones for a given situation.

As coach, let us assume that I interview the director of a company with whom I am preparing a meeting of his board of directors. At some stage, the director refers to his technical director who clearly does not assume his managerial role well, owing to his shortcomings as a manager and the fact that he is new in the company. In this case, I will go through each of the eight zones in turn in my head to illustrate the type of question and intervention that I might use. It goes without saying that this task is not always carried out so explicitly, but if there is a difficulty, it may be necessary to take such a systematic approach.

Zone 1
I clean my spectacles by asking myself whether I have not been prejudiced in my relationship with this director who, I noticed, irritated me. After further analysis, I realise that his personality reminds me of a relative and, because of this, I feel slightly affected in my personal identity envelope.

Without feeling in any way powerless, I am careful not to allow myself to
be led astray by my emotions and prejudices.

At the level of my professional envelope, I may feel affected by my client
who frightens me with his question, because it demands technical knowledge that I might feel that I ought to have. Being affected in my professional
OKness, I have to remind myself that my role as coach is in no sense to
know everything about industrial technology, but to consider myself competent in my job and not required to prove anything beyond a certain point.

Zone 2

I am careful to ensure that my client does not hand me a hot potato by
overwhelming me with his confusion or his anger about the problem. If that
happened, I would be at risk of taking on the role of saviour, then might
become victim and even persecutor. I react by verifying exactly what is his
request in relation to me and in relation to the problem. That is the moment
to quickly establish a mini contract. As another option, I can also let him
know what I feel in our relationship and the unease that I feel as a result.
By trying to make myself an ally at the start, through giving this information, I show my goodwill and embark with him on a process of meta-
communication thus making him aware that in fact his request of me is
unfair and prompting him to recover his position. I have used the grid of the
model for action.

Zone 3

My champion speaks of his colleague with an emotion that is clearly out of
all proportion with the situation. I can invite him to recognise this excess,
owing to the fact that he is upset at present, and the current stressful climate
makes this problem turn out to be the straw that broke the camel's back.
Without going to the point of engaging in therapy, I can help him put in place
some protections in his time management so that his stress is alleviated.

It may be that at some moment he speaks to me about a past situation,
professional or personal, that echoes the situation with his colleague. In TA,
this is referred to as an 'elastic'.

In his professional envelope, I shall be able to help my champion to clarify his definition of his own job and the grieving that remains to be worked
through for him to be OK in his identity as director. Being himself a former
technical director, he doubtless identifies too much with his former job to
the detriment of his current position, to which he should now pay attention.

Zone 4

The difficult relationship that my champion has with his colleague reveals
that he has not found an appropriate management style, and in particular has

not foreseen, in the development of his colleague's autonomy, the necessary stages that will allow him to establish true delegation. For example, he has prematurely delegated a set of responsibilities to him, whereas he ought to have assessed that his colleague needed more time, more information from him, and above all a more progressive and realistic transfer of responsibilities, backed up with real support during that period of transition.

Zone 5
My champion's colleague deserves more understanding of his personality structure and in the identification of his function. My role as coach will be to help my champion perceive this better, by giving him my point of view and removing his 'blind spots'.

Zone 6
Discussion with my champion will enable clearer identification of the specific problem that the technical organisation is causing the colleague, and will help discover the concrete options to be suggested to him. My champion and/or I get our hands dirty.

Zone 7
Clearly, the colleague has an unhealthy relationship with his problem, in this case solving the problem in his department. I will help my champion establish with his colleague a procedure that will allow the latter to have less ambitious objectives, help from outside, protections and permission to take certain initiatives. All of these elements will ensure that the colleague is much less stressed in his relationship with the problem.

Zone 8
I will identify with my client his difficulty in not handling the technical problem in place of his colleague. I will invite him to avoid getting too involved in this matter, to let the grief pass. By proceeding to establish a procedure of a truly progressive delegation to his colleague, he will be less preoccupied on a day-to-day basis about this or that technical solution that, personally, he would have handled differently.

Fish or Fishing Rod

As we have seen from Figure 11.5, the coach may involve himself directly in zones 5 and 6, that is, the champion's colleague or the champion's problem, or he may focus more on zones 2 and 3, namely his relationship with the champion, or the champion himself. See Figure 15.2.

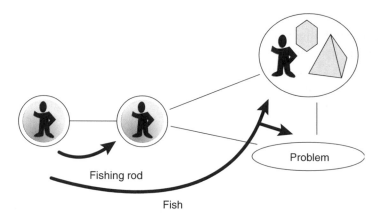

Figure 15.2   Fish or fishing rod

First Case: Offer a Fish

The coach rolls up his sleeves, attacks the problem side by side with the champion and examines the situation that is causing the problem. He helps him resolve this problem or this relational situation by finding out what the options for action are, by offering his diagnosis or point of view, or suggesting some theories or models that will assist him in understanding his reality, so that he can subsequently alter it.

The advantage of this first approach for the champion is that he does not feel alone in his search for a solution, he may sometimes even be provided with a readymade solution. This is often the reason why he approaches a coach or consultant in the first place.

The disadvantage of this lies in the fact that the coach is in danger of replacing his client. Acting in such a way, he risks putting a symbiosis in place, a merging saviour relationship, not realising that he will soon find himself in the position of being both victim and persecutor.

Second Case: Offer a Fishing Rod

While still giving his full attention to the problem in hand, the coach refuses to offer a fish and provide a solution first, but by focusing on his champion and the relationship that he is establishing with him, he offers him help of a quality to enable the champion to come up with his own solution.

The approach has the advantage of empowering the client, and making him recognise that he is OK and capable of finding his own solutions.

The coach will remove his blind spots and avoid putting himself in his client's position. It represents taking the position of a true coach towards his champion, and therefore giving priority to the process of his relationship with his client as opposed to the content of the problem brought to him. This also enables the coach to function usefully, even in cases where he is not a technical specialist in the subject matter. His role also promotes more secure growth for the champion in the longer term.

The disadvantage of this approach lies in the fact that it cannot be introduced too prematurely, especially when the champion has not yet reached the second and third levels of autonomy. So long as the champion is in a stage of dependence or normal counter-dependence (for example, because he is new to this type of problem and lacks basic information), the frustration that results is intolerable. But it is also inappropriate. It is OK for the coach to offer a Parent and an Adult to his champion when the latter has not yet been able to develop his two Ego States in the new situation in which he finds himself. The danger would be for the coach not to perceive this state and to create too much stress and frustration for the champion.

What, therefore, has to be done?

The choice between these two alternatives remains ambiguous. It has to be made according to:

- the alliance for change shared by the champion and coach;

- the champion's stage of development;

- the external situation;

- the degree of urgency or stress on the part of the champion;

- the capacity of both the champion and the coach for tolerating frustration;

- the contract that they draw up in their relationship.

I will give the example of a coaching situation that helped me structure my own thoughts on the question.

It involved a request for help from a director who had to give a presentation to several hundred people. He was required to give a description of his field of activity and to report on the results obtained by his company. This was a problem for him because he was not a particularly good public speaker and, at a deeper level, he found it difficult to talk about himself. However, apart from the training needed for the delivery of this speech in public, I perceived that while this champion was appealing to me as a coach, he was asking for something more than a speech writer. He had come armed with a 10-page document filled with figures and ideas for his speech. At our first meeting, having read his material after half an hour, I gave him this feedback:

'In this text, we have some valuable objective information about the content of your speech. But, overall, this information seems to me to be probably rather boring for your prospective audience and says little about your motivation in managing this department and the quality of the efforts that you have invested in it.'

Surprised and a little taken aback that I was not accepting his request straightaway, this champion replied:

'I am disturbed by what you say, because I have already put a lot of work into it, and I only have ten days before the presentation. At the same time I see what you are saying, it is rather full of clichés. What do you suggest?'

I replied in turn:

'Can you, in five to ten minutes, tell me as though you were talking to your best friend, exactly what it is about your job that makes it so exciting for you; why it is that you are not digging holes in the ground, but you are building a cathedral?'

The champion began to laugh. He had understood. He began to talk on quite a different level; slowly and hesitatingly at first, but with increasing warmth and emotion. After 10 minutes (this went on longer than expected) I interrupted him:

'Well done, that's something else! I think that you have found the thread of your presentation. Shall I reformulate what you have said?'

In the space of a few minutes I related with some emotion, the key points of his speech following the order of the notes and figures that he had given me previously. It was his turn to be surprised and he said:

'Yes, I like that! What do we do now?'

I replied:

'We have just constructed your fishing rod. It's up to you now and I suggest that you continue your speech in this style, with me helping you to maintain the tone.'

In the course of three or four sessions spread over several days, this manager prepared his speech, writing a text that he had scarcely to look at when he came to give his presentation. We produced some slides to punctuate the presentation, but above all he was able to speak from his heart and to convey his enthusiasm. The process was hard for him and for me.

After the event, he told me that there were moments when he had wanted to give up on the whole thing, when he blamed me for 'not doing the job for him, given that he was also paying me for that', he added laughing. But, to conclude, he has several times assured me since that this coaching experience was a turning point in his professional life, in his growth (he has never made a public presentation like it), and in his relationships with consultants that he has used since. He subsequently became a consultant himself, and recently told me that for him this experience had been a model situation that often helped him structure his relationships with his clients. For my part, the experience helps to remind me to refocus my role as coach and be ready to offer either the fish or the fishing rod at any moment, and above all to be careful to optimise this unavoidable ambiguity that lies in the fine choice between content and process.

The Hot Potato

This term (see Figure 15.3) is borrowed from a concept originally put forward by Fanita English, author of the 'episcript' scenario, and which corresponds in TA to the situation where a person transmits his own problem to another person, rather like tossing a hot baked potato into someone else's hands. The terms 'parallel process' and 'secondary process' are sometimes also used.

It goes like this. The champion is submerged in the relationship that he has with his colleagues or his problem and, without realising it, he adopts a similar relationship with his coach. He hands his coach the hot potato. Obviously, at first the coach does not perceive this in these terms. What he sees is some unease in zone 2, that is, the relationship between his client and himself. This unease is located at the process level, not the content level, the psychological level and not the apparent level. In order to perceive it the coach must be very vigilant and used to detecting this invasion that may

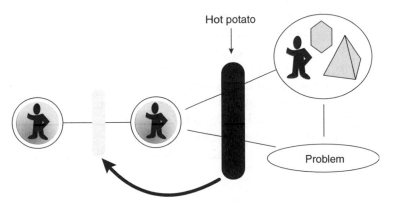

Hot potato

Problem

Figure 15.3   The hot potato

be both subtle and on a grand scale. The client for example may be confused, while at the same time making remarks that appear quite clear in their content. The client does not respond to questions directly and overwhelms the coach by describing the reality in useless detail, without stating what the problem is. The client is seductive or makes implicit threats, leading the coach to understand that he must at all costs come up with a solution or he will be regarded as incompetent.

The client may adopt many ways of presenting himself as the victim, expecting the coach to be his saviour. We know the result; there is a big risk of it turning into mutual persecution.

Perceiving this apparently very simple model allows one to act in a powerful and effective way:

1. By denouncing this phenomenon, the coach is able to enter into meta-communication with his champion. He will make use of the relationship between him and his champion (zone 2), and of the hot potato concept as an opportunity to analyse the relationships that the champion has with his problem (analysis of zone 4 or 8). From a systemic point of view, this analysis process is a particularly useful lever and is a consequence of the process based on 'the whole is in the part'.

    So, in his relationship with the coach, the champion will update all the dysfunctions existing in the system to which he belongs. By being very attentive to what goes on in the relationship with the champion, the coach has a highly valuable field of observation revealing the organisational and relational system in which his client is enclosed.

2. Beyond the work of analysis and meta-communication that allows both the coach and the client to perceive more clearly what is going on behind the relationship problems, the coach will be able to provide his champion with a true model of the way in which the champion may handle, on his own initiative, the relationship problems that beset him. For example, by confronting the symbiotic system in which the champion is enclosed, the coach avoids the risk of being enclosed himself. By exchanging the transactions, by coming out of the drama triangle (persecutor, saviour, victim), by clarifying the request and adjusting the contracts, the coach is not only able to re-establish a healthy and OK relationship with his champion, but also provide his champions with behaviour models that he will himself be able to use in his organisation.

CHAPTER 16

The Ego States

Summary

Each of the Ego States must exist in the champion. The Parent, Adult and Child, and the functional 'sub-Ego States' that they included, each possess a positive aspect and a negative aspect. It is important for the manager to know how to identify the different components of the personality in order to control and limit the harmful aspects, in order to develop his positive Ego States and advisedly take advantage of the whole range of possible options.

We have already referred to the Ego States in the chapter on autonomy, in particular from the functional point of view. Figure 16.1 indicates the different Ego States that we believe necessary for a manager. Note that each state includes a negative and a positive part. We do not propose to embark on a detailed study of Transactional Analysis (TA), but in the following, we amplify the figure with some remarks.

1. It seems obvious that a manager who lacks a State or sub-Ego State runs the risk of eventually being in a serious situation at certain times. The exclusion of some States or sub-States causes the relationships established with this person to lead to compensations in the other person, who may be driven to overinvest the Ego States that are lacking in his protagonist. The result is symbiosis, game playing, drama triangles, and so on.

2. There is frequently a tendency to believe that TA recommends being principally Adult. It seems to us that if the developed Adult of the person is particularly important (that is, the Adult remains functionally in control), it is important in the relationship for the manager to be capable of using the Ego State that corresponds best to his protagonist and to the situation. Apart from his Adult, the manager of a company needs:

   ■ a powerful, positive Normative Parent (who knows how to say no and put protections in place);

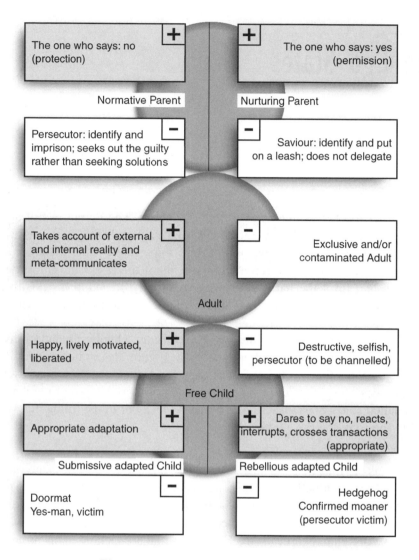

Figure 16.1 The manager's Ego States

- a powerful Nurturing Parent (NP) (who knows how to say yes and grant permissions);

- a Child who is free, lively, happy and motivated;

- a submissive, adapted Child (who knows how to show respect for others and for the values they hold);

- a positive, rebellious adapted Child (who knows not to submit necessarily to the will of others).

3. It is important for the manager to know how to identify the negative areas that he has within him in each of the Ego States and that he might invest in, either because he is carried into his own pathology through stress, or because he is simply not aware of his own self-defence system.

4. After his diagnosis, the coach may use his own Ego States if those of his client are found wanting. He then provides the Ego State that is missing. For example, he will give him a positive Normative Parent model if his client lacks structure or does not know how to say no, or a Free Child model that knows how to express its emotions and be contented. The coach will in addition use with regard to his client the Ego State that his client may have already developed but which he is unable to make use of by himself. He will offer him protections, permissions or information as required.

5. This model of the Ego States may be used both for an individual client and for a team. Indeed, in the dual control work that the coach carries out with the team he supports, he may implement for the team the Normative Parent who appears to be lacking, whether in the team as in its manager, or any other Ego State that is inadequate (Free Child or NP, for example). Similarly, for the team, it is important to spot the negative Ego States that tend to destroy the life of the team.

CHAPTER 17

The Frameworks of Reference

We return to the concept of the framework of reference described in the chapter on meta-communication and illustrated in Figure 3.1. In the case of the coach's grid, it is important to identify whether he is focused, as a priority, on the client's framework of reference (see Figure 17.1).

In fact, this first approach, focusing on the client, will consider that the latter is responsible, has internal coherence, and already has within him the answers to these questions. The coach has chiefly only to create the right conditions that will allow the champion to develop his solutions by himself.

A second approach, focusing more on the coach's framework of references, will consider that the client lacks basic information or the minimum

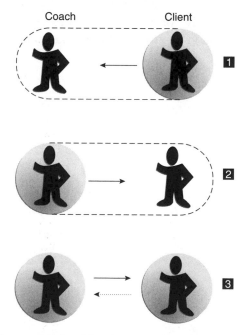

Figure 17.1 The frameworks of reference

necessary competence. Therefore, the coach must provide him with the information (Adult), structures (Normative Parent), encouragement (Nurturing Parent (NP)), energy (Free Child) that he needs. This approach, corresponding to the degrees 0 and 1 of autonomy, may be quite appropriate and OK. It may also be inappropriate and pervert the relationship.

It is very important for the coach to appreciate precisely which of the two approaches is the most favourable depending on the context, while bearing in mind that a third approach, combining the two, is generally the most appropriate. Nonetheless, we draw attention to the following:

1. The novice or uncertain coach tends to use the second approach most of the time, believing that he must provide solutions or 'fish'. However, experience shows that it is a combination of the three approaches that in our opinion reveals the professional. This presupposes that the coach has found his identity, is sure of his ability, already enjoys the confidence of his client, and is neither afraid of silence nor of crossing transactions (in TA terminology) with his client. He may answer a question with a question, or he may sometimes refuse to reply to a question. He may even reply at a psychological level when the client asks him a factual operational question.

2. One of the surprising aspects of this coaching profession is that the more serious and difficult the situation, the more important the champion (in terms of personality), the more the strategic choice proves necessary between one of the three approaches by the coach. Paradoxically, it is most frequently the highest level managers who need to be taken care of the most. Champions at this level have the greatest need for a coach who is resistant and who sometimes refuses to give them fish, because their growth is at stake. The power of these personalities (employers and chief executives) is often such that they have neutralised or terrorised their surrounding resources that might have been able to help them. Sometimes, therefore, the coach, who represents their last chance, must be alert not to allow himself to be destabilised, in the interests of their safety.

CHAPTER 18

The Levels of Autonomy

As a reminder, the reader is referred to Part II, Chapter 5. In the coach's grid, however, whether it concerns the relationship in coaching an individual or a team, we recall that the coach must be careful to identify the level of autonomy at which his protagonist stands, in order to activate in his client, as well as for himself as coach, the suitable Ego States, in terms of process and content (cf. in particular Figure 18.1).

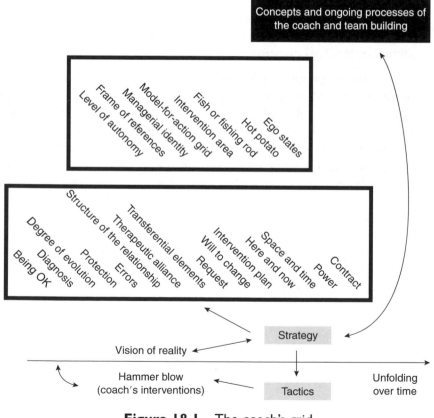

Figure 18.1   The coach's grid

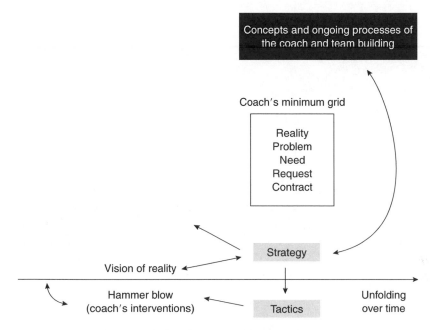

Figure 18.2 The coach's simplified grid

Opposite Figure 18.1, the coach's grid, to conclude Part III, we place the seven previous chapters as the common trunk that the coach must integrate, just as he must integrate the 15 parameters, whether it involves individual coaching or team building. In Part IV, we shall add to this model some elements specific to individual coaching, and in Part V elements specific to team building. From these two parts, we shall produce two subsets that are integrated in Figure 18.2 (the coach's interventions and his dashboard).

In an urgent case where the set of elements in Figure 18.1 appears inapplicable, the minimum grid that can replace the coach's grid and the 15 parameters may be reduced to that shown above.

PART IV

Individual Coaching

CHAPTER 19

Managerial Identity Envelopes

Summary

There are four essential components of managerial identity:

- the person;
- the education;
- the profession (through the various previous jobs);
- the current job.

The coach is especially attentive to these different 'skins', since in the past each may have been the subject of some trauma or inadequate development, possibly constituting deadlock in the manager's development.

We have seen that a manager at the heart of an institution is both a subject of undergoing growth and an object of production. We have also seen how managerial identity results from the dynamic between three components (Figure 14.3): his internal and external recognition and his status (his skin). The concept of the managerial identity envelope therefore corresponds to the different identity 'skins' that the person has been able to build up for himself in the course of his personal and professional history. In this chapter we review the distinctions presented in the development of integrated identities, but in a different way.

In the figure showing integrated identities, we can consider that the different identity levels represent the person's identity in its current components, whereas in Figure 19.1, the diagram of the managerial identity envelopes, appearing like the cross-section of a tree trunk, we find the historic stages in the manager's identity alongside the four major components of his personal history:

- his person;
- his training/education;

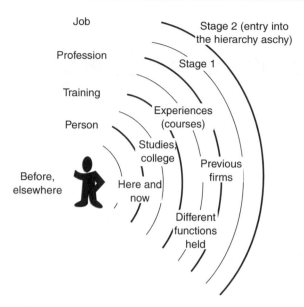

Figure 19.1   Managerial identity envelopes

■ his profession (developed on the job through his various functions);

■ his current job in the present organisation.

From our experience, we have noticed that each of these identity levels may have given rise to trauma or inadequate development. Rather like a scratched CD, a traumatised or atrophied area keeps making its presence felt. The energy linked or bound up in this trauma repeatedly manifesting itself, or the defence mechanism protecting it, will hinder the person in his job or in the future development to which he aspires.

For example, if the person has been traumatised by an experience in a particular job, he is liable to find himself 'reactivated' if asked to do the same job at a later date, or if he has to come in contact with people who do that same job. Since he is contaminated by his past, he will lack objectivity and will be very ambivalent in his present role.

As a second example, we take the case of a person who has hankered after a profession to the extent that one could say it was his vocation. If the training he has been given, for economic or family reasons, is contrary to this vocation, eventually the pendulum will swing in the other direction and, 10 or 20 years later, provoke an existential crisis.

A third example is a direct application of the Peter Principle. The person in his job may have chosen it rationally because of the skills he showed in his previous occupation. However, the gap between his profession and the job may be such that, despite the rational aspect, a reorientation becomes essential. The person has reached his level or degree of incompetence.

Coaching is particularly an appropriate opportunity for listening to and analysing these contradictions and problems that the champion often finds hard to identify precisely, and whose basic causes he has difficulty in determining or accepting. Unfortunately, it sometimes requires a major crisis for the person to go through a grieving process with regard to the apparent advantages of a particular job, and accept to pay attention to his deeper motivations and cease to repress them. To give a recent example, successful sales executives, with correspondingly high salaries, found it hard to see that, deep down, their motivations were driving them to give up their status and jobs in order to become agents for change (trainers or consultants), something more in line with their professional aspirations for human development. Another example would be people who have developed a real aversion to their company over the years, having experienced the world of their company as a place not worthy of their high level of training and their existential aspirations. I recently had occasion to assist a high-level French director with a Harvard MBA, employed as the CEO of the European subsidiary of a multinational company. He was no longer able to bear company life, because he felt himself constantly locked into playing roles. He had to go through a period of personal and professional therapy in order to be able to question his standard of living, his position, how he assumed the risk he was taking as a father, and so on, in order to literally change skin, by moving and establishing himself in Paris as a therapist and consultant, and thus rediscover, after several years, a new enthusiasm for assisting in corporate change management.

While the coach's role is obvious in such situations as out-placement, new job appointment, career planning, improving negotiation skills, recruitment, and so on, his job does not end there. Without acting strictly speaking like a therapist, the coach must pay attention to the deeper motivations of the champion, help him to focus on an existential meaning, make him aware of the protections he needs in order to manage his stress and his time, give him the support and the necessary permissions to reject the over-attractive proposals of headhunters, or to escape from the deadlock resulting from some inappropriate timidity or some routine that the champion has become caught up in. The potential butterfly does not realise that it lives in a caterpillar's skin.

CHAPTER 20

The Manager's Stages of Development

Summary

The linear development of a manager goes through the following stages: professional in a job (often a specialist in a particular technique), manager (in a hierarchy) and leader, knowing that a manager integrates these three stages according to various classifications.

Passing from one stage to another involves grieving processes and reveals a number of pitfalls:

- the threshold of incompetence;

- the lack of training that generally accompanies passing from one stage to another;

- the need for support;

- the ambiguity of the leader stage, centred around the vision and the meaning.

A table allows comparison of the main focus, the advantages, risks, polarisations and thought processes for each stage.

We shall present these stages of development for a manager from two aspects:

1. the specialist, the manager and the leader;

2. the nature and structure of the identity of each of these stages.

Aspect 1: the Three Stages

A little known aspect of managerial development is revealed in a model represented by three stages: the specialist, the manager and the leader.[1]

In fact, when someone has developed an ability in his profession, making him an authority in his field, he becomes the person to consult, the best person in the office or department, the reference point, the expert on the subject. His colleagues will come to him to ask his opinion and they more or less establish him as their leader. From the moment that he has achieved this status, two avenues for development open up for him:

- either he becomes the reference in his domain of excellence (and he chooses to capitalise on his experience in order to become an authority recognised simply through the exercise of his skill);

- alternatively, he may move on to another stage of identity, namely that of manager in the hierarchy. This means that he in fact changes his profession and becomes someone who sees to it that others do what he did before.

We note that this change may be quite appropriate, owing to the needs of the organisation, especially in the case of a person overwhelmed by the demands placed upon him, who can thereby either produce more or because he possesses the managerial qualities that enable him to become the manager of a team. This does however presuppose that he has had a minimum of training through:

- guidance from previous employers;

- a particular technical process;

- self-educational qualities that form part of his potential. Generally, all three factors are involved.

There are however several comments to be made.

Comment I

Moving from the first to the second stage, as justified by the needs of the organisation, may be a major error as the Peter Principle has shown so well. By becoming a manager, the person reaches his level of incompetence. The super professional or specialist may be a very bad manager. Conversely, a very good manager may only be an average specialist. The executive responsible for making the promotion, the person himself and the coach, must all be aware of this factor.

In almost all cases, we see a considerable gap between the time, energy and money devoted to forming this identity envelope of the specialist and the set of elements of this second managerial layer. This is from two viewpoints. In fact, we generally see that the investment made for a person to become a specialist in his profession takes between five and 15 years of training and various exercises (schools, apprenticeship on the job, courses, assignment training), whereas to learn the practice of management, in many cases only a few weeks of preparation are suggested. On the other hand, people with degrees and higher-level education are almost immediately placed in positions of hierarchy, without having undergone, or appreciated the need for, a period of training in the field, something that is absolutely necessary, as much in order to understand the reality of the situation that they have to manage as to acquire credibility in the eyes of their colleagues. In both instances, we have to deal with a blind alley.

We have witnessed numerous examples of such cases in the various organisations where we have worked. In one case, super salesmen became very poor sales directors, and excellent engineers, researchers or people on the ground were overtaken when it was a question of managing the complexity arising from human problems and management problems. Conversely, we have seen senior executives covered with degrees and often justifiably ambitious, either refusing to take risks in an operational situation where they would have to prove themselves in the field (and in doing so not enjoy the credibility to confirm their skill as managers and further their careers), or introducing wayward management systems. This might be described as 'management by five', whereby, through an underhand system of delegation to specialists reporting to them, these bosses, being aware of their own incompetence, make these people answerable, in the event of failure, for decisions that they have not made themselves.

The third stage in this development is that of the leader or strategist. This comes as a radical qualitative change in comparison with the previous stage in the sense that the leader is the person who, in addition to his profession (as specialist) and his role as hierarchical manager, is the one who carries out his responsibility from a point of view of openness; that is, openness in the outer and in-house environment. He must therefore not restrict himself to his expert knowledge, nor simply ensure that the work is done, but he must maintain the coherence between the two previous stages and all the internal and external interfaces that his role integrates in an 'ecological' way. Moving to this stage presupposes a particular capacity, namely:

- management of complexity;

- the capacity to link his job with the company's strategy;

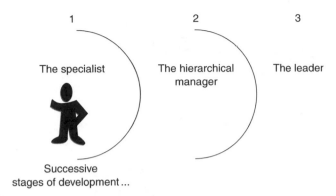

Figure 20.1   The manager's stages of development

■ the ability to communicate these various aspects to others; this is what makes him a carrier of meaning. Note that these charismatic qualities are not necessarily linked to his position in the hierarchy. This ability to endow his work with meaning, to communicate with others, to make links between everyday life and the strategic problems of the company can be characteristics of a trade union official, a salesman or a personal assistant, a secretary or the chairman. For these reasons, we think that anyone can be a leader in a company (see Figure 20.1).

Comment 2

We have presented these three stages in a linear fashion, because they do in fact develop chronologically, generally stage by stage. It is convenient, though, to define these three stages rather as the three constituents to be found in any manager. Every manager has these three identities present in him, albeit with different classifications (see Figure 20.2).

■ *A*: a very good specialist, weak manager and average leader;

■ *B*: an average specialist, good manager and weak leader. This is in particular the middle management leader. As John P. Kotter says,[2] the role of the hierarchical manager lies in the implementation of objectives: planning, organising, controlling, accepting the results; whereas the leader defines the direction to be followed, communicates this to people, inspires and motivates them and creates the conditions for change.

■ *C*: a modest specialist, a limited manager and a person with major qualities as a leader.

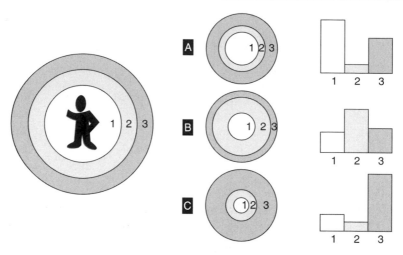

Figure 20.2   Different integrated classifications

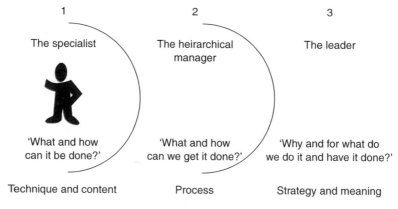

Figure 20.3   Characteristics of the three stages of a manager's development

Comment 3

As we see from Figure 20.3, each of these stages allows us to ask specific questions. The specialist can reply to the question 'what and how can it be done?', the manager to 'what and how can we get it done?' and the leader to 'why and for what do we do it and have it done?' Clearly, a manager is always replying to some extent to these questions.

In terms of focus, the specialist concentrates on the excellence of his technique, and especially on content. He tends to neglect the relationship between his specific field and the environment. However, his field of excellence is incompressible. For example, whatever a client or the salespeople want, he is the one responsible for feasibility (manufacturing, legal, financial, promotional, marketing).

The hierarchical manager must focus his attention more on the relationships between methods, professions, persons, interfaces and concentrate his expertise on what one might call the management of the processes. He may see his role following quite different methods and styles of management, depending on his degree of directivity or his capacity to be an organiser. His excellence is measured by his ability to obtain results from others and by his doing the work himself.

The leader, who has a holistic vision of his job, concentrates on meaning. That is, on the one hand, on the strategic view, and on the other hand, the conditions that must integrate the position he holds and the way that position is organised (both structurally and personally) in order to be aligned with the strategic view.

The tools used in each of these stages may be caricatured as:

Stage 1: the pocket calculator, the shovel, the pick.
Stage 2: the carrot, the stick and the oilcan.
Stage 3: the loudspeaker, the sonar, the telescope and intuition, the ear to the ground.

An example borrowed from the world of music might further help our understanding:

- stage 1, this is the professional/specialist, who in an orchestra would be the first violin, a prima donna or a soloist;

- stage 2, this is the hierarchical manager, who is the conductor (he is not supposed to play any instrument);

- stage 3 would be the impresario or director of the opera.

Transferring the model to the world of the cinema, we would find for each of the stages, respectively:

- the actor or star;

- the director;

- the producer (the latter two are sometimes combined).

Comment 4

We note that passing from one stage to another constitutes radical qualitative steps and situations and, once again, these steps presuppose very

Figure 20.4 Grieving and change in the
manager's stages of development

specific and often poorly recognised grieving. An equally important aspect
in the qualitative change appears through the change in the economy of the
recognition signs* for each of the stages (see Figure 20.4).

A team manager will learn to be recognised for his capacity to get others
to achieve, and abandon the recognition that he received when he was exercising his previous profession. As a reward, though, he will gain satisfaction from the recognition of a team bonded around him.

A leader, in his turn, ought to be able to take unpopular decisions and
accept criticism, distancing and incomprehension from those around him –
the 'loneliness' of the boss. In return, he will have the satisfaction of being
recognised as someone to appeal to in difficult situations, and sometimes
the advantages of the attributes of power, even if they are on occasion quite
burdensome. In our experience, we have encountered all kinds of grieving
that managers had to go through, representing deadlocks until they had been
dealt with. The following are a few recent examples.

▨ An internal consultant of an international organisation whom we assisted
took several months to take on the position of team leader to which she
had been appointed. She had to identify and control the grieving of the
relation of equality and friendship with her peers, accept the recognition
of her superiors, come to terms with herself internally as being competent for this job, despite her own doubts, and accept the frustration that
she experienced in her relationship with her former colleagues, some of

* See Glossary.

whom were jealous, others rebellious, and with whom henceforth she had to deal in a supervisory way. In total, she had to abandon 80 per cent of the profession in which she excelled, namely director of training. It took three to six months, including coaching sessions, for her to identify clearly the different grieving required and analysed from various symptoms. She was able to manage her relationship with her colleagues by means of individual interviews with them, but found it very hard to conduct meetings correctly as team leader. She was either too lax, or she was unpredictably authoritarian. Another symptom that she showed, subtly disguised as procrastination, was postponing a confrontation with one of her colleagues who was clearly creating problems through his wayward behaviour. Not only was she afraid of tackling him, but also after several weeks, it emerged that the real obstacle to her sorting out this problem was principally the risk of breaking the close ties that she had with her former colleagues through sacking this recalcitrant member of the team.

■ Another example is that of the chief executive of a division of a multinational who as leader was obliged to restructure his overstaffed executive committee, cutting it by a half to six or seven, and at the same time dismiss his sales director. Formerly a 'baron' among the others and now 'king', it was a very difficult task for him, as leader, to distance himself from his former peers and face up to the criticism and confrontation due to result from his decisions in his exchanges with this colleague. What acted like a brake was not the fear of the resulting confrontation and conflict, but much more the isolation that would ensue and the loss of the comradeship that he got from his former peers. The dismissal of his sales director is less a test of the relationship that he had with this person and his job than a repetitive situation in which he had a tendency to put himself. This was to hire high-level and high-potential managers as specialists, believing himself capable of dealing with all their dysfunctional traits, and being both saviour and too trusting in his ability to change people (having undergone many changes himself). A determining factor for his decision had of course been the required reorganisation. The main reason for the decision was not the implementation, for the person to be dismissed, of humane and protective measures (out-placement), but the realisation that, for the good of the organisation and for the good of his own managerial development as leader, he needed to become capable of freeing himself from the emotional ties made both at the moment of taking on a colleague and at the moment of deciding to let that person go.

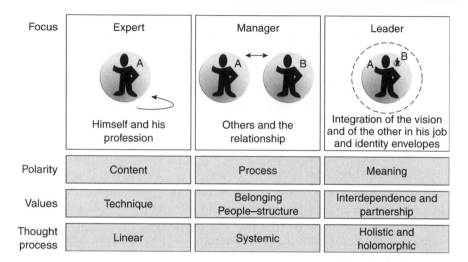

Focus	Expert	Manager	Leader
	Himself and his profession	Others and the relationship	Integration of the vision and of the other in his job and identity envelopes
Polarity	Content	Process	Meaning
Values	Technique	Belonging People–structure	Interdependence and partnership
Thought process	Linear	Systemic	Holistic and holomorphic

Figure 20.5 Synthesis of the three stages of a manager's development

Second Aspect: the Nature and Structure of Each Stage

Figure 20.5 shows how we can distinguish between different stages at different logical levels.

The specialist focuses on himself and on his profession. He perfects his technique.

- The advantage of this attitude is to increase the competence in his job, and to contribute through this to the competency of the organisation. It is an unavoidable stage that must not be cut back subsequently.

- There is the danger that the person may take a narrow view (by not integrating the viewpoints of others and the requirements of the vision). Also, if he feels threatened in his technical identity, he may take refuge in defending his level of power.

- His polarity is the content of the technique and he tries to promote this technique as a value.

- His thought process is linear, in the sense that he tends to consider his technique as external to himself and independent of the relational processes that condition it.

The second stage, that of the manager, is a stage where the person focuses on the array of relationships that he is responsible for within his team in particular, as well as all the hierarchical levels that he has to control.

- The advantage lies in the management of complexity, the mutual understanding and the opening up of everyone's framework of reference.

- At this stage, the dangers are that technical values will be forgotten, and secondly, navel-gazing and showing a preference for confluent belonging, or an exaggerated solidarity to the point of neglecting what is going on outside the team. The manager would prefer to be liked by his colleagues rather than cut loose and forced to make painful decisions.

- The polarity is the conduct of the processes. The values advocated are membership, solidarity, communication, effectiveness and operational results obtained.

- The thought process is systemic in the sense that the manager is aware that technical values are not enough and the operational results depend on the interactive processes between departments, hierarchical levels, solidarity and integration of different points of view and consensuses, even more than on each individual's technical excellence. Group cohesion is as valuable as the individual.

The third stage, that of the leader, focuses on taking into account the vision that he embraces like an identity envelope, taking into account the other's position and skill and integrating them into his own reference framework (cross-functional integration) and seeing to it that his position and managerial identity envelopes are maintained at a level consistent with the vision.

- The advantage of this stage is of course that its aims are to make every manager a 'builder' of the company and every 'stone' to be positioned according to the vision of the 'cathedral' and the location of the other 'stones'. It implies assimilating the complexity that integrates the vision of others, and above all a meta-position that allows a shared vision, implying in addition a true surpassing of his own initial vision (as we have seen in stage 6 of Figure 5.4).

- The risk of this stage is that one of the three poles might be exacerbated, to the detriment of the others; such as being too focused on the vision and forgetting one's own technical responsibility, or being too focused on listening to others and on cross-functionality and forgetting the vision.

- This stage is polarised on the concept of meaning, involving investment in the vision, sharing this vision, communicating the vision, the objectives, the values and everything that we have discussed under the heading of the Minimum Cultural Envelope (MCE). The values placed at the forefront are obviously complexity, interdependence of the different elements that make up the reality of the organisation. The latter are the external reality (locality, clientele), internal reality (different departments, the organisation) and the people, all viewed as a partnership to be optimised depending on the levels of autonomy of all these elements.

- The thought process is post-systemic, that is, holistic or hologram-like. As in the human body or in a hologram, each cell carries information about the whole body or about the complete holographic image. In terms of identity, the manager knows that by contributing to the visions he is developing his peers and himself.

To summarise, it seems important to note, once again, that these three stages each have to be experienced gradually and must be integrated. Furthermore, what is experienced in management, with its ambiguities, contradictions, constraints, specific stakes in the organisation field and in the economic environment, is related to the dynamics of an individual's development at the heart of any human community. We shall give three metaphorical examples to illustrate.

Some Metaphors

Example of a Couple

The two individuals forming a couple, as a first stage, may each develop individually, find their own identity, improve their skills and talents, and so on. At a second stage, only possible when they have both reached a certain degree of individuation, they can develop as a couple by focusing more on the relationship and system that they form. At a third stage, there is the identification and investment that each puts into the alliance through their mutual faithfulness and common values, through their contribution to building a heritage that is material, emotional, cultural and spiritual, all the while developing this identity envelope which is the couple that they form. Of course, all of this is based on the assumption that each takes account of the other, contributes to the other's development and, paradoxically, through surpassing themselves, contributes to their own individual development.

Mystical Metaphor

The hermit who prays in his isolated retreat only finds meaning and coherence in his attitude when in the third stage of development. This is because he considers that his identity is not reduced to his own individuality, but that he is a member of the 'mystical body', actively involved and responsible in the communion of saints and his attitude. Far from being selfish and withdrawn, he is on the contrary a member that through his faith and action acts as an intermediary between the divine and the human. Therefore, by giving himself over to what he believes to be his religious destiny (if he is a Christian, it is the body of Christ, if he is a Hindu, the universal Self, etc.), he participates in the messianic role, contributes to the salvation of humanity and fulfils himself paradoxically through this surpassing of his own individuality.

The Therapeutic Community in US Prisons

During the course of my experience and training as a consultant, I worked for a few days with groups of prisoners in therapeutic communities in Arkansas prisons. The working methods developed in these communities were a combination of approaches used in drug addict groups and 'hard' confrontation techniques used in TA, a treatment developed by Martin Groder. What struck me in this work with long-term prisoners, apart from a development of their individual identity that could be achieved through traditional therapy, was that there was a very strong emphasis on the community aspect and on the implications of each person's individual behaviour. For example, if one of the members of the community stole another member's soap, this act was identified as materially of little importance, but of extreme importance in terms of meaning. At the next session of the group, the prisoner was accused by the whole community of being responsible through his action for attacking the climate of trust and the law of the community as much as for damaging the relationship with his comrade and sabotaging his own individual development, his system of values, beliefs, emotions and behaviour. Gradually, the prisoner became aware that his identity was not simply the product of an individual ego, and he could only develop as a free being, worthy of being given his freedom, once he had accepted that each of his actions portrayed his identity as an individual, as a relational being and as a member of the human community.

To conclude, as we shall discuss later in the development stages of the team, the concept of managerial development, essential for the coach to have in mind, must respect each of the three stages that we have described, as an extension to the concept of interdependence. The coach must integrate them in a coherent way and above all be carrier of a managerial anthropology whereby individual success cannot come at the cost of an anthropology and code of ethics within which the manager develops his talents in a process of individuation (this corresponds to stages 0, 1 and 2 of the levels of autonomy). This process can only flourish if he integrates (stage 2) a development of his capacity to manage relationships and processes (the 'individual', focused on himself, becomes a 'relational being', with belonging and solidarity: a 'person'). Finally, when focused on meaning, after developing the preceding stages, he links up content, processes and meaning. He becomes capable of identifying himself with the meaning, and revealing it to others. Beyond relationship, he becomes capable of 'sharing' himself, of managing this communion, and this rallying, in others. If he sees himself as a carrier of meaning, he will to a certain extent have to experience, know, integrate and harmonise within himself these three stages of development.

CHAPTER 21

Content of Coaching

At the point we have reached in this book, we are able better able to appreciate the complexity of the act of coaching – the range of instruments used, the understanding of every parameter, mastery of each technique, intra-psychical work, acquiring corporal culture, field experience and the capacity to manage a relationship of support. These are the factors that have to be taken into account.

Nonetheless, we believe that it is possible to distil four main aspects, identifiable in terms of behaviour, that constitute the content of coaching, apart from the management of the relational process between the champion and the coach (the model for action grid, handling the different types of contract, etc.).

1. The coach listening to the champion.

2. The coach's contributions.

3. The coach's interventions.

4. Modelling (see Figure 21.1).

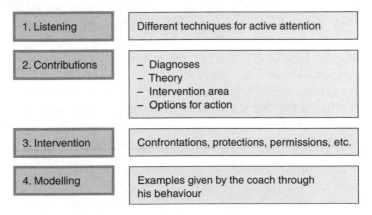

Figure 21.1   The four elements of content provided
by the coach through coaching

Listening to the Champion

As we have already seen, between 30 and 90 per cent of the quality of coaching depends on the attention of the coach. This presupposes a behaviour where the coach is capable of keeping quiet and using the different ways of paying active attention in order to perceive his client's framework of reference, and a behaviour that gives the client the feeling of being understood, respected and supported. That also implies an attitude of empathy and availability, supported by a positive attitude of 'I am OK and so is he/she' and the belief that, whatever the client's level of autonomy in his potential as a champion, and thanks to the coach's support, he is on the way to resolving, progressively and by himself, his own problems.

The following are the traditional techniques for paying attention.

- *Silence*. We recall that to be capable of being silent assumes a whole set of attitudes:

  - leaving room for the client to speak, and more specifically being able not to reply to certain questions;

  - 'crossing transactions' (TA term)

  - not breaking a period of silence;

  - above all being able to trust himself as he trusts his client, in order to avoid adopting a saviour approach.

  It is therefore a question of managing the ambiguity of the fish and the fishing rod. This silence is far from being the attitude of the enigmatic sphinx and the 'neutrality' that psychoanalysts are accused of, but is much closer to a benevolent and active presence, offering the client protections and permissions so that he can develop his own thoughts, words and actions and, progressively, his solutions. Keeping quiet in an empathic attitude does not mean abandoning the client, on the contrary, it is recognising his own force and saying to him 'I am not bringing you a fish on this topic, but I am still there to help you on your way. If it is really necessary, I will bring you a fish, but my first task is to be your facilitator or partner and not only to be a provider.'

- *Questions*. Through posing open questions, the coach will invite the champion to recall aspects that belong to the client's reference framework and about which the coach has no idea. Through closed questions (choosing between two alternatives), he will help him to clarify his thoughts and adopt a position. Through specific questions, he will help to refine his client's map of reality's 'territory'. Open questions are on the side of non-directivity, whereas closed questions show a contrary tendency.

- *Clarification.* A question such as 'what do you mean by ...?' will help to clarify the team's or the individual's interpretation of a given term or concept.

- *Reformulations.* The statement 'if I understand you properly, you are saying that ...', is not a gimmick, it allows the coach both to verify what has been said, and to reassure the client by giving him an external sign that he has understood, and above all to stimulate him to further develop the map, without making external contributions to what the client has said.

- *Confronting emotions.* This is the most delicate and difficult technique to implement, but it is certainly one of the most powerful. It bears witness to a high degree of empathy and presupposes in the coach an ability to perceive not only the operational level of the discussion, but also the psychological level of his client. For example:
  Coach to champion: 'When you tell me about this problem, I have the impression that it is very important, and that you are indignant (or sad) about what happened ...'
  This intervention will cause the client to embark on a discussion that is full of his feelings about the matter (yes, I am indignant, or sad, I've got reason to, etc.) and thereby free himself of the energy attached to such emotions. In Transactional Analysis (TA), it is well known that the person who speaks is not only a rational Adult, but his energy is often blocked in his Child and his Parent.

To conclude, the coach must be prudent and not hurry, nor be driven by the belief that he has to provide a fish. On the contrary, he must remember that his attention is the prime condition allowing his client to emerge from his confusion and pass through a primary process and into a secondary process (that is, help the client to adopt a 'meta' position with regard to his problem) and finally initiate a process of autonomy for his client.

The Coach's Contributions

We can list four main types of contribution:

- *Diagnoses.* Here it is a question of helping the champion draw up a precise map of the territory, that is, to define the reality (what's there, the problem, the need, etc.).

- *Theory*. Providing the client with the information necessary to be able to define the reality (the relevant technical field to which the problem relates, the area of management, leadership, procedures, communication).

- *Areas of intervention*. Determine with the client precisely where the problem lies and in which area one should intervene.

- *Options*. Examine with the client, or suggest, the options available for action.

The Coach's Interventions

The coach's contributions are not simply in paying attention to contributions of content. The coach is ultimately supposed to intervene in a number ways that will obviously alter the relational process. Nevertheless, in terms of content, the contributions will often form the essence of a coaching interview and will at least constitute what the champion takes away with him from the session.

- For example, it may happen as a confrontation. The client will therefore be able to identify that in his behaviour he was mistaken about an important aspect of the problem or of the psychological elements that prevented him from identifying or dealing with the problem.

- There may be a protection. The coach will put his client on guard against a danger or a behaviour that he will then be able to identify and therefore avoid.

- For example, a permission. In terms of content, the essence of the session will emerge from an intervention and attitude on the part of the coach that encourages the champion to take a calculated risk or give himself permission to do something that, psychologically, he had forbidden himself to do, either through simple fear, or through inhibitions caused by past traumas.

Modelling

Through his attitude, that is, through an internalised and silent behaviour, or through demonstration (outward behaviour), the coach will offer his champion a model that the latter will internalise, consciously or not. The support given by the coach through this modelling will provide the champion with a very precise reference in a real situation. A typical example of this modelling is where the coach refuses to accept a hot potato brought by his client, thus putting an end to a chain of symbiotic relationships. This shows his client how, when back on his ground, he too can refuse to take on problems that are not his, but which he previously tended to assume in the role of saviour.

It seems to us that any coaching interview includes these four possible ingredients, either individually or combined. It is therefore useful for the coach to bear them in mind, especially if he has in front of him a champion who knows little about the coaching procedure and does not really know what he wants from the coach. With a view making a contract that often remains implicit, the coach may then suggest one or other of these elements of content. For example:

Coach to champion: 'We only have thirty minutes for this interview, would you like us to have a period during which I just listen to you, or I help you to define the problem better, or more specifically would you like today to define three possible choices for your meeting tomorrow? Shall I make some theoretical observations about the problem, and perhaps point it out to you if I think that you have a personal blind spot owing to your depth of involvement in this situation? What would suit you best, given that we cannot cover everything in the space of half an hour?'

CHAPTER 22

Coaching Process Alongside 'Appraisal Interviews'

Summary

The coaching process aims at separating out what is often bound up with the annual appraisal interview, which covers:

- the assessment of the past year;
- the setting of objectives and decisions relating to the variable parts of salaries or increases.

This process is established in several stages through:

- a phase of preparation and announcement of the procedure, individually or collectively, taking into account the company's resistance to this type of exchange;
- an individual interview for setting objectives and the development of the minimum cultural envelope (MCE), taking account of everyone's level of autonomy;
- one or more subsequent interviews;
- an appraisal interview.

Process for a Manager's Coaching of a Subordinate

In this chapter, we shall present the constituent type element for a specific coaching relationship, that of a manager with each of his subordinates. The previous chapters have focused on individual coaching as an internal or external consultant and how it can be practiced in regard to a client. The hierarchical manager may of course adopt this approach in the context of his own management. However, on the one hand his operational responsibilities for his colleagues do not allow him to have the freedom of an official or of someone outside the institution and, on the other hand, the weight of the relational hierarchy 'contaminates' the different aspects of the coaching relationship that he can have with his subordinates. In this chapter, we simply wish to sketch out the elements of a procedure that allows the manager to introduce a minimum structuring of his relationship with his colleagues in the spirit of coaching (see Figure 22.1).

Phase 1: preparatory phase

1. Announcement of the formal and informal procedure over the year
2. Request to prepare objectives
3. Definition, as coach, of one's own objectives

Phase 2: individual appraisal or object-setting interview

1. Announcement of the procedure for a year; this year: development year
2. The individual's perception (representation system):
   - team
   - himself
   - getting acquainted
3. Our reciprocal perceptions: strong points, points to be improved
4. Definition of his objectives and their context (team's objectives)
5. Help that he requires:
   - field work, financial, personnel, technical
   - from me
   - from experience
   - from hierarchy / senior staff
6. Training and development
   - courses
   - training positions
   - travel, visits
7. His suggestions
8. Mutual strokes (signs of recognition)
9. Assessment of the interview process

Phase 3: follow-up interviews

Measurement of the level achieved

Phase 4: appraisal interview

See phase 2

Figure 22.1   Coaching procedure alongside the appraisal interview

We suggest four phases that represent a minimum procedure to cover a year. In fact, we believe that a manager who wishes to practise coaching with his colleagues owes it to himself to hold at least four fairly formal interviews during the year.

Note that in the majority of cases, the only formal procedure that exists in companies is the annual appraisal interview. Moreover, even if it is conducted carefully and rapidly, this interview has a tendency to combine three objectives:

- a dialogue between manager and subordinate relating to the assessment of the year and a reciprocal evaluation of their performance;

- possibly set next year's objectives;

- a more or less discussed decision taken by the manager on the allocation of a possible bonus or changes in salary.

Without wishing to enter into detail that lies beyond the scope of this book, our recommendation is to separate these three elements so far as possible and to deal with them at separate interviews spread over a period of time.

The four phases of our coaching procedure are as follows:

1. Preparation phase and announcement of the procedure;

2. An individual interview for setting objectives and developing the MCE;

3. One or more subsequent interviews along the way;

4. An appraisal interview.

Details on the Four Phases

Preparation Phase and Announcement of the Procedure

As its name indicates, this phase is concerned with establishing contact between the manager and his subordinates, individually and collectively. This contact is the opportunity to announce implementation of the procedure, to explain the spirit behind the work, and allow them to appreciate its ambiguity (Managerial Identity Development [MID] is of course involved), without neglecting to take into account operational constraints, and without being able to reduce one polarity to the other. It also has to be understood that the approach is not merely quantitative, just setting quantified operational objectives, but much more, as we have recalled with the Ouchi banking example, implementing via operational objectives:

- a common MCE;

- a coherence of behaviour;

- verifying shared values;

- experiencing interdependence and reacting and being proactive together in the face of the reality within and outside of the team.

Occurring possibly at different times, this phase aims at giving information, inviting colleagues to draft out their objectives and their views on the entire department and present their individual vision, removing resistance, objections and questions about this procedure and providing models, and so on. In fact, it is a support process that may upset the culture of the organisation that the people belong to, and which must be done with prudence, consistency and without haste.

I recall the amazement and indignation of a high-level manager of a multinational when faced with this kind of somewhat brutal attitude from his American boss, who had requested him to produce his objectives for the following year. He saw it as an aggressive, controlling attitude, casting doubt on the climate of mutual trust, an attitude that this French manager, living in a strong contextual culture, was unable to integrate.

Individual Interview for Setting Objectives and Developing the MCE

Phase 2, focusing on past or future objectives, must be structured according to the level of autonomy of the two partners, and needs to change as they evolve towards reciprocal interdependence and delegation. It includes a certain number of elements that we have listed in Figure 22.1, not as a rigid procedure, but as a checklist to avoid any major omissions.

Note that this interview is designed to disentangle the three relational levels that exist between a manager and his subordinate:

- the hierarchical or institutional level that, by its nature, includes non-symmetrical elements of dependence, since the boss by definition has greater responsibility than the subordinate;

- the operational level in which it is desirable for the manager's six Ego States and his subordinate's to be active and able to communicate in every possible combination;

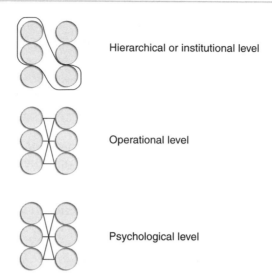

Hierarchical or institutional level

Operational level

Psychological level

Figure 22.2   The three levels of the boss–subordinate relationship

- the psychological level, where it is desirable for the flow of exchanges between the six Ego States between manager and subordinate to be at its optimum. When this flow and this separation are achieved, there is optimisation of the two partners' energies. This means that trust and transparency are shared at an optimum level (but not maximum). Finally, we recall that exchange of 'signs of recognition' and a climate of mutual appraisal contribute to making the two partners feel united, grateful and respected (see Figure 22.2).

A Follow-up Interview Along the Way

This phase, repeated as required, aims chiefly at providing a marker, depending on the events, the level of autonomy of both partners, on the nature of operations and the agreed contract of delegation.

Appraisal Interview

Over time, this phase can be exchanged with phase 2 and the same comments will apply.

We note that the decision made by managers to embark on processes of this type, far from being a waste of time, prove to be a very valuable investment for the progressive implementation of delegation procedures. This process can warrant the manager's meeting each of his colleagues for an hour or two per week, up to the point where he only meets them at their request. This reflects our strong view that a manager can only delegate effectively after progressively managing the stages of autonomy, in the role of enabler and teacher. Finally, we believe that this process is very beneficial to the manager because it leads him progressively from the role of specialist in a profession to that of hierarchical manager to the role of leader, as we defined it earlier.

PART V

Coaching a Team: Team Building

CHAPTER 23

The ORT Model (Operations, Regulation, Training)

Summary

In this spiral model:

- 'Operations' means the work of team building, focusing on highly operational problems.

- Regulation means taking a break during the phase of operations, in order to make adjustments. This ranges from 'sharing of representations' to 'resolution of conflicts'.

- Training means specific contributions and exercises.

The coach must continually integrate and adapt all three phases to the situation.

The process of growth fostered by team building can be regarded as a spiral revolving around three polarities, operations, regulation and training, which are always present to varying degrees (see Figure 23.1).

Sometimes the focus is on operations and it is often there that the coach must make contact with the team for the first time. This is in order to get to know one another, discover people's characteristics and become aware of the climate, character and customs of the group, its major stakes and its culture. Although at first it may appear somewhat lengthy and wasteful, this time is in fact a necessary and valuable investment to the extent that it allows the coach to pitch his interventions at the most appropriate level. Being focused on operations, the engagement in team building gains in credibility and appears as what it aims at achieving ultimately in every case, namely helping the team become more successful. We shall therefore begin with the problems that it is concerned about. This is often necessary when first faced with the multi-faceted resistance in a team towards any examination from outside and the related threats of change.

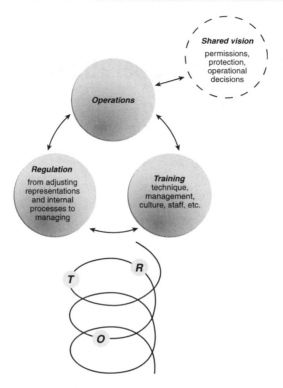

Figure 23.1   A team's growth process

Sometimes the focus is on regulation, because the operations phase has run into an obstacle or because a specific time has been allocated for it (for example, a day devoted to reflection) or because it is found necessary to resolve some conflict.

Sometimes it will focus on training with the aim of adding contributions or training in particular skills.

In all cases, the team-building coach must take care to ensure that there is a link between these three poles. Being present in the normal life of the team can be very useful, even if, at most, he only intervenes for a few minutes during the day. In fact, some simple feedback given to the manager during a pause may enable him to avoid going down the wrong path. The simple and brief contribution of a methodological concept may alter the whole dynamics of a day.

Embarking on a team-building operation may occur via one of these three entry points, depending on the circumstances.

Entry through Training

This may be done within the team in the company, or externally. Members of the operational team may for example participate in an introductory seminar on coaching and team building, either individually, or in pairs. In this inter-company situation, they can enter the culture of coaching and team building, assess its value and plan with the consultant an intervention that would take place within the company. Another approach is to hold an internal conference or a day of reflection involving all or part of the operational team. This could be a conference lasting several hours or a day divided up into periods in which the coach(es) presents models of action and experience with other clients, alternating with periods in which the team examines its vision and other topics that concern it. Through this sharing, the manager, the consultant and the members of the team enter into the culture of coaching and team building, identify the problems or the intersection points on which it is useful to spend time, perceive more clearly how a coach's support can be profitable for them and possibly decide on another meeting or on the implementation of a period of continuous support.

The advantage of entry through training is that it is relatively fast, it allows for a collective decision by the team and not simply the boss, and it quickly articulates the dynamic of the partnership in which on one side the operational team works on its real problems and on the other side the coach helps out with his contributions and facilitates the processes.

The disadvantage to be avoided in this approach is the danger that the team may ask for a theoretical presentation of the coaching and team-building culture and criticise it intellectually, thus masking its resistance to actually invest in it. There is also the risk that the team will be reticent, owing to some lack of confidence in the boss's intentions or some mistrust at the presence of any outsider, or purely and simply through resistance to change for all kinds of reasons. The danger of this approach is that understanding what coaching and team building are about requires a minimum of experimentation.

Entry through Regulation

By regulation, we mean the whole range of processes from the simple sharing of representations in which everyone develops and presents his or her vision of an element or problem, up to a process for managing a difficult conflict, requiring the presence of a mediator.

In the first case, it is an approach to prevent a conflict that may be experienced by the participants in different ways. It implies improving an already satisfactory working system. Introducing coaching and team building can therefore be likened to a trainer working with already successful athletes.

In another case, we are rather in the world of emergency medicine, fire-fighting or hostage taking. Here it is a question of an on-the-spot request where the coach's role is experienced by the participants in a completely different way. The main problem is the partners' accepting the coach in his role as mediator.

This type of gateway can therefore be used in an emergency, in the case of managing a conflict, with all the protections and permissions that are involved, or it may be the result of a far-sighted request from a manager aware of the value of investing in coaching and team building. An operational manager who is putting his team together or going through a major phase of his own development may correctly see how important it is for him to adopt every means of optimising success at this stage.

The advantage of this entry method is that, in both cases, a decision is made by at least one of the major decision makers, and there is a clear request. The danger is that, if we are simply sharing representations, the team members may not see the usefulness of the investment, or, in the case of a serious conflict, the coach is seen not as a mediator but wrongly as the company's dirty tricks specialist (or at worst as a potential executioner).

Entry through Operations

When a major event occurs in the operational life of a company, inviting a coach may be justified on the grounds of the extent and complexity of the change imposed by operational life, whether a merger, the launch of a new product, a restructuring, a new appointment or a reconfiguration of the market. Entering a process of coaching and team building includes defining the operational objectives to be achieved, at the same time as reaching an agreement on the coaching and team-building process. In practice, initiating this new collaboration implies the coach's progressive participation at several operational meetings of the team. For an executive committee, for example, there may be an operation review, a preparatory discussion, a strategic decision, a communication meeting or a meeting focusing on a specific operational problem. The coach must carefully weigh up his degree of participation, keeping a low profile when first attending meetings, so that he can absorb the minimum cultural envelope (MCE) of the team that he meets, and in order not to disclose his view of the support role of coaching and team building until he has had the chance of perceiving this MCE.

He will need to know about the team's operational objectives, its values, its experience, its stage of development, its capacity for recognising the value of coaching and team building, its degree of resistance and its requirements.

We have described these three polarities for the purpose of educational clarification. It is quite clear to us that company situations always include a mixture of all three aspects to varying degrees. As a coach we have to manage these complexities; that is our job. We are not consultants focusing on the objective and external problems of the people before us, we are not trainers who must contribute by optimising an educational process, nor are we simply facilitators or mediators in a conflict. In all cases, all of these functions must be integrated to some extent simultaneously by 'wearing a different hat' and 'playing the accordion' (constantly varying time management), and also being chameleons that adapt continually according to the information of the moment. Therefore, at a given meeting the coach will have to take into account the operational objectives and contribute towards the team's gaining a better consensual vision. On another occasion, he will have to intervene in the management of a relational process among the team members in order to avoid or outflank a conflict, and then, a few minutes later, be ready to deliver a short but all-embracing piece on a management or cultural concept in order to help the group progress further in its identity or in solving its problems. It's a great job, isn't it?

CHAPTER 24

Development Stages for Teams

In this chapter, we shall present model 1 of the six development stages of the team, followed by model 2, the collection of individuals, the group, the successful team. Finally, we make the link between these two models with that of the manager's development stage.

Model 1: the Six Stages

We shall describe each of the six stages in a linear way for educational reasons, knowing that passing from one stage to the next constitutes an advance. However, we can see, in this model, as in several of our preceding models that:

- each stage is OK and represents a necessary stage to invest in;
- according to the principle that 'he who can do the most can do the least', the further one progresses from 1 to 6 the more one increases the team's operational resources and its ability to be successful;
- depending on the situation and the people involved, it is quite appropriate to go back to a previous stage that one has already experienced, either because the situation does not allow consultation due to the urgency, or because new members have to be integrated into the team;
- a process of spiral growth is completely desirable, once again, where it appears that one is going through a similar stage, but this time, at a different level of consciousness.

Stage 1

The characteristic of this first stage is the flow of information and decisions coming down from manager A to his colleagues B, C and D (see Figure 24.1).

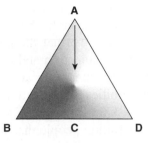

Figure 24.1   Stage I

This may correspond to the quite natural phase in the setting up of a team in which the head recruits colleagues, as in when a company is created. This is frequently the case with a one-man business. It applies also of course to free-market professional firms that are established around an original founder. However, it may also reflect a regressive situation where the circumstances, or the personalities involved, have contributed to create a situation in which the boss is relatively dominating, either because his level of competence is too far removed from that of his colleagues, or because his management style is autocratic.

▪ The role of the manager in this stage, if in the context of a natural stage, will be mainly to define the framework, to vitalise the team and above all to create the relational conditions that allow the colleagues to find the support they need to take on their position (level 0 of autonomy) and at the same time be assured that a development process for their autonomy is announced (from levels 1–4), with the ultimate prospect of delegation, and that level 5 (the level of meaning) can be set up at the same time as level 0 (see Figure 6.4 and following).

▪ The dangers of this period are to be found in the fact that the manager and his colleagues are installing a system and a representation of their relational reality in which might enclose themselves in the long term, without providing for this educational process on either side. This generates what is referred to as a homeostasis, namely a stable system from which it is very difficult to free oneself despite apparent changes.

▪ The coach's role is mainly to perceive the manager's blind spots, help him to define each person's needs, including his own and above all to ensure that the manager fulfils his strategic and operational roles, does not delegate prematurely and at the same time adopts the type of relationship necessary for level 0 autonomy. This is not guaranteed, since some managers are averse to giving clear orders (positive critical Parent) or giving clear permissions (Nurturing Parent (NP)). But, more especially, the coach's role is to help the system establish itself, not become locked in homeostasis, so that the partners enter straightaway into a position of meta-communication and anticipate a growth process such as for example that of the model for autonomy development. While taking into account his affinities, his sensitivity and emotions, the manager will find it useful to ask the coach to help him avoid going down the path of narcissistically recruiting people that sing his praises like a band of cronies, but help him choose colleagues that are different from him (in particular by compensating for his weak points) and at the same time set up relational processes, a common meaning, a sufficient minimum cultural envelope to prevent these differences from becoming a source of conflict, but rather a complementarity aimed at synergy.

Passing from stage 1 to stage 2. Here the task is to create conditions under which colleagues will be able to speak up in front of their manager. This implies two factors, mainly on the part of the coach:

- the manager has to accept contradiction, embark on a process of true autonomy development that is somewhat like giving up control. In some cases the coach has to establish with the manager a real confrontation contract that allows him, while protecting the manager and himself, to establish before the group the fact that one can have a different point of view from the manager's, without that being a danger. In fact, at stage 2 the psychological and operational levels are strongly imbued with the relational symbiosis resulting from the hierarchical dimension. The coach must make it possible to move on from this stage, first by opening up another type of behaviour in the manager, namely adopting a more Adult stance and positioning oneself before Adult people, even if they still lack some qualities and hold some fears;

- as for the colleagues, the coach must facilitate their speaking-up in the group. In some cases, when managing the group process, he has to see to it that everyone is able to express himself. This implies a satisfactory degree of individual trust with each member, and may often require prior individual interviews.

Stage 2

- As shown in Figure 24.2, this stage deals with how the team members express themselves vis-à-vis their boss. It is an experience that corresponds

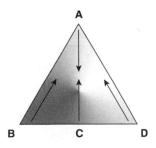

Figure 24.2 Stage 2

to their contribution to elaborating the decisions, going beyond their roles as simple performers. At a psychological level, they must be able to confirm their specificity and difference in comparison with their boss. This being either because they are more competent in their profession, or because they have a different vision that must necessarily be taken into account.

■ The manager's role corresponds to stages of levels 1, 2 and 3 of autonomy. That is, while assuming the operational responsibility that is his own, he allows his colleagues to speak up, and even to generate and create a desirable climate of trust themselves.

■ The dangers of this stage relate to the manager's role, if he has not adjusted to his colleagues' capacity for speaking up:

– either because he prevents them from speaking owing to his overbearing personality;

– or, the opposite, if he prematurely delegates his own responsibilities.

Another danger is that the manager may feel challenged at a psychological level and placed in a drama triangle with his colleagues, faced with the aggression that they show, like hedgehogs, to prove counter-dependence (level 1 of autonomy).

On the side of the members, there is the danger that they remain inhibited yes-men (level 0), or they experience their counter-dependence stage by swinging back and forth in aggression, becoming hedgehogs (level 1 of autonomy). They either reject any intervention by the manager out of rebellion, or they want to prove to him that they are right, or more often, they express themselves through having 10 to 90 per cent of their energy consumed by contradictory feelings, and of course fear too.

■ In this situation, the coach's role is mainly to help the partners adjust to each other so far as is possible. This entails preparing the agendas, talking with the different partners between meetings, acting as 'sherpa' at top-level conferences, freeing the team manager from managing the processes. He therefore helps the manager to avoid combining all roles such as: operational responsibility, responsibility for meetings, and chairperson and manager in order to leave him the role of hierarchical manager who arbitrates as a last resort. The coach will see to it that each team member can express himself. Depending on the nature of the meeting (see Figure 2.2 ORT), he will focus mainly on the sharing of representations (see next chapter).

Passage from stage 2 to stage 3. When stage 2 is completed, and the relationship between the manager and each of the team members is such that there is a true exchange, there often remains the task of making the colleagues work together, and for there to be some horizontal passing of information from B to C and C to D and reciprocally. It is desirable for the coach to seek out all the different operational situations outside team meetings, to invite dialogue between the participants, such as preparation, projects to carry out together, sorting out conflict between pairs, work in subgroups and so on.

Stage 3

■ What characterises this stage is that team members have already discovered their identities sufficiently to dare to express themselves in front of their boss. However, each person's territory is not yet sufficiently defined for people to speak freely within the group. Having passed through the two preceding stages, each member of the group has found a modus vivendi with the boss, to the extent that, during the meeting and outside, they are able to communicate (see Figure 24.3).

■ The manager's role is chiefly to arbitrate between the different functions and different persons, to make sure that everyone speaks up, and to adopt a star-shaped method of operating. When everyone expresses his/her views, it is he who acts as arbitrator. The most frequent dangers of this situation are that decisions are for the most part taken outside the meeting, in a one-to-one manager–subordinate context, or between two colleagues alone. What is said during the meeting is mainly the communication of a point of view or the official announcement of a decision, the key

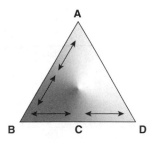

Figure 24.3   Stage 3

elements of what is at stake having been dealt with outside the meeting. This development stage leaves much unsaid in the team.

■ The coach's role is mainly to optimise what occurs between the unsaid and the explicit, knowing that not everything is transparent yet and that the group's maturity ranging between the four first levels of autonomy is not sufficiently advanced to allow complete transparency. Together with the manager, he will manage through his understanding of the situation the levels of meaning that can be tackled, and not hesitate to initiate numerous informal dialogues before or after meetings, by himself with the participants, or in face-to-face discussions so that suitable adjustments are made for each of the partners.

Passage from stage 3 to stage 4. The coach focuses on the transversal exchanges between team members, and he tries to create two types of situations:

■ formal or informal teams, bringing together several colleagues B, C and D on a project to be managed together, such as a change process, and so on.

■ with the manager's consent, to set up team meetings without the boss, in order for the team to learn how to operate without him.

Stage 4

■ The characteristic of this stage is that decision-making and information circulation begin to occur during meetings and, even if the presence and hierarchical role of the boss remain quite evident, there is greater transparency and sufficient confidence for people to be able to broach levels of meaning other than those concerned with strictly operational matters

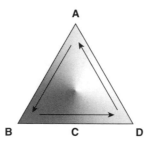

Figure 24.4 Stage 4

(see Figure 7.7). Each person's territory is respected, decisions begin to be made interdependently, and the boss plays his role of arbitrator without affecting what people say through his presence. There is solidarity in the team (see Figure 24.4).

- The manager's role is to invite the participants to make their views known to their colleagues and not only to him. He encourages them to meet outside his presence and to make decisions on matters that have been discussed collectively. He also invites them to announce externally, either individually or collectively, the decisions made by the team.

- The dangers of this stage are that the manager may find it hard to accept this phase of autonomy in the team in relation to him and be anxious about the meetings that take place without him. With regard to the coach, he may take umbrage at his progressive role as co-pilot and question the trust in the alliance for change to which he agreed. By insidiously questioning one or two of his team, he risks perpetuating the symbiotic system of stages 1 and 2, either at his own initiative or because the participants themselves prefer to return to the relative comfort of these stages. The partners then run the risk of inciting the manager to conduct separate interviews, to discuss matters that ought to be decided upon at the collective meetings.

- The coach's role is one of meta-communication both during and outside the meetings, in order to restrict the unsaid to the maximum and to cause it to emerge progressively at the meetings, and to manage in particular the interface between manager and subordinates, mainly regarding the meetings without the manager. Through his consistency, the protection that he provides, his concern to consider each and everyone and the signs of communication that he gives, he contributes to creating the conditions of trust required by the team at this major stage.

Passage from stage 4 to stage 5. In this stage where the team begins to operate while setting aside the boss's hierarchical role, the coach, who up until now has often played the role of process leader or conductor, will increasingly remain in the meta-position, inviting the participants, in turn, to conduct the meeting.

Stage 5

■ The group usually operates like a quality control circle and, as we have shown in Figure 24.5, rulings by the hierarchical manager may still occur but are the exception, because the participants are most frequently located in positions A', B', C' and D', that is, in a circular energy flow. Each uses his three Ego States, leads the team in his turn and feels free to intervene at any level of meaning (operational, psychological, strategic, identity, power, meta meaning). Return to position A, B, C and D remains possible and desirable in certain cases, but it is no longer a structural factor for the identity of the persons. In terms of levels of autonomy the team members live chiefly at level 3 of interdependence.

■ The manager's chief role is to pass from A to A', in other words, from the hierarchical role to that of simple participant, and locate himself as much as possible in A', the position of a member of a quality circle. In terms of content, his role is to be more focused on the eight other levels of meaning than on the purely operational level, and he can play his role of coach for the team fully, because he will have delegated the majority of his operational responsibilities to this end. He gives each of his team the opportunity of surpassing his role as guardian of a profession (technical specialist) and even of manager, and becoming member of a team

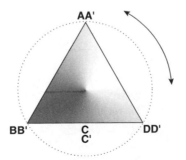

Figure 24.5 Stage 5

in which each person is united and focused on interdependently made decisions and in which each can be carrier of the decision collectively vis-à-vis the outside world. It is no longer a question of the participants finding their individual identity or of even making decisions together, but of collectively implementing the vision.

■ The dangers of this stage are that the group members confuse the second and third levels of autonomy and, under the pretext of interdependence, try to take all the credit, not because they want to increase their territory, but because, as a result of the encouragement to take the initiative, they believe prematurely that they can replace the manager. The other danger for the manager is that he may too soon delegate all his responsibilities and neglect an aspect of the 'immaturity' of one or more of his team members.

■ The coach's role is to remain chiefly in the meta-position and no longer conduct the process. However, he will need to review the different levels of meaning addressed by the content of the team's discussions and, by focusing on the development stage of each of his champions, spur on in them those qualities that need to be developed or strengthened. He will thus help the group to meta-communicate about the way that each member performs through increasingly sophisticated group processing regulations.

Stage 6

■ As Figure 24.6 shows, the distinction between the hierarchical relationship and the participants has become completely blurred, meaning that the united group, where each member has integrated his vision as an element of his identity, operates, at the very least, like a quality circle.

■ One cannot speak of this stage as the final one, because in the spiral process (see Figure 24.7) it only represents one aspect of the life of the

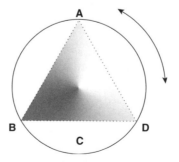

Figure 24.6 Stage 6

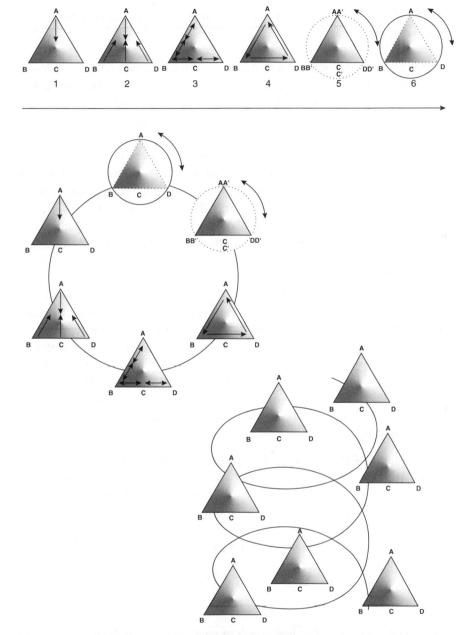

Figure 24.7 The process of the six stages of model I for team development

group. However, in the first phase where a team passes through the six stages, stage 6 constitutes an important qualitative change compared with the previous stages.

A second characteristic is where the group knows how to decide, even in the absence of the manager, and can function without difficulty in infinitely variable ways. That is, in the absence of several team members, it can make decisions of a quality consistent with any decision that would be made by the complete group. There is an atmosphere of trust and transparency, and the group is sufficiently mature to know that the participants at the meeting will wait for a particular member to be present if they think it useful, but will not in any way try to take advantage of someone's absence in order to push some matter through. Each member of the team is sufficiently a 'carrier of meaning', not only for the team but also for the organisation, for any member in turn to be able to conduct the meeting without being challenged.

- It is in this phase that the manager is able to realise most fully his potential as a leader, unencumbered by the operational aspects and the management of his team's processes. It is this stage that he can delegate fully to those of his colleagues who have thoroughly integrated the fourth and fifth levels of autonomy, that is, the levels where they can take care of the group (4) and be carriers of the meaning and mission of the team (5). Finally, thus freed from day-to-day management through this delegation, he can concentrate fully on strategy and on his role as trainer of a team of champions.

- The dangers of this stage are that it might be implemented too soon for some of the team members, or that a backwards move, required by circumstances or the weakness of one of its members, obliging the manager or one of his colleagues to return to a previous stage, is experienced by the team as a traumatising event adversely affecting the quality of trust and the partnership already established.

The coach's role in this stage is not to withdraw but to make his presence felt in three areas:

- he can become the individual coach of each member of the team on some particular aspect;
- he can act with full authority as an interface for the team with other teams or the remainder of the organisation;

- he becomes a valuable sounding board for the team, which regards him much more as the person who reflects feedback back to them by virtue of to his detached position. The sharing of his own MCE with the MCE of the team is of such a quality that they will be able, in the partnership, to communicate and understand one another with great subtlety.

Model: Collection of Individuals, Group and Effective Team

In this second model, different from the previous one, we shall concentrate on other parameters that make up the team, and in particular give priority to the identity aspects of the team members and the points where they have to focus their energy. At the same time, we shall pay less attention to the relationship with the leadership.

First Stage: Collection of Individuals

- At this stage, the team members (Figure 24.8) are in a phase where they are focusing on their identity and their individual jobs, typically when a team is being put together. Alternatively, having found it difficult to find identity and territory, they have focused on the maintenance of their territory and the promotion of their own individual profession within the group. To compare this with a government situation, it would be like newly appointed ministers promoting their ministries, seeking out an identity, boundaries and territories, or ministers whose portfolios have been established for a long time but who are concerned about preventing others from encroaching on their patch.

  This stage is normal and necessary to the extent that the uniqueness of each team member must be defined, as will his identity, which is often

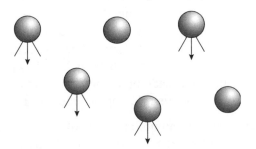

Figure 24.8   Stage of a collection of individuals

linked to missions and precise territories, and that the means given to each member (techniques, human resources, finance, etc.) have to be continually optimised.

■ As we shall see from Figure 24.11, the thought process that prevails at this stage is chiefly linear, where each specialist, focused on himself and his job, tends to regard the problems he addresses as objectives, without paying much attention to the type of relationship he has with the outside. Managerial development concentrates on skills with an emphasis on content and considers that values are technical values. The team member tends to identify with the team, even to the point of being its vassal.

■ Belief and position in life. The partners can experience this stage as necessary and positive. They can be in the following individual life position: Me +, You + the others. Me as member of the team 'I am OK', the other members of the team are 'OK', and the people outside are also 'OK'. However, it is possible and very often occurs that this stage, where each individual needs to position himself and find identity and territory, unfolds in a partially negative life position: Me +, You − and the others −. This is where everyone fights for his territory and is at risk of being in a winner–loser position.

■ The dangers of this stage lie in the team members' closing up in relation to the other members' jobs. Each person is concerned with finding his own identity and protecting himself, rather than with communicating and exchanging. In the case of a team that has existed for a long time, feudal systems may well have become established. This is especially likely if the team leader has already changed several times and if minimal conditions of trust and solidarity have not been created, or if the team has experienced repeated trauma.

■ Of course, the manager's role varies according to the dynamics of the team. He does not need to operate in the same way if he is creating a team from nothing. Or he may have joined an existing team, being himself drafted in from outside, or he may be promoted among his peers as leader of a team to which he already belongs. For restructuring purposes, or because of conflict or other reasons, he may have had to take on this role in an original team, often made up of people who belonged to it at different periods in the past. His role appears threefold:

– first, to create the minimum conditions of trust between himself and his colleagues and between the colleagues themselves. We may recall the two or three first stages of the previous model;

- second, to handle the identity problems of each of his colleagues in terms of skills, responsibility and means. Another way of formulating this is to recall that the model of the nine levels of meaning allows identification of how power issues are often no more than defences intended to protect the eight other levels of meaning that people are unable to deal with adequately (cf. Part II, Chapter 7). (It can be a big project, can't it?)

- third, to implement a team-building process, alone or with outside help, in order to guide the team through to stage 2 and then on to stage 3.

■ The coach's role in this stage is to create the conditions for an alliance with the manager, and with the team members, that does not threaten anyone, and allows the various partners to approach their way of working with a view to bringing change and growth if they wish (which may not always be the case). First, his role is to personally carry out a minimum feasibility study, to put any necessary protections in place, such as for example a progressive sequence of meetings, individual interviews with each participant if necessary, securing the manager's assurance that he is prepared for a progressive but difficult road without resorting to repression, and verifying the minimum compatibility of the partners' MCEs. It is important for him to establish as soon as possible that he is not the 'bringer of solutions'. Simply by his presence, and the investment it represents in terms of time, energy and money, and thus of the team's will to change, the coach can help the different partners, and of course the manager, to define their request to move towards a contract without any aggressiveness, by remaining firmly in the position of mediator and facilitator. This very process (initial meeting, evaluation of the situation, agreement to move to a contract) is already in itself the beginning of a team-building process.

Passage from 1 to 2. The main criterion of this will be to define the boundaries of the group. It has to be established who belongs to this group. This may not be immediately clear; there may be several hierarchical levels or people (secretaries, personal assistants, etc.) who do not hold the same status and knowledge, especially when all members of a group are brought together at a first meeting. There is a delicate decision to be made, because of the danger of defining a membership that might be called into question later and prematurely cause conflicts. On the other hand, deciding upon too restricted a group may generate a feeling of exclusion on the part of those who are not included. Through this work, the team's system of operation can be analysed and beyond this the status, role and identity of everyone. When a management team is involved, the distinction between a strategic committee meeting, operation review meeting, communication meeting, objective-setting meeting, and so on, must be handled with care on the first occasion. Before any of these first meetings can be set up, there must be detailed individual preparation with each team member and particularly beforehand with the director to define the identity and membership of each person. It should be remembered that the passage from 1 to 2 cannot be achieved at once. It can only be the result of a progressive transformation through successive cycles, implying that the new identity characteristic of stage 2 will not appear for several weeks (or even months) after a complex process.

One of the main roles of the coach is to create a sufficient degree of trust with the participants, evaluate the level of motivation for a growth process, and see to it that the team members have the capacity to carry out the grieving required by such a transition.

Second Stage: Cohesive Group

At this stage:

- the boundary defining team membership becomes clear;
- the leadership is confirmed;
- the identities and energy of each participant are altered.

Each member of the team has found his identity and his territory to a sufficient extent, and if there are still sometimes some debates about these territories, the energy is focused much more on mutual attention, understanding of the necessary complementarity and a much more systemic thought process. In fact, each protagonist is aware of his interdependence with the others and that if he makes a decision without considering the others' point of view, and without the others feeling respect, he will cause rejection that will be harmful to all. The team's spirit is focused on the process going on between the members. The team's values become relational and consensus values and the members' identity is more an identity defined in relation to the group and the solidarity of its members (see Figure 24.9).

The positive aspects of this stage are that the participants develop in a relationship of solidarity that goes beyond the quality of interpersonal relationships because they feel themselves to be responsible carriers of the decisions made by the group. Pursuing the government metaphor, they are more 'united minister members of a government' than 'ministers with tenure of a ministry'.

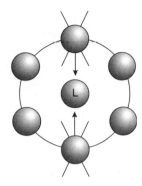

Figure 24.9 Cohesive group stage

- Belief and life position. Belief can again be + + +, but if the group slips to a negative side, it risks positioning itself in a form of collective self-ishness where the beliefs will be + + −. In this case, identification in the group risks being very exclusive and generating relationships that lead progressively towards the drama triangle with people outside the group.

- The major dangers in this stage are that on one hand, the values of soli-darity and membership cause the group members to lose their individual voice, the group solidarity becomes oppressive, an individual or a minor-ity is oppressed in the group, and the apparent consensus does not take account of each person's real uniqueness. On the other hand, the danger of this solidarity, if it is excessive, would be the group's closing in on itself and losing contact with external reality, all in the name of solidar-ity; examples of this might be forgetting the law, the market, other mem-bers of the company, showing preference for seniority to the detriment of resources needed by the team.

- The manager's role is of course similar to that in stages 3 and 4 of the previous model. He must invite discussion in the group, having first as much as possible positioned himself as a simple participant and only assuming his hierarchical role to the extent necessary for operational life and for the growth of the group.

- The coach's role is to make the team members focus not on the content, skills and a linear mode of thought but, while still accepting these reali-ties, adopt a meta-position and develop competencies and a sensitivity with regard to a systemic way of thinking, a true mutual attention, skills in managing processes and in promoting the quality of relationships.

The passage from 2 to 3 is a progressive qualitative change in the form of a spiral. However, it may be characterised by the fact that the manager, the participants and the group will radically change identity through focusing on the vision. This transition is therefore allowed mainly by the link between sharing each person's representations and co-elaborating a vision with a view to sharing it. Ultimately, this implies not only clarification of this vision for everyone but a type 2 change, that is, merging out of homeostasis for the participants, and challenging the culture, for them to change individually and structurally their process for defining reality. In other words, as we described in the discussion about the MCE, they access a capacity for understanding the mechanisms for autonomy, meta-communication, growth, meaning and change.

The team's passage from stage 1 to 2 and the educational and transformational processes that they experienced before this stage will condition this transition. The 'butterflies' of stage 2 already know that they are not 'fat caterpillars' as in 1, and the coach must remind them that they have yet to experience an equally radical transformation in order to move on to stage 3. In terms of autonomy level, it is level 5 where identity and action are to be defined by meaning, as a priority in comparison with the four preceding levels of autonomy.

Third Stage: Effective Team

■ This stage is characterised by the fact that the identity of each participant, like that of the team itself, is defined by his/its relationship to the shared vision, what may be also called the meaning (both significance and direction), or MCE (since we know that it is not simply a question of operational objectives but also of values and behaviours, in short, what defines a culture). In fact, having already to some extent integrated their technical competence and their capacity to be mutually receptive, the team members are focused on developing this shared vision and the continual readjustment of everyone's role and of the team's role to this vision of itself; a vision which is constantly updated according to the evolution of the surrounding reality (see Figure 24.10).

■ The thought process, as we have seen in the manager's development stages, becomes holistic and like a hologram. The team members, who had already at the preceding stage begun to constitute a 'collective body', take on as an element of their individual and collective identity the mantle of the shared vision of the team or the organisation. Thus, as Figure 22.1

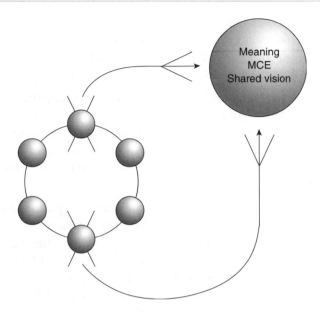

Figure 24.10 Effective team stage

shows, each team member integrates the other's uniqueness into his identity. For example, the sales director will have assimilated the constraints of production into his own approach. However, in addition, everyone will place his own job in a position consistent with the vision.

In a way, each team member becomes a leader, not in the sense of someone who is overdeveloped in comparison with the others, but as someone who is 'a carrier of meaning', capable of showing others the 'stars' to be followed. The values of this team are beyond techniques and the relational system, focused on coherence with regard to meaning; and the identification is made on belonging to the 'whole', encompassing the team. It is like a hologram or the cell of a living body, where each element becomes a carrier of information about the whole organisation, even including information about the external environment.

- In this model, the beliefs and life positions are quite likely to be +++. However, dangers of perversion remain present.

- The risks of this phase are as follows:

  - First danger. An idealisation of the relationships in such a way that the two preceding stages may be experienced as not-OK, and this stage not be seen, as the result of a form of asceticism where everyone must bring into play great vigilance, strategic awareness, grieving that must always be completed, a process of structural transformation, mutual attention and management of the parameters of change (I must listen to the other person while asserting myself).

– A second danger lies in the very significant and always tempting gap between discussions and the internal reality of experience (the real intentions) of everyone. The attractions of power remain, and although in a way a point of no return has been reached owing to everyone's demands and awakened consciousness, it is never possible for there to be complete transparency and the return to square one is potentially present.

– A third danger is an angelic, utopian and idealistic position of the team, both outwardly and inwardly, that does not take account of the development stages of the partners who cannot always understand or experience this qualitative degree in relationships. We should not forget that, as with a chain, the strength of the chain is often reduced to the value of its weakest link. This is why the passage to this third stage and the teams' solidity implies an educational process that cannot be carried out without some significant investment, of time in particular.

■ By definition, the manager in his identity is the person responsible for the team, especially if a management team is involved. He must have integrated the different levels of growth (linear, systemic and holistic) mainly if he is the founder of the company. On the other hand, perhaps he lacks the capacity to manage the educational process that will allow him to transmit to others and acquire either the managerial role or the role of leader. Moreover, he will experience the paradox of every educational process that consists in revealing the vision, while leaving others to find their own way to it. It involves managing the paradox of 'I will teach you to manage by yourself'.

He has to handle the five levels of autonomy with his colleagues, whereas he may have some very important shortcomings himself. These shortcomings may be even more serious in someone who inherits an institutional situation that he has not created. His chief role will therefore be to endorse the role of the major person responsible for the vision, and allow his team members to contribute both to the development and to the implementation of this vision. In fact, the more he allows everyone to contribute to the development of the strategic vision, the more he creates the conditions for motivating its implementation.

The second aspect of his role is knowing how to surround himself with the right people, that is, selecting and then creating the conditions for the development of his colleagues while at the same time being able to remove himself if necessary. Being the carrier of meaning and supporter–trainer, his apparently simple role implies that he has had to completely assimilate the complexity of the cultures that he must master. However, he does not need to be a superman. On the contrary, his attitude should be one of humility, where he assumes his own qualities, recognises his limitations and is sufficiently ontologically solid to be able to rely on colleagues more competent than him in their fields, confident that the delegation and synergy that he establishes will carry him along with the flow. Management of this complexity implies that he sees the value, apart from humility, in surrounding himself with competent advisers and especially a coach, whom he can trust.

▧ The coach's role. In this stage, the coach has progressively abandoned his role of facilitator and pilot of the group, and focuses on a relationship of interdependence with the group members in a role where, mainly from a meta-standpoint, he helps the team to manage the complexity and centres fully on being the trainer of already highly performing champions (see Figure 24.11).

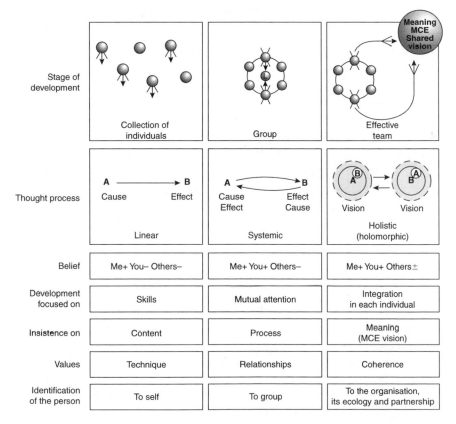

Figure 24.11 Stages of team development

Figure 24.12 summarises the characteristics of these three stages. It is clear that, as with all the preceding models, progress evolves in a spiral.

We see here the need to develop consistently the combination of technical development and content, hand in hand with the development of processes and belonging, and to reframe through an integration with the concepts of meaning and partnership. Finally, in Figure 24.13 we see the concordance between the three models, namely the development stages of the team (models 1 and 2) and the development stages of the manager (cf. Part IV, Chapter 20).

The purpose of Figure 24.13 is to show the different matches between the different models, but also to recall that team building assumes a parallel cultural development for each team member, and to show that the support dynamic for the team is completely dependent on the change operated in each link in the team's chain. We know from experience that for a row of 10 cars to advance smoothly as a group, the speed is governed by the slowest and that the convoy will be slowed by the individual brakings of each car. The coach's role is therefore greatly assisted if he is able to combine individual coaching with team building.

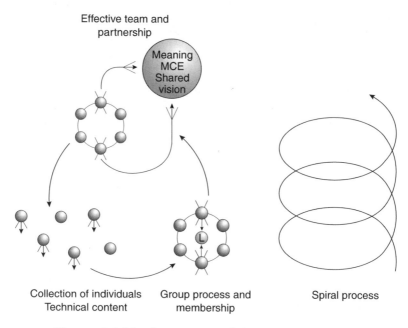

Figure 24.12 Integration of the three stages in a spiral process of growth

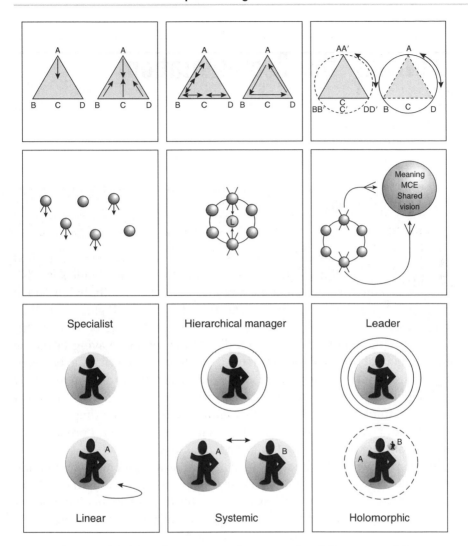

Figure 24.13 Comparison between the different models

CHAPTER 25

Clarifying the Representations

Touched by blind people, an elephant might be described as a tree trunk, a large leaf, a snake, a wall ....

In this chapter we should like to discuss a far too widespread method whereby, without being aware of it, people talk 'over other people's words', and at the same time present a method that is fundamentally based on the concepts of meta-communication. The first diagram of Figure 25.1 illustrates what happens most of the time at meetings. On the pretext of efficiency, people tend to plunge into a discussion without having taken the time to think about what they want to say, without structuring the proceedings with some visual aid or a proper agenda. The usual result is a relatively undisciplined group dynamic in which everyone uses the group to construct their own thinking, and invests much more energy into putting over their own point of view than into trying to reach a consensus, or a proper clarification of everyone's point of view and an assessment of these views.

The apparently quite simple method that we provide includes a minimum of investment and structuring, and presupposes sufficient discipline and cultural envelope on the part of the participants for its implementation. For this reason, it may be useful to have an organiser at the start. The procedure follows the three stages described in Figure 25.1.

1. Prior Individual Reflection (PIR) is a very important stage where each person is obliged to reply to questions put by the organiser, or to work out his own thoughts on a given subject, stimulated by the silent presence of his colleagues and the immediate prospect of expressing those thoughts in front of the group in conditions of protected communication. The others who will undergo the same exercise may not talk among themselves and must adopt an attitude of active and positive attention.

    Whether it involves the perception of the team's objectives and strategy, thoughts on the vision, or each person's position with regard to a

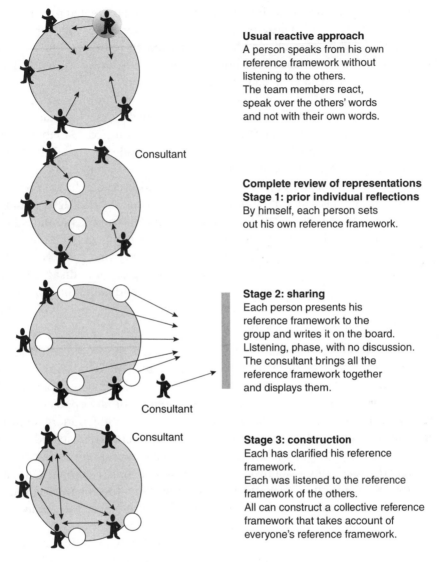

Usual reactive approach
A person speaks from his own
reference framework without
listening to the others.
The team members react,
speak over the others' words
and not with their own words.

Complete review of representations
Stage 1: prior individual reflections
By himself, each person sets
out his own reference framework.

Stage 2: sharing
Each person presents his
reference framework to the
group and writes it on the board.
Listening, phase, with no discussion.
The consultant brings all the
reference framework together
and displays them.

Stage 3: construction
Each has clarified his reference
framework.
Each was listened to the reference
framework of the others.
All can construct a collective reference
framework that takes account of
everyone's reference framework.

Figure 25.1 Clarifying representations

particular problem, the team members' level of reflection on each of
these points is often very varied. Moreover, when sharing takes place in
stage 2, it is disturbing to see major gaps in content between the participants, either in the quantitative objective elements, or in the way
they regard the problem, as well as the angle and culture that they reveal
at this stage.

2. It is important to provide for a very structured and protected time period for listening. Each participant is invited to prepare a slide or transparency and to present it without discussion from others. Only questions to facilitate understanding or clarification are permitted. The timing of the manager's address must be carefully judged, because his presence may influence the presentations of his subordinates. In certain cases, it is preferable for him to speak, to allow the others to react to his suggestions. On other occasions, in order to encourage co-elaboration, it may be better for him to speak towards the end of a round-the-table presentation, without necessarily being the last speaker.

When this second process is completed and everyone has expressed himself and has felt that he has been listened to, one can detect qualitative advance in the team's communication. This process represents a 'performance' for the team members and it often appears that the team members are clearly experiencing this for the very first time. By itself, this process marks the transition from the agreement–disagreement position to the agreement–disagreement–misunderstanding position (see Figure 5.6). It enables the team members to be 'anchored' in the meta-communication position.

3. If the two preceding stages have been respected, the work of this stage can take on a quite different dimension, because many misunderstandings can finally be removed. Since everyone's point of view is perceived better, the quality of the discussion, the strength of any opposition, the quality of the ensuing decisions and consensus are much more significant. This does not mean that the relational problems are resolved, quite the contrary. Everyone's expectations have increased and, consequently, managing this process demands much greater vigilance, attention and willingness to co-operate. It is clear that this stage of cultural development marks a point of no return for the members of a team.

We would point out that we have only sketched very broadly the principles of the method; it includes numerous techniques, depending on whether the context is a meta plan, a quality circle, whether there are stages for sub-groups, or whether it is a meeting for reflection or decision-making.

Finally, as a guide, we suggest that a three-hour meeting, devoting two hours to the three parts of phases 1 and 2 and leaving only one hour to phase 3, is likely to be much more productive than one that uses the pseudo-method at the top of Figure 25.1, on the pretext that there is insufficient time to structure the process. For many years, we have used it in its most sophisticated and varied forms (creativity sessions, meta-planning methods, group quality circles, the most up-to-date developments in group working, such as Shiba 'affinity diagrams', etc.). It is not our intention to produce a handbook of group techniques, but to set out some fundamental principles that govern any approach to team building.

We would refer the reader to the book, *Transformational Leadership* (by Alain Godard and Vincent Lenhardt, Palgrave, 2000, pp. 84–6), where this approach is described from another point of view. I have been inspired by different approaches to group working and, in particular, by Peter Senge's recommended approach in the 'fifth discipline', and by what he refers to as 'dialogue' (a kind of organised group working that aims to respect everyone's reference framework while at the same time generating a synergy between participants).

What I therefore describe as 'sharing of representations' allows one to approach situations for constructing shared visions, transcultural encounters (at times of mergers, for example), conflict resolution, co-construction by different categories of players in a company and 'confrontation groups' in Organization Development.

It is generic in the sense that it represents for the coach the common denominator of all regulation in a group.

CHAPTER 26

The Circle of Trust

As we see in Figure 26.1, this circle comes into play through a spiral process and is built up over a long period of time. Being more easily destroyed than constructed, it is the *sine qua non* of a successful team.

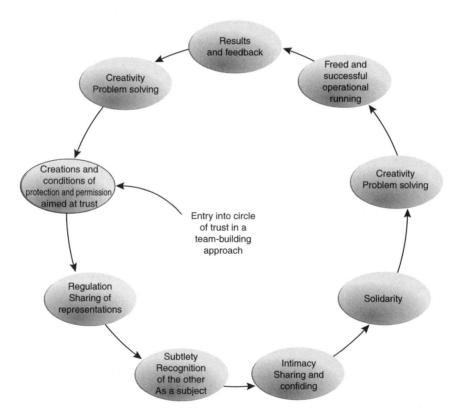

Figure 26.1 The circle of trust. Launch of a team-building operation and establishment of protections. Start of intervention with operation, regulation and intervention

Depending on the degree of trust placed in the manager, and then in the different team members and/or vis-à-vis the consultant–coach, the effective work of team building is able to make headway.

While being viewed as a process of growth in an ascending spiral, it can equally be conceived of as a descending process that could be described as a circle of mistrust.

For me, this diagram represents a synthesis of various influences that have made their mark in the course of my work on corporate team building and in my experience as a therapist.

1. Reading Ouichi's book, *The Z theory* (InterÉditions), made a strong impression on me. The comparison of the cultures of Japanese and American companies where Ouichi underlines the extent to which for the Japanese the culture of group working, the concept of consensus (through the Rungi procedure), the culture of life-long employment, and so on, create conditions for sharing and openness that are greatly superior to those of Americans and, beyond, Westerners in general, who are much more branded by an individualistic culture. William Ouichi notes in particular how Americans are at pains to keep to themselves the finer points of their skills (their know-how, their individual competitive added value) as a condition of their individual employability.

2. The set of protections and permissions that will create trust work towards what William Schutz developed so well in his work on inclusion and control as a prelude to 'openness'. It is clear that the management of successful teams takes place when the managers have emerged from the three modes of coercion, compromise and complementarity in order to enter a mode recommended by Schutz, namely that of openness, in which the participants may express their fears and needs, and set aside their masks, defences and rigidity.

3. My reflections based on my experience as a therapist, on numerous sessions of team building and in parallel with Bertrand Martin,[1] who within the framework of the EVH Association (Entreprise vivante par et Pour des Hommes Vivants) correctly insists on the concept of depth, have shown me how much the fact of appealing to the positive facet within myself and within the other person (which I refer to as the Princes' alliance) generates a high level of co-operation in a team and the capacity for the players to dedicate themselves to the common good. Once this has been experienced, it can never be forgotten. What might be called the trust expressed in the dynamic that exists in an 'alliance' beyond and through the players' commitment to a solidarity, even a communion, of wills combines to bring about an exponential productivity.

CHAPTER 27

Communication, Meta-communication and 'Over-communication'

Summary

Communicating is not a linear process. It implies adopting a meta-position ('communicating about the way we are communicating') and, because of the complexity of communication, it involves making a considerable investment in order to check that the messages have got through, and that they do not generate amplifying or controlling feedback that distort them.

This is the required 'over-communication'.

Only after successful meta-communication and 'over-communication' can we conclusively claim to have communicated.

Once one has embarked upon a systemic or holistic way of thinking, it becomes impossible to regard communication as a linear process. It becomes clear that, in order to communicate properly, to understand one another across different cultures, in order to delegate (the result of a complex process, not an 'objective' procedure), to ensure that decisions made are adhered to, for the declared consensuses to be real, it is essential to enter into meta-communication and even 'over-communication'. This requires three specific elements:

1. Each message sent must result in some feedback to indicate to the sender that the message has been received.

2. Communication of this message causes a dialogue about the differences in the reference frameworks between sender and receiver. It is not sufficient for the message to be simply received, it must not provoke any resistance on the part of the receiver, even if it has been understood, nor should it provoke any active or passive counter messages that start any contrary or divergent behaviour different from what is expected.

3. 'Over-communication'. This is confirmation that the loops of communication and feedback have been completed, especially when several people are involved. It is perhaps to meta-communicate with each person, or even act as mediator or conciliator among them, since otherwise the message would only strengthen divisions. The process of 'over-communication' can sometimes surprise people, and at first cause annoyance, since the sender is seen to be too scrupulous and obsessive. However, if he does his work with patience, without aggression, showing recognition and consistency, this leads to a powerful climate of trust. Such investments in 'over-communication' are outward signs of communication that provide the partners with an up-front reassurance of preventive care, in case of conflict or chaos (cf. Figure 27.1).

Many examples can be given from the world of business. Partners may be inclined to interpret the frustration that they feel, from a position of paranoia, from the fact that there is a garbled message or a breakdown in communication (a letter or a person arrives late, information is missing and so on). Meetings, trips, the importance and always random quality of secretarial support, the complexity of the stakes riding on encounters, all make this attitude necessary, especially in the case of a team meeting where there is so little time available for everyone to be together. Hence the 'Sherpa' role of the coach before summit meetings.

Another example from the author's personal experience relates back to his presidency of the European Association of Transactional Analysis (EATA) from 1982–84. He was responsible for a team of 20 administrators from European countries representing 11 different countries, many communicating in a quite basic form of English. Countless decisions had to be made by the board of directors whose representatives were not necessarily the

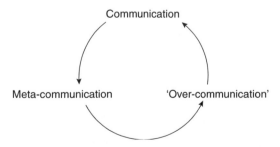

Figure 27.1 The necessity of meta-communication and 'over-communication'

decision-makers in a given country and where the trust between the different countries was relatively tenuous, since each had in turn found themselves faced with *faits accomplis* and situations where decisions were made suddenly without each country having had the time to understand and assess what was at stake.

1. Before every board meeting, the author spent hours on the telephone, not only talking to the board members, but also to the presidents of national associations who did not attend these meetings. He had to explain to them at length, each in his own country, the ins and outs of the agenda, get their opinion and reassure them that no decision would be made on any matter not listed on the agenda.

2. During the meetings, he kept strictly to his word. After the meetings, he re-explained things over the telephone and confirmed what had been decided.

All this took considerable time, but after a year it led to a climate of deep trust between the different countries and the generation of a model (the creation of a MCE) that lasted throughout the life of this board of directors.

Perhaps this small example reminds the reader of some similar experience in his/her professional career.

CHAPTER 28

Mine, His, Yours, Ours, Mine

Summary

In a team, integration of the following three dimensions:

- myself;

- the other person;

- the team as a constituent entity of myself, can be determined from this question: 'Is this problem mine, his, yours, ours or mine?'

This is a small, but representative model of systemic, even holomorphic thought, for each member of the team, as well as for the manager or the coach.

In this chapter, we shall show how the triple vision, the linear, the systemic and the hologram-like, can be very practically integrated into a process of coaching and team building. We use a simplified example.

Suppose that I am 'A', the member of a team, simple participant, coach or manager. During the meeting 'B' behaves in a way that is disturbing, because he insists on pursuing a delicate matter, and also because he clearly puts an exaggerated amount of energy into it. He talks for a long time ('Is this too much?') and in a way that reveals a position that is both defensive and a little aggressive. After a few seconds, I can come up with the following five questions in order to decide on the most appropriate way of intervening (see Figure 28.1).

Is This My Problem?

'B' annoys me through the content of his question and the process irritates me. Instead of intervening compulsively, I adopt a meta-position and ask myself whether, in fact, what I am feeling relates to some personal psychic experience, meaning that this is not B's problem but mine. Generally, I do

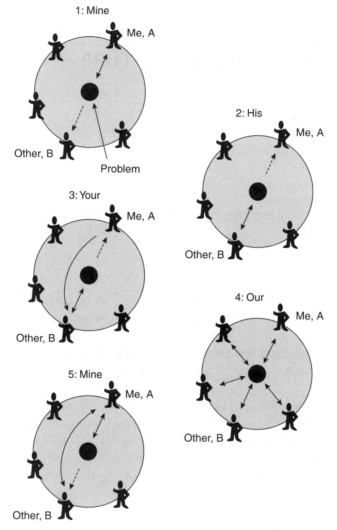

Figure 28.1   Mine, his, yours, ours, mine

not like being attacked, or I do not put up with personalities like B's
(a throwback to someone in my past with whom I never did settle the
scores), I find contradiction hard to bear, and I do not like time being
wasted. In other words, through making this reflection instead of intervening, I have begun by cleaning my own spectacles. If I do not see well, and
I say to myself that I need to control my frustration or that this points to a
problem that I need to deal with elsewhere, then 'It is *my* problem!'

Is It His/Her Problem?

Having cleaned my glasses and accepted to control my frustration, I think about what may be going on for B at the psychological level (cf. the nine levels of meaning). I tell myself that the energy he puts into handling the problem comes from his trying to deal with a psychological problem that has nothing to do with me, or that would be too difficult to handle in the context of the team. I avoid intervening as Saviour, and since I judge that it is more appropriate not to confront him about his behaviour, I accept my frustration and I allow the process to play itself out in the group or vis-à-vis myself. There is no danger, and the time spent on this process may be the best way of managing the situation. It is urgent 'to do nothing' and I wait, since 'It is *his* problem'.

Is It Your Problem?

In terms of the previous question, I see that, at one of the nine levels of meaning concerning B, it is important to remind him of his responsibility, either for reasons of protection or permission. It is not appropriate to deal with the problem in the group. I therefore make the choice of addressing B and telling him 'It is *your* problem'.

Is It Our Problem?

Having dealt with the three previous questions, it may turn out that the point of the debate is located on another level. In fact, the problem brought forward by B is the 'voice' of the group, that is, either at an unconscious level, or at an operational level, he brings to the forefront an element of reality that the group was unaware of but which concerns them. For example, B has just met one of the team's clients and this problem might concern each of the members and does not arise from something dysfunctional in B. Without discounting the first three interrogations, it is appropriate at this moment to make the group aware that 'It is *our* problem'.

Is It My Problem?

After dealing with the four cases up to this point, I can conclude that, whatever the replies given so far, it is becoming important for me to intervene, because it seems clear to me that I am responsible for the fact that the team or a given member is dealing with it in public and I should not remain passive in my relationship with the team. I therefore see to it that the team deals with this situation raised by B and it becomes my problem to ensure that the team resolves the matter.

This simplified example shows how to involve oneself personally as group member and how to manage relationships between individuals. Personal involvement in the team testifies that my identity integrates all

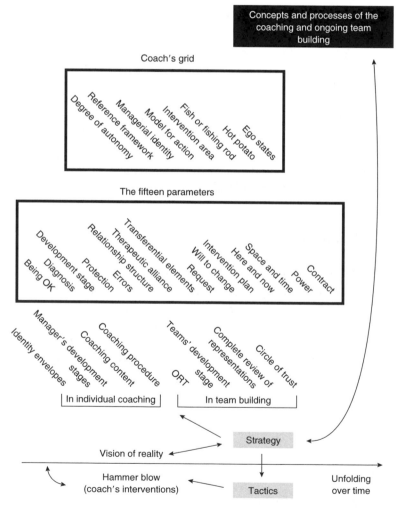

Figure 28.2   The coach's interventions and his control panel

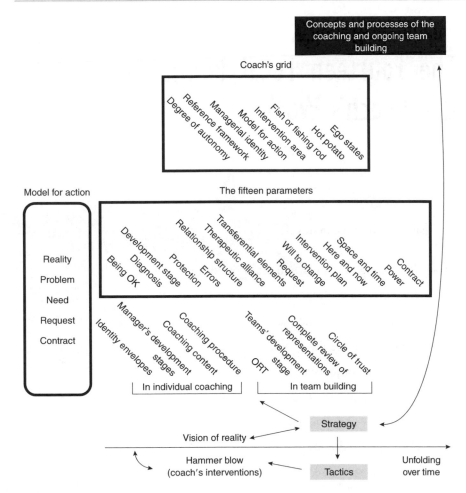

Figure 28.3   The coach's interventions and his simplified control panel

three dimensions: self, others and the team as a constituent entity of myself. Welcome to systemic thought!

As we have seen in Figures 14.2 and 18.1, we can now combine in one diagram all the categories of intervention discussed in the book, to provide a concise 'tool box' (see Figure 28.2).

As in Figure 18.2, we can use the model-for-action grid as a useful simplification of the 'tool box' (see Figure 28.3).

The Fourteen Focal Points in the Coach's Work

What a fine profession this is!

1. Combining coaching and team building
2. Relationship with the manager
3. Relationship with the members of the group
4. Attitude outside the group
5. Optimising objectives
6. Ambiguity of the coach's status
7. Optimising the coach's role
8. Modelling and compensation
9. Transitional symbiosis
10. The coach's responsibility
11. The manager's final decisions
12. Coaching process
13. Coach as carrier of meaning
14. The coach's autonomy and partnership

1. Combining coaching and team building
Now that we have presented more specifically both coaching and team building, we can recall (as shown in Figure 0.1) that the optimal use of these techniques is achieved when they are combined. That is to say, when a manager approaches his coach for both personal coaching and for the coaching of his team. This involves alternating individual interviews with him, with

the members of his team and the meetings with the complete team. Of course, the nature of the work with each of these poles varies depending on whether it is combined, in which case it is interactive, systemic and holistic. The coach's many-faceted role is that of a trainer, a sherpa (the person who arranges summit meetings), a confessor, a comforter or an initiator, a mediator, moderator, trainer, adviser, facilitator. Isn't that a wonderful job?

2. *Relationship with the manager*
Before, during, between and after each meeting or set of meetings with the team, the coach needs to pay close attention to his relationship with the manager, in order to sustain and optimise the 'dual command' arrangement with him. Sometimes he has to sit in the pilot's seat; sometimes he is a navigator.

Through his empathic and responsible attitude, he can perceive and name the problems, constantly suggest solutions, meta-communicate, perhaps even confront the manager and in all cases maintain contact and conditions of permanent and mutual trust.

3. *Relationship with the group members*
The situation to be managed by the coach is clearly complex. He has to establish a relationship of trust with each member of the group, listen to requests, prompt latent requests to emerge, measure the satisfaction or dissatisfaction, invite feedback and constantly adapt his work to the situation. It is important for him not to be biased but capable of confronting both the group members and the manager. It is also important for him to be able to abandon an agenda item if necessary in order to manage a group process. Conversely, he may have to refuse some requests, and structure the group according to its level of autonomy. In all cases, he must maintain the same degree of empathy at the individual level as at the entire group level. He needs to manage the complexity (levels of meaning, chaos, mine, his, yours, ours, mine, content–process, meaning, etc.) and the systemic dimension of the situation.

4. *Attitude outside the group*
Rather like in the films of Max Ophüls, the key moments in the life of a group occur in the staircases or during an interval. The unsaid often emerges during meals, trips together or at various informal moments. The coach therefore needs to be vigilant, alert to the 'unexpected' and constantly inviting feedback from team members.

5. *Optimising objectives*
In addition to managing group processes, one of the coach's essential tasks is to update and optimise the agenda, constantly taking account of the

team's vision, objectives and ultimate goals, and of the multiparty contract between the organisation, the manager, the team and himself. What are the objectives of today's meeting, given the situation, the operation's objectives, the objectives of the team and the objectives of the institution? These are the questions he must keep asking himself and putting to his clients.

6. *Ambiguity of the coach's status*
The coach lives in ambiguity so far as his status is concerned, both in relation to the managers and in relation to the team and the organisation. He is paradoxically on the outside and at the very heart of the levels of meaning of the situation. He has to manage the different parameters we have encountered, while respecting the degree of development of the group's cultural envelope. He must accept all the ambiguities we have mentioned (fish, fishing rod, content–process–meaning, intervention, observation).

He must respond to an explicit request, but reframe it in relation to the implicit and latent request. Moreover, all this he must do with a profound respect for the group's identity and autonomy.

7. *Optimising the coach's role*
He must constantly integrate and choose between an interventionist attitude (where he suggests solutions, confronts the group members, gives out fish), his role of listener and welcomer (he manages processes, he speaks from a meta position, he facilitates speaking), and interventions of an educational type or offering a mirror image (in which he gives information, presents theoretical models of management, culture and communication).

8. *Modelling and compensation*
Through his attitude and behaviour, the coach acts as a model for the team and for the manager. At the same time, he has to compensate for certain shortcomings in the team or the manager, and in particular activate some deficient Ego States in the group, as we have seen earlier. For example, he can offer a structure (normative positive Parent), permissions (positive Nurturing Parent), and allow emotions and the unsaid to be expressed (positive free Child).

9. *Transitional symbiosis*
We have seen that the hierarchical and institutional relationship between the manager and his colleagues runs the risk of seriously interfering with the group's operational life group and their psychological experience. By guaranteeing the management of the group process, the coach can temporarily relieve the group manager. This can be described as a 'transitional symbiosis'

on the part of the coach, allowing the manager to relinquish for a moment his role of locomotive engineer in which he is in danger of remaining trapped, and the group members to stop acting as wagons. All partners become 'self-propelled'.

10. *The coach's responsibility*
In terms of investment level, the coach must be aware that his degree of watchfulness must be at least comparable with the team manager's. If he is not 'caliph in the place of caliph', it is important for him to feel as responsible as the manager.

This level of investment is necessary for the team, more or less unconsciously, and at least the manager, to feel sufficiently taken care of and able to maintain with the coach a true 'alliance for change'. This also allows the manager to hand over control more easily and accept any confrontation from the coach, which he finds difficult to accept from his subordinates.

11. *The manager's final decisions*
The adviser is not the payer. While he certainly feels himself responsible and very committed, the coach gains from not forgetting that ultimately it is the manager who has to answer for the decisions and life of the group. He must avoid substituting himself for the manager and show full respect for any decision made by the manager at any time.

12. *Coaching process*
It is for the coach in his support role to be responsible for providing information, and suggesting a structure for the relationship most suitable for developing the coaching and team-building process. It is therefore up to him to arrange meetings, ways of working with the team and the manager and make adjustments or provide solutions so that the process is adapted. All without replacing his client and removing his responsibility for his original request (a tough job!).

13. *Coach as carrier of meaning*
Since he is the manager of ultimately, an educational process, the coach knows that he must look after the different stages of autonomy to which his support must lead. By his presence, he acts as guarantor that the meaning (values and objectives) of the action is respected. In a way, he plays the role of vestal virgin or guardian of the holy flame. By his presence, he gives his support to the processes under way. It is for him to judge if they are compatible with its values, at the risk, if not, of becoming partisan, or of taking part in manipulations and losing all credibility for his role as facilitator and mediator.

14. *The coach's autonomy and partnership*
Both in relation to his clients and in relation to other consultants called in by his clients, the coach sets out to establish partnerships, in other words, a relation of autonomy within interdependence. If the 'meaning' must be constantly present, it is his responsibility to lead his clients towards autonomy, where they are capable of solving problems by themselves and are ultimately brought to the point where they are able to manage without him.

Having respect for his client's request, it is appropriate for him to be the first to fix the duration of his intervention activity.

APPENDICES

Coaching and Team Building — Fad or Serious Trend?[1]

In France we would need one coach for every fifty inhabitants! (V. Lenhardt, Consultant and Coach, Chairman of Transformance)

Summary

The threefold change in the corporate environment, its organisation and the people who work in it, means that traditional solutions of training and consulting become inadequate.

Coaching and team building are professional levels of support aimed at developing the individual. They offer the players a new vector for a change management that shows contextual intelligence and is extremely personalised.

This approach, which is followed by internal or external consultants for their clients' or by manager–coaches who become resource staff to provide better support for their colleagues, presupposes a professionalism, a code of practice and a training process that includes a high degree of personal commitment.

The requirements in companies are becoming significant and are now no longer restricted to top management. These needs have progressively generated demand and supply, to the point where something that first appeared as a fad, now in fact demonstrates a serious trend in current and future management towards these true and unavoidable tools for success.

New Support for Today's Changes

The business world is undergoing a threefold change:

1. The change in the environment, society and the business context through globalisation, financial pressures from takeover bids and the stock exchange, restructurings, acquisitions and mergers, the range of new technologies, contradictions and crashes in the old and new economies, all elements that no company can remain immune to for its survival and even more so for its employees.

2. The change in companies, which under these pressures are now increasingly forced to be on strategic watch and to be permanently reconfiguring themselves. The organisation structures become increasingly complex and create contradictions for the players.

    The matrix and network structures of hierarchy combine with management that is more and more transverse and organised around ephemeral projects. The parameter of speed weighs more and more on their strategy, the financial burden means that years are now reduced to quarters and the organisation struggles with constraints that are both short and long term. No organisation can any longer function without integrating the different parameters of complexity, these being uncertainty, paradoxical aims, ambiguity of jobs and permanent dual constraints for the players.

3. The change in the players themselves who, with these changes and the emergence of new generations, are no longer guaranteed employment, and are faced with opportunities that a few years ago were unimaginable. Some examples are the possibility of creating one's own start-up company, becoming CEO at the age of 25, being no longer obliged to carve out a career, having completely legitimate individual aspirations and being able therefore to obtain jobs or a position that the preceding generations could not even imagine since it is now possible for anyone to create in his own home a single-person global company, using a fax, computer, mobile telephone and Internet connection.

Coaching and Team Building

This set of changes means that the traditional methods of support, such as training, advice on business organisation and conventional change management, while they are still useful, are no longer sufficient. Methods of support that are both personalised and fully adapted to the situation are becoming increasingly necessary.

My experience as a consultant, trainer, change agent, therapist and teacher led me to discover in the Anglo-Saxon countries during the 1980s what was involved in coaching and team building, and to identify the new pathways and in 1988 to write the first articles in France on the subject. Coaching and team building constitute two key levers in the set of vectors in managing change that allow the development of collective intelligence. The need for permanence and growth in companies can no longer depend on the actions of a single director who on one side thinks and decides and on others who implement his decisions on the other side. The learning company is emerging, in which everyone thinks and operates and where all the players become agents of knowledge and learning processes and where each individual tends to become a 'carrier of the whole'.

Some Definitions

■ Coaching may be defined as a helping relationship, designed to allow a player to find his own solution, in his job and his professional problems, with the aim of being both operational and furthering the development of his managerial personality. While coaching is the term generally used for a one-to-one relationship, when a team is involved, the expression used is team building.

- In both cases, it is a question of a philosophy, a managerial anthropology, an attitude, behaviours and procedures.

  Such philosophy and anthropology include beliefs about the human being, according to which if he is capable of the worst, he is also capable of the best. If one tends to see first his difficulties and mistakes, there is at the heart a 'champion', 'prince' or 'princess' that can be activated and brought forth in an appropriate way. Each player is capable of changing on condition that he receives the right help, and also participates in his own change.

  From this philosophy and anthropology there flows an attitude; that of the coach, who is a kind of trainer of a champion or champion team, and who generates a Pygmalion effect. For, while he witnesses the current objective performance, he sees beyond it to identify and awaken the potential in the champion or team so that it can be actualised.

- The behaviours also gain from being professionalised because a fundamentally paradoxical relationship is involved – helping a person to manage by himself. It is the entire process of the person's educational support and development which so far as possible tends towards an approach where it is preferably the person himself who must find his own solution and not the coach who hands it to him on a plate.

- Finally, there are the procedures. In the professional world of organisations, these approaches will assume budgets, documents and operational procedures that set down the way to establish contracts between the person being coached, the company managers who control the budgets and make the decisions and the internal or external coaches. When the manager himself wishes to play the role of coach with his colleagues, he will progressively set up a regular support system and ways of establishing objectives and common decisions in which, beyond delegation, the principle of subsidiarity will be implemented. The manager–coach will consider that his colleague is the one who has the information, motivation and capacity to take decisions. It is up to him as a manager–coach to create the conditions where this energy, this creativity and this motivation can be exercised. He therefore becomes a resource person, who facilitates the growth and empowerment of the colleague.

Uniqueness of Coaching and Team-Building

The two approaches are different from:

1. Traditional training, in the sense that it is less a question of acquiring skills or knowledge, but more that of generating a dynamic in which the person develops his own solution.

2. Consulting, in the sense that in coaching, the reference framework of the coached person will be the site of endogenous development; there will not be work and solutions brought in an exogenous way through consulting and advice.

3. Therapy, because, in coaching, the focus is more on the present and the future, and on being very careful regarding work on the unconscious, on regression, past history and emotional and bodily work that is more especially the field of therapy.

However, being both a 'field' (area for intervention: a kind of helping relationship) and a 'method' (aimed at an endogenous development for the coached person), coaching sits at the frontier of these different areas and must take account of the person as a whole. It is therefore important for the coach to know about these fields that we have described in order to be able to distinguish between them. His support role therefore presupposes mastering a complex range of related competencies.

The Types of Coaching

▪ Support while the person goes through a period that is more or less clear, more or less difficult and where, without setting a very precise objective, he/she will progressively find room for dialogue, accompaniment and elaboration.

▪ Crisis management. When a decision has to be made rapidly, or an obligation arises somewhat unexpectedly and, in the weeks or months following its appearance on the agenda, the person has to face up to this situation. It is valuable for that person to have room for reflection, feedback and help. Coaching may well be suspended once the event has been worked through.

▪ The third form of coaching, the most frequently encountered, is coaching for performance. For the person, this consists in envisaging a period of coaching based on a managerial situation. This could be taking up a new position, a restructuring, setting up a team, launching a product or a complex project, preparation for an overseas posting, and so on, and here the coaching process will initially include a highly operational phase.

In all cases, the coach will have to establish with his client what type of support is required:

▪ is it support aimed at type 1 change, that is, focusing mainly on managing elements exterior to the manager or managing his behaviour?

▪ or is it support aimed at a type 2 change, that is, beyond external changes and behaviours, is it a question of reconfiguring his beliefs, values and possibly his systems of representation of how he perceives the company, management, how he learns to manage increasingly complex processes, how he builds for himself a new identity as a man of resources?

The Coach's Code of Practice and Skills

We can appreciate the complexity of the problems posed since they touch on the managerial personality and perhaps even deeper aspects of the person, as well as the environment. This complexity makes it a requirement for the coach to have a sound knowledge of the mysteries of the management and of the company as well as knowledge of the aspects of personal development and even of therapy.

It is therefore important for the coach to have undergone the necessary work on himself, to have learnt to clean his spectacles so as not to be influenced by his own problems. He is thus able to provide support for his client because he is well distanced from his emotions and affects and transferential phenomena. It is also important for him to know enough about therapy in order to avoid practising it on his client and be able to refer him elsewhere, since as coach in his present remit he is not in a position to practise, even if, in another context, he might envisage doing so.

It is therefore important for the coach to have integrated:

- A sound training and competencies that include sufficient experience of the corporate world, and experience and training in helping relation.

- A minimum of personal therapeutic work so that he can maintain a correct distance and a thought-out code of practice to ensure that he retains an ethical position.

- A space for control and supervision, to ensure that he has the means to avoid going down too many blind alleys.

Choice of Coach

The manager is faced with the question of how to choose his coach. This can be done through assessing the objective elements of the person's competencies and the extent of his integration of the elements that we have described, but also through very important subjective criteria. The quality of the relationship and trust that the client may have with regard to the coach will clearly be a determining factor and includes an unavoidable non-rational element.

Fad or Serious Trend?

The term coaching currently flourishes in the media and figures prominently in the range of professional services, both internal and external, offered to companies, as well as in the concept of the manager's role. This popularity might suggest that it is something of a fad.

After more than 20 years in this profession, during which time I have been involved in the training of several hundred coaches over long periods and have encountered numerous cases of companies where coaching was required, I am convinced that coaching is a serious trend.

In fact, there has been a serious decline in the benchmarks offered by the traditional institutions, such as the family, education, the company (as an institution that in the past offered stable employment and the possibility of a long-term career) and other organisations such as religious institutions, the armed forces, and so on. So, in this huge reconfiguration of the business world environment and of the players' individual positioning, the traditional solutions of training and consulting become very inadequate. People see, on the one hand, major changes being imposed on them and on the other, opportunities opening up, offering them a freedom that is difficult to manage and an invitation to responsibility that is even harder to take on fully. For each player, the needs become vast. Not only does he want to ensure the permanence of his professional career, he also wants to achieve significant development. He needs to find a means that is both very individualised and based on a full understanding of the situation, something that only coaching, and its extension into team building (through the management of his colleagues), can provide.

What manager or what team can claim not to have the potential to develop and not to dream about the objectives that high-level athletes or sports performers set for themselves in order to maintain their competitiveness and their growth?

This leads me to assert that in France there would need to be one coach for every 50 inhabitants, not only for the business world, but also for schools, hospitals, community life, local authorities, and so on.

Here is an approach with a fine future ahead of it!

The Manager's Personal Development[1]

Summary

The potential and the limitations of an organisation are predetermined by the potential, or limitations of the chief executive. Focused on his managerial development like a lobster relying on its shell, he may dangerously fail to invest in his own personal development.

Training, consulting, help from his peers, coaching, clubs, all provide useful resources. Nevertheless, only through opening up to personal development or to therapy (defined as both the analysis of his past and history and the construction of his deeper identity) will he condition the core of his growth.

This is of course not obligatory. However, such an investment is an invaluable source of development of the chief executive's potential, from which his colleagues and more especially his company can benefit greatly.

The Stakes: the Lobster Complex

The question of personal development for CEOs becomes unavoidable in a world where the environment, the structures of companies and organisations and the managerial situations are changing at a rate unequalled to this day. My experience as support consultant for change, as individual and team coach, as intervener at many employers' associations and in addition as therapist and educator, has caused me to be faced with extremely varied situations. From my numerous encounters I have seen how the development of the chief executive's potential and limitations becomes a major stake in the organisation for which he is responsible. The potential and the limitations of the organisation are determined by the potential and the limitations of the chief executive.

Whether he be entrepreneur, manager, social representative, company founder, divisional head of a large group, head of a small or medium-sized company or industry or of a multinational, in every case he is confronted with his ability to change personally in the face of the chaos, stress, uncertainty, the complexity of the stakes and the multiplicity of the relationships that he must tackle. I know of no such executive who is not threatened by what I call the 'lobster complex'. In fact, the lobster, with its shell, can manage without a spinal column, but once its shell is removed there remains nothing. In the same way, if one compares the status and power of the executive to the shell that can protect him, he runs the risk of being constantly trapped by a defensive attitude in which he may be tempted to enclose himself. He needs to build his spinal column that can represent his 'ontological security' (see Note 1), without which he will be plagued by his concern to protect his territory, his status and power. He will be unable to dedicate his full faculties to others, because of his basically defensive position. I have met many 'lobsters' in the companies that I have worked with. Directors who, through their capacity to manage their stress and their composure, have moved beyond their role of decider to become men of resource for their environment or carriers of meaning, completely transform their relationship to the company and become, for their partners or colleagues, sought after beacons and leaders.

The Chief Executive's Situation and Paradoxes

The chief executive risks allowing himself to be enclosed in several paradoxes. The more he is in difficulty; the less he can show it. The more he grows in importance, the more he feels obliged to manage by himself. The more responsibilities he has, the more he fantasises and others fantasise about him. Stepping down from his pedestal becomes difficult and, even when he sincerely wants to, others may not bear the fact that he has doubts, and so the paradox of isolation overtakes him. The more he is alone and needs help, the less he is able, paradoxically, to ask for it. Therefore, the question of the help he needs for himself and for his development becomes vital.

What is his job? Whatever his level, after education, training and/or various experience, the director finds himself in a job that is different from the position that was more or less clearly defined by the person who engaged him, if it was a manager's position, or the position that he gave himself if a company founder or public company director. In fact, he finds himself in a complexity that requires him to deal with a multiplicity of stakes; those external to the company (the environment, finance, markets, competition, etc.) and within it (the operation of the company, with all the technical, human, financial and managerial aspects).

He cannot be competent in every field and be:

- the specialist experienced in one or more professions;
- the executive capable of managing the process of aligning and implementing the coherence of the complete system;
- the leader capable of defining the objectives, values and aims in action, in short, the visionary guide of people.

The Answers Offered

The three most traditional answers are training, consulting and the hierarchical approach, or dual or collegial management.

Training

By training, we mean especially the elements of continuous and specific training. For chief executives, attending a training programme such as offered at summer schools, in

MBA or CPA courses or in more or less tailor-made programmes, presents unequalled opportunities for improving one's resources and acquiring both managerial and technical skills to help advancement. Apart from acquiring new skills, retraining and opening up to the outside are the principal advantages. The chief executive thus gains a permanent meta-position and a receptiveness to change that are definitely the most important secondary benefits.

However, the workload, the pressure of time and the difficulties in finding oneself with course attendees who are not at the same level or do not have the same concerns, often mean that executives deprive themselves of access to training that their colleagues on the other hand do benefit from.

Consulting

Recourse to consulting on strategic, financial, market-related, legal matters, apart from the purely technical assistance it affords, can clearly provide an irreplaceable opening up and yield true development for the manager who acquires new ways of thinking and thereby broadens his managerial consciousness.

Dual or Collegial Management

A third form of resource is dual or collegial management, which entails for the manager having recourse to his hierarchy or his different partners and, for the public company manager to his shareholder. Fortunately, he is sometimes able to find, for example, in his supervisory board of directors some support, strategic distancing and a co-operation that represents a true alliance. The manager tied to day-to-day operations and to the work pace can therefore find in his main shareholder, an extremely valuable source of distanced, objective views, support and broadening of the strategic vision and of the financial, media and public environments.

Conversely, the shareholder will find in the manager an understanding of the technical, and the professional, stakes that might otherwise escape him. The outcome can therefore be an enrichment and an extremely fruitful managerial development from this two-way interchange.

In the growing complexity of organisational settings, previous methods prove increasingly inadequate because the executive must ultimately find his own solutions, and it is a highly individualised support that will perhaps be the most valuable, namely coaching. This is the help provided by an internal or external supporter in order to resolve professional difficulties with a view to securing lasting development for the person. In fact, the function of the coach, which incidentally could be provided by those in the preceding categories, has the unique quality of offering the executive room for reflection, feedback, for developing scenarios, removing blind spots, testing out new ideas and even protection (he is warned of the dangers) and permission (he is encouraged to complete the stages and free himself from the fear and doubts holding him back); all of these will help him develop progressively and find his own solutions. This is indispensable, because a readymade solution or a decision coming from outside obviously does not have at all the same force and weight as a solution that has been internalised and decided by the very person responsible for its implementation. Hence the rise of coaching and our claim that it has reached a point where it now represents a strong trend.

Among the other resources available for the development of executives, there are of course the employers' associations, now in growing numbers. We could mention the French Association for Progress in Management (Medef), made up of more than 250 clubs, each consisting of about 20 chief executives. This model was developed for the second and third levels in the corporate hierarchy, called the GERME club, which is run on the formula of monthly meetings, generally with an outside expert speaker. Such meetings provide an opportunity to meet other executives, to step out of one's isolation, to gain knowledge of what is new, as well as question invited speakers about their chosen topic. Among other clubs is the Baltimore Club, led by Philippe Le Roux, offering a meeting place for chief executives ('Quadra') of leading companies in their field. This club follows a similar and especially successful philosophy. The club headed by Bertrand Martin (founder president of EVH, 'Entreprise Vivante par et pour des Hommes vivants') operates in a similar way, but focuses on an in-depth consideration of the place of the chief executive and man in general within the company; in time this contributes to the construction of a real identity. Gradually, the executive perceives just how much the development of his company occurs through the development of his employees and himself, and vice versa, his development occurs through the company's development.

Managerial Development and Personal Development

Apart from the formalised situations that we have just described, the most important factor for development is of course the practical experience (or expertise), that is, the set of situations that the executive faces and the way that he acts, reacts and 'pro-acts' in these situations.

As one might say in the arts world, 'the expertise is the only thing that cannot be learnt'. One has to experience the real world. The fact of having been appointed when a company is in full development or in a crisis, or during a split-up, a merger, a takeover, and so on, can be unmatchable. It is clear that this managerial situation alone will have had an unparalleled effect on the managerial and personal development of that executive. No school could have provided that.

My experience of major business schools has shown me that the transfer from theoretical teaching to the case study method and then on to the handling of real projects is an irreversible step, as, for example, is the case with Groupe HEC Entrepreneurs, headed by my colleague and friend Robert Papin. Others may also quote as an example the fact of having been the number 2 or a close colleague of a 'model-setting' chief executive, such as the top figures of industry, retailing and the service industries. To have worked in the wake of an important boss may in fact be the best school and the best way, not only for integrating skills, but also for seeing the world, and reacting and growing up as a man. Is it really only a question of managerial development? Where does personal development begin and what does it consist of?

We can use a model to define better what we mean by personal and managerial development. It is our reference to the spinal column of the identity (see Figure A2.1).

By managerial development, we mean specifically the three domains of professional development, managerial development and organisational development.

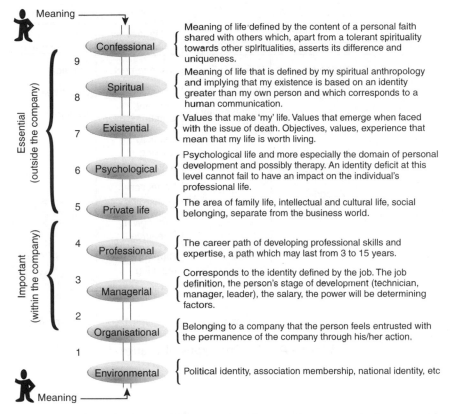

Meaning ——————

Confessional — Meaning of life defined by the content of a personal faith shared with others which, apart from a tolerant spirituality towards other spiritualities, asserts its difference and uniqueness.

9

Spiritual — Meaning of life that is defined by my spiritual anthropology and implying that my existence is based on an identity greater than my own person and which corresponds to a human communication.

8

Existential — Values that make 'my' life. Values that emerge when faced with the issue of death. Objectives, values, experience that mean that my life is worth living.

7

Psychological — Psychological life and more especially the domain of personal development and possibly therapy. An identity deficit at this level cannot fail to have an impact on the individual's professional life.

6

Private life — The area of family life, intellectual and cultural life, social belonging, separate from the business world.

5

Professional — The career path of developing professional skills and expertise, a path which may last from 3 to 15 years.

4

Managerial — Corresponds to the identity defined by the job. The job definition, the person's stage of development (technician, manager, leader), the salary, the power will be determining factors.

3

2

Organisational — Belonging to a company that the person feels entrusted with the permanence of the company through his/her action.

1

Environmental — Political identity, association membership, national identity, etc

Meaning ——————

Essential (outside the company)

Important (within the company)

Figure A2.1 The spinal column of meaning and its nine levels of identity

Professional development is the total professional capacity acquired by the person through his training and technical ability, including everything that constitutes his intellectual and experimental history and that has added to his knowledge and practice.

Managerial development is everything that is memorised from the experience of the status and different positions that the person has held. In particular, the way in which he approaches his current position and the related stakes.

We call organisational dimension the degree of belonging to the organisation. Of course, similar professions and similar positions vary considerably according to the organisational context in which they are located and which conditions them.

The chief executive's development is clearly focused on all three identity levels. However, when speaking of the executive's personal development, we are referring to the person as a whole, including the other identity levels, each of which has its own unique quality, a different type of level, its own logic. It is important not to mix the important with the essential, but to integrate each level rather like a spinal column that is only as strong as its weakest vertebra.

When speaking of the executive's development, we should restrict ourselves to this aspect of developing the important, but certainly invite the executive to welcome what

Internal (invisible)			External (observable)	
Deepest structure	Deepest structure of the person	Attitudes	Managerial behaviour	Manager's environment
The Prince Toujours à developper to be developed	His defence system and his wounds His former decisions His history His unconscious His body His emotions	Beliefs Values Representation systems	Management style Listening Communication Capacity for working in a group Protection/ permission Order giver, Resource Carrier of meaning	Strategy Structure System
Type 4	Type 3	Type 2	Type 1	Type 0

Figure A2.2   The types of change

we developed with Bertrand Martin (see Note 3), after discussions with Olivier Lecerf (see Note 4), which was to ensure that the 'essential was placed at the heart of the important' and to guard against a development of the executive in his professional, managerial and organisational functions that would make him schizophrenic and separate him from his personal dimension. We think that without combining the levels, the person in a company must develop a coherence and an equilibrium that takes account of every facet of this reality. We recall Stephanie Covey's metaphor of the goose of the golden eggs. If one expects the goose to produce beautiful golden eggs, it will be very important to look after it before caring about the eggs.

We now need to define the levels of change that may be touched upon in this development (see Figure A2.2).

The Levels of Change (see Note 5)

Reference is made here to concepts developed in *Transformational Leadership, Shared Dreams to Success*.

Talking about the executive's development will be very different, depending on the levels of action and of development that one focuses on.

We will look at the level that I call level 0, which is the manager's environment, consisting of his strategic thinking, the changing of structures in his care, the implementation of new systems and what concerns him more directly, his managerial status. It is clear that all actions of this type can contribute to his development and well-being, and will imply the development of his skills, and so on.

At level 1, we find the managerial behaviour. We refer to what the systemic approach calls type 1 changes, that is, the attention paid to behaviour. It involves its improvement through paying attention, better communication and the ability to use different managerial methods and to establish new relationships, ensuring that the management style is more facilitating than directive. Here again, the different development methods that we have mentioned, such as training, consulting, coaching, and so on, will be very fruitful. It should nonetheless be noted that a type 1 development might be relatively superficial and mainly consist of a 'control', not allowing the person to change sufficiently in depth to be credible and, to prevent his more profound, impulsive behaviour pattern, from returning as soon as the situation becomes a little too stressful.

Level 2, corresponding to a type 2 change in the systemic approach, is the level of attitudes. For the chief executive this calls into question a deeper set of elements including his beliefs, his values and above all his representation systems. Included in the beliefs are those that govern his life, work, people, difficulties and the fact of being OK or not OK, the fact of trusting or not trusting, and so on. Such values include clearly the basic choices in one's attitude to work, money, success, fellow workers, power, and so on, and all of these obviously have a profound effect on one's behaviour. The systems of representation constitute a subtler element of the attitudes. All the executive's management actions will be conditioned by these representations. For example, it depends on whether he allocates greater priority to technical content or to processes, or regards the company like a mechanical entity or as a closed 'bowl' with himself on the outside instead of seeing it as a system from which he can never completely extricate himself and which is conditioned by his presence. Our many years of experience in supporting teams and individual executives have shown us that the educational process and development of the executive's representation system are absolutely essential.

We now come to level 3, that of deep structure, which could be described as the 'character' and which in fact represents the structured organisation of the person's defences and unconscious beliefs, developed over his entire history and in particular during his childhood (thanks Doctor Freud!). It is clear that the business world is not a place where this can be analysed even if it is the place where it is displayed! For practical reasons first, and then ethically, it is not appropriate to turn the company into a place for therapy.

Nevertheless, the chief executive's managerial and personal development can gain considerably from taking this dimension of personality into account and from working on it in a venue other than those already indicated. This venue could be a place of therapy or personal development in the sense that being separate from the company, and protected by confidentiality and by a clear distinction from the organisation's stakes, he can express himself openly to a therapist, analyst, trainer or adviser, by lowering his defence system in order to free himself from it (see Note 6).

We know many chief executives who have opened themselves to this dimension and generally as a result of repeated negative situations. They understood very well that depriving themselves of this realisation and self-appraisal would not allow them to progress and solve their problems. For all that, we do not think that every executive must take this route, simply because such an investment is demanding in terms of time, energy and money. As with any well-managed investment, it can be of immeasurable value for the well-being of the person and, as a consequence, for his company. When the subject arose (often raised by them), with chief executives whose transparency, self-appraisal, openness and trust were clear, I have frequently had occasion to suggest this dimension and to advise an approach of this type outside the company or outside the coaching venue.

We can also add a fifth realm (level 4), which would constitute the deepest and most intimate development of the person, to which we refer generically as the 'prince' level. It is in fact the most intimate part, beyond the defensive and blocking system of any human being; the unconditionally positive part that exists in every human being, at least such is our belief (see Note 7).

Being trained in humanist psychology and personally committed to a Christian spiritual approach, I cannot look at a human being without having this belief and this basic trust. In other works, such as *Responsables Porteurs de Sens* and *Oser la Confiance*, I have expanded on the issues. In my experience as a coach and in my own personal work, it has become clear to me that the development of this positive part of us is perhaps precisely the place, the cornerstone of the entire architecture of a person's identity.

In any event, it is important for the chief executive to learn to make contact with this part of himself, whether it implies a value rooted in a humanistic view, in political hopes or beliefs or whether it is nurtured by a spiritual life, through meditation or prayer or belonging to a particular faith. In all cases, we believe that the executive, like any human being, can only gain from recognising this dimension deep within him which is undoubtedly the only one where he may find rest for his soul, a prerequisite for the rest of his spirit and his ontological security.

We note that the role of the coach is based on the Pygmalion effect, well known in educational psychology: that is, the impact of one person seeing in another, beyond his current performance, the potential that lying precisely in that deeper part of himself. Through the quality of this perception and the trusted granted by the coach, the person would then be able to gain strength and rediscover in himself the strength and resources that he might not otherwise have dared to assume by himself.

Personal Development and Identity Construction

To conclude, we see that, in the face of the stakes that the chief executive must take into account, the result of this managerial development work is largely conditioned by the inner development of the person, which we call personal development in its broadest sense. The important depends on the essential. We cannot overemphasise the value of realising this.

I should like to underline two aspects of the development of the chief executive's identity:

- its complexity and its ambiguity;
- its recursive dimension (that is, through the development of the other person the executive develops himself, and vice versa).

The Complexity of this Development and its Ambiguity

The chief executive, who gives orders and has the duty to be a competent strategist, leader, manager, and so on, must in fact endorse a responsibility up until the end of his mandate vis-à-vis his shareholder and his employees. He has to assume all roles: order giver, arbitrator, referee, controller, and so on. However, in this world of complexity, he risks locking himself into the role of expert or hierarchical manager and therefore impeding the development of his colleagues and not being the resource that others need. He therefore needs to learn to manage processes rather than content and to support people. If he has been coached to become in turn a manager coach, to become more a manager of cross-company projects, co-ordinating and facilitating processes, while surrounded by people often more skilled in their field than him, he may become a resource person.

On the other hand, there is a need to integrate this third dimension of the 'manager who is a carrier of meaning', that is, the person who can create and co-develop with his colleagues one or more shared visions, and who, while still able to show the way, can be receptive to the faintly emerging signals from his colleagues in order to reconfigure the vision on a permanent basis.

The manager in his job therefore has to integrate permanently these three dimensions and the contradictions that go with them. Is it for others or for him to decide? Is it for the others or for him to listen? Is it he who has the initiatives, or must he leave them to others? Meanwhile, he arbitrates and takes the difficult decisions that he alone, through his status, has the skill to take. In order to come to terms with the complexity of these roles, he will have acquired an inner freedom that can only be attained through an intense period of personal development work brought about by his experience of life or through work on himself. The manager has the heavy task of integrating these three identity levels, while remaining Manager as Order Giver, Manager as Resource and Manager as Carrier of Meaning (see Figure A2.3).

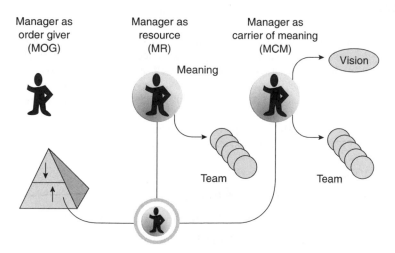

Figure A2.3   Manager's identity levels

Appendix 2

The Recursive Dimension of Development

The act of developing oneself will be greatly enriched by the way the executive has been able to develop and support others. As the philosopher Emmanuel Levinas has reminded us, otherness lies at the heart of our ontology. In other words, our capacity as a relational being is a constituent of our own individual identity. We are relational beings and not isolated individuals. We cannot dissociate personal development from attention to developing the capacity to listen and to accept another as a person. So, the chief executive's personal development will be achieved as much from the attention he pays to his colleagues' development as from the time spent being listened to and developing himself individually. We see that beyond the individual development of this person, the capacity to contribute to the development of others in an individual relationship as well as in a collective relationship will be the very measure of his total development. This puts the importance of the chief executive's development into perspective, which, as stated at the outset, is the measure of the development we might expect in the company in his charge.

Biography

Vincent Lenhardt, consultant, founder president of the firm Transformance, HEC (Paris), MBA Chicago, therapist and teacher, is a former president of EATA (European Association for Transactional Analysis). A trainer of coaches and consultants, he has assisted numerous chief executives as well as national and international company teams. He is author of several books and articles on management.

Notes

Note 1. For me 'ontological security' is the state of serenity, doubtlessly always relative, but real, which a manager might experience once he has sufficient confidence in himself, in his life and in others, to accept himself as he is, unconditionally. That is, without continually believing that he has to prove his skills, power and importance, or responding to an irrepressible need to be liked. He knows enough about himself and, without pride or vanity, he has an inner security that means that he is no longer dependent on what others say. He is complete as an individual, aware of his limitations; he gives himself permission to act, hence his 'authority'.

Note 2. Clubs:

- APM: 6, avenue Marceau – 75008 Paris. Tel. 01 40 70 15 93
- Germe: 15, rue du Puits – 17460 Chermignac. Tel. 05 46 74 75 66
- Baltimore: 12, rue de l'Église – 75015 Paris. Tel. 01 56 77 01 77
- EVH: 22, allée de Chaponval – Les Tuileries – 78590 Noisy-le-Roi. Tel. 01 34 62 66 78

Note 3. Cf. Oser la Confiance, co-author with Bertrand Martin and Bruno Jarrosson, INSEP CONSULTING Éditions, 1996.

Note 4. Cf. O. Lecerf, Au risque de gagner, Éditions De Fallois.

Note 5. Cf. Transformational Leadership, Shared Dreams to Success, A. Godard and V. Lenhardt, Palgrave 2000.

Note 6. We can perhaps define more precisely what I call personal development and therapy.

Personal development

In-depth therapy and treatment of the unconscious	Various therapies	Personal development	Coaching	Managerial development

I place 'personal development' in the restricted sense, as shown in the above table, *between* the fundamental approaches to the unconscious such as psychoanalysis, various therapies that take into account the person as a whole in his/her situation, like the humanist and systemic therapies on one side, and on the other side, coaching and training. These are the areas where, without necessarily going to a great depth, the person develops his sensitive awareness, his creativity, his skills and his well-being. These could for example be courses or sessions on massage, oral expression or expression through movement, yoga, writing courses or artistic activities, and so on.

Therapy
By therapy we define four domains (apart from medicine or paramedical activities), as shown in Figure A2.4.

1. Psychoanalytical approaches whose field is mainly the consideration of the unconscious, and whose aim is the release from unconscious blockage and access to one's deep motivation (Freud, Jung, Lacan, Adler, etc.).

2. Humanist psychology approaches whose fields are integration of the body, emotions and cognitive and behavioural realms. Examples are bioenergy, Gestalt,

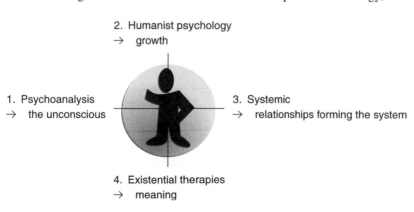

Figure A2.4   Types of therapy

Transactional Analysis, neurolinguistic programming, psychosynthesis, and so on. Their purpose is to restore the person's responsibility for his/her life and growth, in addition to healing the symptoms.

3. Systemic therapies that are less concerned with the person's intrapsychic life than with the organisation of relationships within the system of which the person forms part. Their purpose is to restore in the system its capacity for self-regulation and to succeed in identifying its problems and solving them. The best known approach is that of the Palo Alto School.

4. Existential therapies focus on the access to the meaning of existence but less in terms of causality (the answer to the question 'why?') than in terms of purpose (the answer to the question 'for what?') and on the choice of values. Victor Frankl and Logotherapy is without doubt the best reference.

Note 7. We refer to E. Berne's metaphor in 'What do you say after you say hello?'. E. Berne, founder of Transactional Analysis (TA), refers to the frog that we have become through the weight of the bad influences and decisions taken in childhood, whereas the Prince/Princess that we really are only seeks to be transformed again through the therapeutic process.

In the Prince, depending on our beliefs, whether existential, spiritual or based on, we can distinguish different and specific identity levels.

The Creation of Value through Meaning[1]
Source and Function of the Collective Intelligence

Preamble

What are the basic elements that allow a company to lay claim to the description 'advanced company'? Drawing from their extensive experience as consultants, Manfred Mack[2] and Vincent Lenhardt,[3] both directors of the advisory firm Transformance, present their thoughts on this subject. By examining in depth the concepts of meaning and value, they put forward the case for a collective intelligence based on a global approach, integrating what they call 'the new paradigm of complexity', which leads to a true 'profound reconfiguration of both the cultural and organisational systems' of companies.

Introduction

Based on our experience as consultants and support accompanists for company executives, our plan is to present some characteristics of what we refer to 'advanced companies', along with the elements to be taken into account in order to ensure permanence and implementation of profitable growth.

The stakes: the company's positioning and identity
Nowadays, the stakes for any company, whether private or public, national or international, are bound up with the fact that it operates in an uncertain environment that forces it to adopt a position that, from both the strategic and internal dynamic points of view, may be characterised as 'advanced'.

It is not sufficient simply to adopt a cost-cutting approach. One has to look to a new representation of the environment, markets, the positioning of the company, its identity and management techniques. It is therefore a question of 'getting out through the top', in other words, focusing primarily on the elements that influence the factors highest up on the profit and loss account, namely the creation of new activities and the dynamic of the players who contribute to that rather than only studying short-term profit, however necessary that may be.

Rigorous management of the accounts must subscribe to the creative dynamic of visionary strategies. The high-speed train of the pessimistic accountant who, only looking at costs, must abandon his straight and narrow thought pattern, based on certainties, pressure and fear, in order to find fulfilment (without losing his rigour or realism) by climbing into the rocket that leads to the possibilities, albeit uncertain, of infinite space.

There are three corollaries to these stakes: a new relationship with the client and the environment, a new approach to the management of change and the acceptance of complexity.

The customer's delight

In the relationship with the customer, first of all, it is no longer enough to have an active attitude of doing a good job, or even a reactive attitude (responding to customers' claims, providing after sales service, etc.). It is only through the company's dedication to 'delighting the customer', in addition to providing the products, taking into account a spirit of service that if possible integrates a complete function, that goes beyond the latent request of the customer, that the company will be able to position itself as 'unique' to the customer who in turn is regarded as 'unique'. Upstream, the assumption is that the company is in close contact with its environment (customers, suppliers, local communities, social partners, shareholders, public authorities, etc.) and with its internal players (staff, managers and directors) operating as a collective intelligence, in processes that are increasingly transversal with management on a project-by-project basis and through networks (with a minimum of imposed hierarchy). The company then becomes focused on the 'creation of value' for all those involved – customers, internal players, suppliers, shareholders and situational contacts.

This new perception constitutes a profound change. We recall the metaphor of the frog quoted by Peter Senge. If one puts a frog in a pan of very hot water, it immediately jumps out. However, if one puts it in a pan of cold water that one gradually heats up, the frog will not move and will eventually be completely cooked without trying to escape from the pan. This metaphor applies to any company that does not perceive in time the faint signals that come from outside or inside, indicating the need for major change.

Cost reduction will certainly be an element of the necessary change, but much more important will be the continual strategic deployment and the cultural change that the company will have to implement. The stakes go beyond simple 'innovation' in the sense of new technologies or the creation of new products. This involves adopting ways of creating value, conceiving new activities or new professions and developing key competencies in the organisation (macro-competencies) necessary for the future.

An integrated approach to change

For change to be successful, one must avoid separating, on one side, strategic thinking and development, and on the other, consolidating the company's strategy. It boils down to unifying this dynamic thinking and the mobilisation of all players to work towards this vision and macro-competencies. This will allow them to appropriate the stakes through empowerment and thus all become strategic players. In short, it involves moving the players from the system of obedience to that of co-responsibility (see Figure A3.1).

Our job as a consultant, charged with setting up learning organisations, team-building processes and manager coaching, is to make use of these different vectors in order to

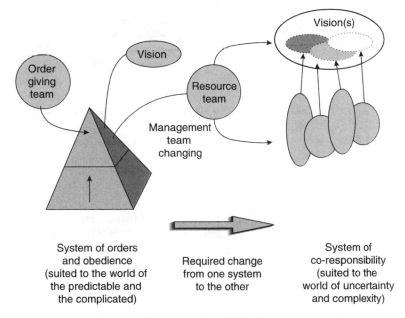

Figure A3.1   A new logic

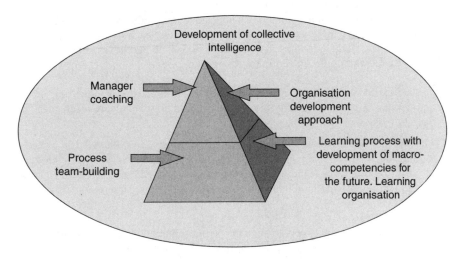

Figure A3.2   Development of the collective intelligence, an integrated approach

allow the company to grow, evolve and sometimes make that true leap of change towards this very dynamic – that of advanced companies.

This integrated approach allows the development of a collective intelligence that is in itself a motor for change (see Figure A3.2).

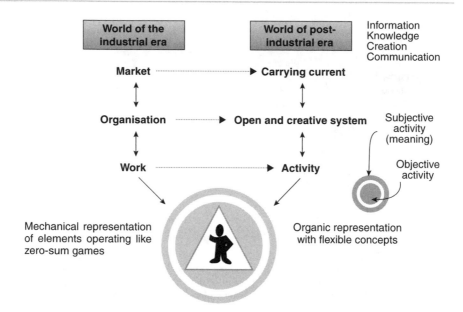

Figure A3.3 The players caught off-balance between two worlds

The context of complexity
This evolution occurs within a context that appears increasingly like that of complexity.

In fact, every company operates in two worlds at once, each of which clashes with the other and places the individual and collective players in paradoxes, dual constraints and unavoidable ambiguities (see Figure A3.3).

- The industrial world and its system, where work, organisation and the markets are perceived as realities, obviously moving but quantifiable, relatively mechanical and operating like zero-sum games.

- The post-industrial world, also called the era of information, knowledge and communication creation, where work is handled rather like a portfolio of different types of activity (cf. Charles Handy[4]) where the organisation is transformed into an open system, with poorly defined boundaries, and markets are regarded more as carrying currents.

This situation forces managers to align their representation systems with those of the complex reality of which they are part, and from which they cannot completely extract[5] themselves. The Cartesian reality logic of planning, forecasting and targets must not be abandoned, but rather transformed into a logic of the complex and the emergent according to a constant constructivist practice.

Our goal is to present our thoughts on these various emerging aspects. We shall examine them on the basis of four main ideas:

1. It is up to the management teams to generate around them organisations capable of prospering in the new environment. How must they operate in order to succeed?

We recall here the principle of recursive causality that is perhaps the cornerstone of a new paradigm.

2. The new organisations operate according to a different system from those that preceded them. What are the characteristics of this new logic? How can they be translated into actual practice that can be seen in the companies we consider advanced? Here we touch on the concept of learning organisations and co-evolution.

3. At the core of the new system there appears a highly developed capacity, namely collective intelligence. What are its essential elements and what is the procedure for its further development? We examine here the concept of emergence and self-organisation.

4. The different systemic processes that characterise the operations of advanced companies must also be applied in approaches to the management of change. How can the different ideas be for company evolution be articulated using the new logic of 'getting out through the top'? We shall describe the different facets of an integrated approach.

How Successful Teams Function: the Recursion Principle

In order to guide the company towards new ways of functioning, the management teams themselves must operate differently. They need to progress from an approach based essentially on the content of action to a way of working that integrates process and meaning. This evolution entails a new representation of the company and of the types of causality that constitute its activity.

Integration of the Trilogy: Content, Process and Meaning

Let us take the example of a manager drafting a memorandum.

Content
If this manager focuses on the concept of 'content', that is, trying to reply to the questions what? where? who?, he will draft his memo as an expert, putting all his care and skill into it and seeing to it that it is clearly understandable to the people involved, and so on. However, even if he has taken the trouble to inform himself about the context in advance, he runs the risk, albeit with the best of intentions, of discovering that his document recommending the 'best' technical solution will not be taken into account and the solution not being adopted by his colleagues simply because it is not *their* solution.

Process
If this same manager broadens his approach to integrate the concept of process, knowing that it is vital, then how does he reply to the question? What is more, while keeping the fullness of his previous approach, he will be operating according to a 'process–content' model in which the process comes first, without abandoning the knowledge and demands of content. He knows that, with a view to the ultimate implementation of solutions by his colleagues, it is infinitely preferable to create with them conditions of trust, and zero-contempt as a consequence for a collaboration, or even co-creation, of the

Content	Process–content	Meaning–process–content
Manager "Order-giver"	Manager "Resource"	Manager "Giver of meaning"

Figure A3.4 The manager's levels of identity

solutions that they will have to implement. To do this, he will question them and invite them to find solutions to the problem with him. By doing his best in this preparation work, depending on the circumstances, the personalities involved, the degree of co-operation possible and the urgency, he will aim to turn himself into a 'resource manager' as opposed to an 'order-giving' manager, expert and/or hierarchical manager. He knows that a solution will infinitely be better implemented if the person has developed it himself and knows that he can at least collaborate on it or take credit for it.

Meaning
Finally, if the manager goes even further, he will have to manage the trilogy of 'meaning–process–content' by handling these parameters in that order so far as possible, and responding first to the question of the 'meaning', that is, the question 'for what?' and 'why?' (the aims, the stakes, the vision, strategy, priorities, importance or urgency). If he has been able to discuss the company vision with his colleagues, and depending on their personalities, their degree of development and the context, create the conditions under which they feel themselves to be co-managers of the company, he offers room for the creation of identity and co-responsibility that radically alters the very nature of the relationship between the team members. He then becomes a manager who is a carrier of meaning, that is, someone who will create the conditions to allow the different players present to gain access to the meaning that they assign to their own actions, even if they need some temporary help from him.

Figure A3.4 illustrates the sequence we have described.

Representation of the Company and Causality Types

Integration of the trilogy of 'content–process–meaning' corresponds to an enlargement of the field of consciousness that at the beginning focuses on the part (content) and then progressively includes the whole (meaning).

In order to be complete, this evolution must include the dynamic element, that is, the way in which the forces present act upon one another.

Let us take this time the example of a director who is a member of the management board assigned to implement several groups of projects.

Linear causality
If the director operates in a Taylorian way by focusing on the technical content, he will nominate the members of the project groups, place a manager in charge of each group,

install deadlines, assign a schedule of specifications and launch the operations, having perhaps first carried out a benchmarking study. He will place himself in the position of manager order-giver, aiming to delegate to his project heads as much as possible the responsibility for the implementation of these projects, ensuring that they have what they need and establishing meetings for them to report to him at different stages in the project.

By operating in this way, without necessarily considering all the consequences, he acts as though he regards the company as a 'mechanical' entity, with the group project operating within a 'glass bowl' and himself on the outside of it. He sees the causality system for which he is a carrier as a 'linear' causality. A (linear) is the cause of B (those who are in the bowl) that is the effect. The part can be isolated from the whole, even controlled by an external hand; the bowl does not interact with the observer.

Circular causality

If this same director realises that management of these project groups could not be done without real strategic and operational support from him, he will progress to a method leading him to intervene in the interfaces upon which the group and the remainder of the company rely, all the while knowing that the internal functioning of the group was largely conditioned by its environment. The players involved would in fact be put permanently under a dual constraint: do they answer first to their hierarchical director, or to their project head?

He will be putting his role as an order-giver in second place compared to that of the resource manager who first conducts an educational and supportive process for the internal life of the project groups, and to that of facilitator–sponsor–arbitrator with regard to external interfaces.

He concludes that the project groups are not isolatable glass bowls and moves to a view of the company as a 'system', all of whose elements are interactive and where the causality is circular before being linear. A is the cause of B, which is the effect, but which is also the cause of A in turn, with A becoming the effect of B. Every action leads to a feedback effect in a circular cycle, with the result that, very quickly, one does not know 'who started it', whether A or B was *the* instigator; both become cause and effect at the same time.

Recursive causality

The next stage of awareness consists of ensuring that the aims of the projects are explicitly linked to the aims of the company, and that the members perceive that the success of their project is a condition for the success of the company. On the other hand, it is necessary for the members of the management committee and those responsible for the major policies of the company to include the stakes of the company within the stakes of each different project. Hence the necessity for close communication between the players and co-developers of the levels of vision. The group project is in the company, and the company is in the group project!

Being responsible overall for the projects, the director must position himself so as not to be the sole member of the management committee to become a resource manager. All members of the management committee and the governing board, as an entity, must act as 'resources' and learn to place themselves 'at the disposition' of projects in order to resolve within the management committee itself, any cross-company difficulty that might arise from any latent 'disputes between project heads' preventing proper

Representation of the company	Mechanical	Systemic	Holomorphic
Type of causality	Linear	Circular	Recursive

Figure A3.5 The three causalities

interaction between members of the project groups. Hence the dual need for cohesive teamwork at the management committee level (and perhaps at other intermediate levels), and for a true identity change in the directors, individually and collectively, so that they learn to become resource managers without losing their skills as order-givers and their responsibility to control. The management committee is in the project group and the project group is in the management committee. Therefore, the different players have to learn to change identity in order to experience this 'holomorphism'[6] of the company (each entity having the form of the whole) and travel at ease through this reality that belongs to the world of complexity, namely recursive causality. The company is in the person and the person is in the company. The manager generates the company, which, in turn, nurtures him. The whole is in the part and the part in the whole. Each management act, whether individual or collective, can contribute to advance or block the company.

A – the part – is the cause of B – the whole – which in turn becomes the cause of A.

A – the part – and B – the whole – are each in turn and at the same time, both cause and effect and, as we already knew, more paradoxically included one in the other.

Figure A3.5 summarises this parallel evolution of the company representation and of causality types.

We have devoted space to discussing the anatomy of these developments, because in our view it is essential to understand these before examining the particular characteristics of advanced companies.

The New Thinking of the Advanced Company: the Concept of Co-evolution

As indicated in the introduction, we find ourselves in a transition phase between two eras: the declining 'industrial–commercial' era, and the developing 'creation–communication' era. The majority of companies today have a foot in each era. It is not easy for these companies to establish where they are on this transitional path. In fact, the tectonic shock produced by the meeting of these two continents creates innumerable upheavals: restructurings, social plans, raised levels of unemployment, all obstacles to be overcome by a company that wishes to advance.

The companies that we describe as advanced are those that have deliberately swung towards the new era by basing their operation on a completely new thinking. We shall describe their characteristics.

Broadening the Limitations of What is Possible

Advanced companies, the ones that get out through the top, have from the onset a frame of mind that permanently points towards widening the limits of what is possible. We have already alluded to the fact that these companies no longer think in terms of work, a narrow and outmoded concept, but of 'activity'. They no longer regard the organisation as being fixed and closed, but as an 'open and creative system'. They no longer see themselves as fighting to gain only parts of a limited-size market, as in a zero-sum game, but growing by being swept along by the buoyant 'strong currents' that they have helped to create.

We can point to such spectacular examples as the success of Microsoft, based on its position on a strong current comprising all the new tools for communication. In fact, Microsoft not only sensed the emergence of this current, but itself made a bid to adopt it, carry it off and expand it by bringing in a veritable constellation of other players.

To provide another illustration of a giant of industry that was able to reconfigure itself brilliantly by locating itself on the buoyant current of added value in services, we can mention General Electric, whose director, Jack Welch, claimed forcefully that 'markets are the very measure of our dreams' and not restricted to the space of zero-sum games.

Community of Players Dedicated to Creating Value

The *raison d'être* of advanced companies is no longer to produce or sell a product or service but to create value. Few companies have truly integrated the subtleties of this new concept. Creating value, in the sense that we mean here, is simultaneously improving the economy of the players who make up the system and the economy of the system in its totality.

The advanced company considers 'value creation' to be an array of relationships constructed between a community of players with itself positioned at the heart of a system where its own competencies (macro-competencies) mesh with those of other partners in order to create a value configuration that it would never have been able to be created alone. In such a group, the partners can be complementary providers for customers or suppliers.

The example of IKEA is a perfect illustration of this approach. IKEA's concept is to 'co-produce' modern design furniture that is simple and attractive, with its customers. The customer accepts that he must assemble the furniture that he buys as flat packs, in exchange for which he is rewarded with lower prices. IKEA saves on the cost of assembly, storage and transport. To construct its system, IKEA has recruited a network of successful suppliers around the world, who agree to manufacture designs produced by a team of high-level designers put together by IKEA. These suppliers benefit from a guaranteed flow of work and can also take advantage of the various services offered by IKEA, such as advice on training, connection to the information network, and so on.

Pro-active Networked Organisation

The organisations of advanced companies are the antithesis of the traditional pyramid structure. They go beyond decentralisation (smaller pyramids within the larger) and even matrix organisation (co-existence of horizontal and vertical responsibilities) in order to adopt flexible forms, capable of being permanently reconfigured around key processes or projects, thus federating multiple competencies. These are networked organisations, but of a special kind.

The 'cells' of the network are the individuals and teams that must self-regulate and synchronise their intelligence and actions to work together to achieve the goals of the systems. The performance of the system is a function of the equal dynamic relationship between the cells (parts) of the whole network. It is also a function of the energy that the system can mobilise, being itself conditioned by the degree of initiative, commitment and motivation of the players. It goes without saying that the advanced companies have established managerial and organisational systems that empower the players and distribute power and autonomy, precisely judged according to a policy of co-responsibility or empowerment. However, in conformity with the principle of recursion, they go even further. By creating a shared vision, that is inspiring, worthy and demanding, the management team provides everyone with a picture of the future of everything. Each person can thus adjust in relation to this common vision and be nourished or motivated by it. In addition, each person's action can progressively enrich the global vision (the whole).

In this respect, the Swiss company, Landis and Gyr, a specialist in energy control systems, is an interesting example. This company has built a vision around the concept of 'exceptional value for the customer'. This vision has allowed the company to transform itself in a few years from a manufacturer of thermostats into a service provider whose aim is to conceive and implement complete energy management systems that allow its customers (hospitals, large hotels, retail parks, residential apartment buildings) to achieve substantial reductions in their annual energy costs.

The Company as System that Learns and Constantly Reconfigures itself

In a world of perpetual change, acquired positions do not last. The communities of players are dedicated to the creation of value, operate like pro-active networks and must continually reconfigure themselves, even if certain parts of the system, such as its basic core, may retain some relative stability over time.

Continuous reconfiguration implies the identification of new opportunities, the perfecting of new solutions to extract value from these opportunities, the development of new knowledge and its dissemination among the players in the organisation, and, finally, the integration of its knowledge that is then transformed into competencies, and even into macro-competencies.

This sequence, designed to stimulate the evolution of the creative capacities of organisations, is in fact a cycle of apprenticeship that operates within any company. What distinguishes the advanced companies, is the fact that these processes are made explicit and conscious, leading them to be envisaged as a system that learns.

Figure A3.6 Recursion and creative co-evolution

Apprenticeship becomes a central preoccupation and is practised actively in every part of the company.

Apprenticeship as we understand it covers a very broad range of activities, including exploration and discovery of new territories, experimentation, problem solving and the development of competencies. It occurs at several levels: knowing how to do it, awareness and thought process (questioning mental representations). It also applies simultaneously to individuals, to teams and to the organisation as a whole.

We think that creation must also be included in the act of apprenticeship, so that the company must not only promote the idea of learning but also that of learning to create, a topic that we shall return to later.

Finally, advanced companies discover that one of the most productive forms of apprenticeship is that which is practised between the players, who learn from each other. This is why the communities (or networks) dedicated to the creation of value are also learning communities; partners and customers learn together to create value to the benefit of each person and of the community in its entirety. They become jointly involved in a process of creative co-evolution in which each, by evolving, helps the other to progress. This principle is similar to recursion in that it integrates the idea of reciprocal progress. Figure A3.6 summarises the two principles.

These two principles lie at the heart of the system for operating an advanced company. They both call for what becomes the supreme capacity of any company, namely collective intelligence.

Development of Collective Intelligence: Principle of Self-organisation

Nowadays, many books and research writings refer to the collective intelligence, but authors rarely provide a concrete definition of it.

Definition of Collective Intelligence

For us, a definition of collective intelligence can be assisted by comparing it with centralised intelligence. Traditionally, companies have operated on the basis of centralised intelligence. Top management made all the decisions, implemented them by giving orders and directives, verified that these were carried out and, if necessary, took corrective action (the system of obedience).

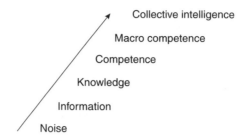

Figure A3.7 From noise to collective intelligence

Collective intelligence is distributed throughout the whole of the system. The 'central' organism (management team) retains part of it but so do the other players (system of co-responsibility and subsidiarity, but different from delegation). The system functions through the combination of the individual intelligence that merges into a total intelligence that is much greater than the sum of the intelligence of each individual.

A company that sets out to give life to a community (often adopting several organisational methods and tending towards the network), which is dedicated to creating value, can only operate through the presence of the collective intelligence. The latter figures as a kind of meta-capacity; it is the highest capacity of the company. Therefore, if one sketches out the hierarchy of the elements that make up the cognitive spectrum, collective intelligence is located at the top, as shown in Figure A3.7.

This supreme capacity of collective intelligence is integrative, which implies that it brings into play not only intelligence from the head (rational thought), but also intelligence from the heart (intuition), that is, the sensitive perception of feelings, needs and expectations of others.

Based on these elements, we suggest the following definition: 'Collective intelligence is the dynamic of co-responsible players who are culturally (soft) and organisationally (hard) interconnected in an alliance focused on shared visions.'

We spell out below what we believe is essential for each of the terms used:

▪ Dynamic. A process in constant flux that cannot be stopped or described in a fixed state. This causes much frustration and discomfort that gives rise to much reticence.

▪ Players. It is useful to wean people away from a system of passive obedience that is only active or reactive, and progressively leads every member of the organisation towards becoming proactive.

▪ Co-responsible. There is a vast distance between the process of liberation and the promotion of individual rights and the logic of responsibility and the free interiorisation of stakes and duties. The great Viennese therapist, Victor Frankl, talking to a group of Americans, said that there was a whole continent to cross. In the east of the United States, there was the Statue of Liberty, but there remained the country to be crossed before building the Statue of Responsibility in the west.

▪ Interconnected. The players need to be linked together. It involves moving from a collection of individuals in a community to the stage of a successful team inspired by a common spirit.

- Soft. This is the change and the agreement of the representation systems involving the players. Do they speak a common language? Do they have the same cultural envelope, made up objectives, values, competencies, language, experience and spirit of conviviality?

- Hard. This involves making the management systems consistent (recruitment, organisation charts, pay, information and control systems, etc.), along with the means of communication (electronic mail, etc.).

- Alliance. We are referring to the rational and irrational agreement between the parties who accept their differences and remain faithful to the relationship, allowing them to pursue a common path, despite the contradictions, suffering and frustration.

- Shared vision. This is an agreement on the aims and stakes that allow complex systems to function and give meaning to the movement and to the grieving periods that have to be borne at each stage of change.

Simplified Diagram of the Functioning of Individual Intelligence

It is useful to look briefly into the way that individual intelligence functions, before we address the specific characteristics of collective intelligence.

Intelligence can be seen as consisting of five essential functions, as set out in Figure A3.8.

We describe each function separately, but it is their interconnection that constitutes intelligence.

- An instrument of perception (hearing, seeing, receiving signals) that allows knowledge of the external reality to be gained.

- A central system that thinks, evaluates, chooses, and at a more sophisticated level, gives shape to concepts and organises elements of knowledge into categories that make sense. According to various experts, including F. Varela, the mechanisms of choice operate through a phenomenon of entering into resonance.

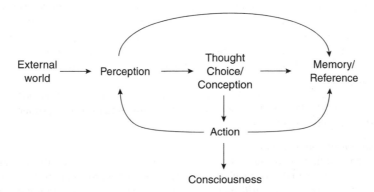

Figure A3.8 Connection of the five functions

▨ A memory function in which knowledge of information is stored at more or less conscious levels. This memory contains the set of representations as well as reference elements related to the system.

▨ A system that translates the choices into action (implementation of decisions). Note that the action is at the same time an experience whose returns alter the perception and are recorded in the memory.

▨ Consciousness, this capacity, only found in human beings, allows us to observe ourselves functioning and thinking. Not only can the system think, it can also think about its way of thinking. It is through the function of 'consciousness' that intelligence is able to assess its effectiveness.

Teachings from the Sciences of Complexity

Our understanding of collective intelligence is enhanced by taking a brief detour through the new teachings brought to us by the science of complexity.

Phenomenon of self-organisation
Every company operates as a complex adaptive system that functions according to a method found throughout nature: self-organisation.

In the interest of simplification, one can say that a self-organising system operates without the need for a central regulator (the boss). The different elements of the system regulate one another according to certain rules, often 'compressed' into an organising principle that guides the regulation of the system.

The science of complexity teaches that a system emerges during a phase of 'trial and error' during which the players jointly seek out approaches that work the best, with the latter regrouping to allow one or more organising principles to emerge; these in turn act retrospectively on the behaviour of the players.

A capitalist company or a democracy are examples of extremely developed types of organising principles. They contain within them rules of operation that govern in the first case a type of company, and in the second case, a model of society.

Phenomenon of emergence
This is one of the most important teachings from the science of complexity. We shall see that it contains the key to understanding the specifics of collective intelligence.

Emergence is a phenomenon whereby a global dynamic (or organisation) is created spontaneously as a result of the initially random interactions between players. The global configuration that results is not predictable from the initial behaviour of the individual players.

Emergence is the basis of all creation. The new form created is not a simple rearrangement of existing elements, but a real transformation that produces a new, completely original totality.

Phenomenon of a higher order
The human intelligence, through the use 'consciousness', has the ability to evaluate if the system that it regulates is, or is not, operating according to an appropriate organising principle. In fact, in a world that is continually becoming more complex, a given organising principle may, at some stage of its existence, be overtaken. It is as though it had reached the limits of its capacity to face up to situations.

Collective intelligence will then generate a new, more developed organising principle that will be in a position to handle more complex situations. We can say that the system has reorganised itself at a higher level of order or at a higher level of complexity. This is a basic concept. In fact, it can be observed that every living system tends to evolve towards a higher level of order. We are in the presence of a basic law about the evolutionary direction of the universe.

Specifics of Collective Intelligence

At the first level, it is possible to imagine collective intelligence as being the capacity (for a group) to work together to activate the five functions described in Figure A3.8.

Therefore, the group would be capable of having a collective perception of making common choices (or creating new ideas), and building a collective memory that would store common representations. In addition, the group would have a collective consciousness.

Without going into details of these different operations, we are above all interested in a central aspect of collective intelligence, namely the one that makes choices (taking a decision, setting objectives, etc.).

Once again, process develops according to the degree of advancement of the company, Figure A3.9 illustrates.

Therefore, an essential aspect of the collective intelligence is what we call the 'learning and creative dialogue' that feels its way forwards, exploring possibilities until

	Traditional company	**Company in transition**	**Advanced company**
Type of intelligence	Centralised	Multi-level	Collective and shared
How choices are made	Choices made and imposed by top management	Choices made in a participative way, even negotiated Often, top management decides and a section of the players finds itself in the minority	Choices made via a learning dialogue (feeling the way) The result emerges (higher level solution) All players unite
Political principle	Authoritarian centralism	Democracy	Creative co-evolution

Figure A3.9 The different types of intelligence

through emergence new choices are produced. By nature, this type of choice includes an important element of creation. It is also through dialogue that advanced companies create their vision of a desired future. This vision, shared because it is created through dialogue, then serves as a collective reference allowing future knowledge to be structured and further developed. Collective intelligence cannot develop without structured and shared references (meaning). The shared vision structures the collective intelligence and also forms part of it. The recursion is located in the very construction of the collective intelligence. In a way, the big circle is closed.

Organisational Conditions Necessary for the Development of Collective Intelligence

We believe that there are three organisational conditions absolutely necessary for the development of collective intelligence.

- The management team must demonstrate a long-term political will to provide the necessary combination of 'protection' (to avoid pitfalls) and 'permission' (to permit initiative) in this important approach to change. Their clear personal involvement and example are necessary to lend credibility to the implementation of new practices.

- There must be active, in-depth learning processes working to renew the knowledge, methods, competencies, behaviour and culture.

- There must be support (coaching and team building) that the players need (in their changing identity, values and jobs) in order to sustain and feed this dynamic. This can be provided by the managers themselves (resource managers and managers who are carriers of meaning), by internal agents of change (trainers, co-ordinators or consultants) or by external professionals (it is sometimes essential to call in those who are outside the glass bowl).

Implementation: an Integrated Approach

Our thoughts on the ideas presented and our experiences have led us to devise and adopt an integrated approach whose objective is simultaneously to conduct the change and develop the collective intelligence within the company. This approach includes a number of stages that sometimes follow a chronological order, but more frequently follow a spiral path, that is, some stages are revisited at different levels and with different implications; they are also recursive, in the sense that each stage includes the stakes of everything.

Those players who have already made up their minds and have reached a high level of experience and motivation can complete some of these stages very quickly. For others, the amount of time it takes can vary and depends on the maturity of the players as much as on the factual context in which the company players are located.

Raising Consciousness

This is our name for the time period, of variable length, between the moment when one or more players in the company perceive the necessity for change in their organisation and for themselves, and the moment when those who decide, who are not always the same players, come to a decision and manifest a political desire to carry forward and implement such an approach.

Frequently, it may start by a player reading an article or book, or attending a conference, or even more so, by managers talking to others who have had similar experiences. For a decision to be taken on implementation, it is generally advisable to plan for a phase to increase awareness, alleviate fears and uncertainties and carry out a full informing and updating exercise for those involved. The managers who embark on such an approach will need to weigh the stakes carefully, the work involved, the necessity of their own personal involvement, failing which the operation may come to nothing and may even generate more frustration and loss of motivation in the long term. We would warn managers against the 'freezer effect', where well-intentioned directors launch themselves into an approach with enthusiasm, but do not fully appreciate that their role is to support, protect and encourage a process that will include stages that are inevitably sensitive and perhaps difficult for all players to experience, including themselves. This is because, when one has stirred people from their relative passivity by inviting them to empower themselves, the problems are exposed to the light of day and it becomes dangerous to send the players away in silence. One can defrost once, but not twice!

Strategic Diagnosis

It is not about complete strategy development in the classic sense of the term, but about a dialogue between the principal internal players and, for example, the support consultants in order to explain the main strategic axes, perhaps validate them or reconfigure them, so that these strategic axes are linked through a 'learning process' to the prospective construction of the macro-competencies of the company and create a favourable environment for the establishment of a collective intelligence. This work leads to the joint conception and engineering of the stages and organisational processes to be used throughout the rest of the implementation.

This diagnostic stage is often a decisive stage in regard to the players' understanding the stakes, a 'dialogue' process, team cohesion and the beginning of learning processes.

Launch with the Decision-makers

This phase can be developed with all or part of the management team or possibly by pilot groups, sometimes even by a set of work groups that assess the strengths and weaknesses of the company and share in its stakes. Bertrand Martin, in his exemplary experience as chairman of the French subsidiary of the Sulzer group, proceeded in this way, an approach that very quickly brought about an early and global mobilisation of the company.

We do not propose to list all the elements that go to make up this stage. We will simply recall that it is convenient to work on the following points.

- Sessions on regulations and team cohesion: sharing of perceptions, dialogues, conflict resolution, and so on.

- The choice of operational projects, most often involving cross-company jobs and departments, to ensure that the approach to collective intelligence is completely in step with the reality of the stakes and perceived as such by staff and management.

- The choices of the first learning processes, such as collective learning expeditions, competition benchmarking, experimental sites, awareness seminars, cultural changes, and so on.

Dynamic Deployment

Once the core of decision-makers has launched the approach in the terms we have described, the question arises of the deployment and participation of the whole of the organisation, so that it can become an open, creative and learning system.

Sometimes it will be an approach from the management committee and going from the top to the bottom (top-down) progressively broadening the previous work with levels $n-2$, then $n-3$, and so on. Sometimes, one will start with groups and pilot tests and make a round trip by going up and down the hierarchy to secure its acceptance and endorsement of these experiments in due course. In certain cases, we recommend implementing an 'action-painting' approach (like a painter who just uses paint without first drawing lines), which affects various parts of the company at the same time and mobilises horizontal as well as vertical forces.

It is also possible to bring into play processes that strongly involve the intermediate hierarchy, because that is often the part of the company most resistant to change. Whenever it is possible, a general mobilisation of the company is obviously the most desirable choice, as known examples have shown. We mention again General Electric and the 'work out' approach, and also Bertrand Martin's achievement at the French subsidiary of Sulzer.[7]

Four deployment vectors can be applied in an integrated way:

1. The sharing and 'co-development of visions' by giving preference to a conception of the vision that we will describe as 'porous' or 'cordial', in the sense that it must not be a readymade 'pill' that everyone must swallow, but much more a collective reflection on the different stakes and the positioning of the different operational actions carried out by the players and their coherence in regard to these stakes.

    We mention of 'porous' visions because, if management has to define a framework, it must welcome and absorb everyone's ideas like a sponge. Similarly, the visions are 'cordial' because, like a heart, it must be alive and moving, and function like the diastolic and systolic rhythms of the heart as it sends blood into the limbs through the arteries and pumps it back, enriched through the veins. A vision must be a living, collective dynamic, the sum of the different projects and processes that it is charged with inspiring, illuminating and guiding.

2. Work on the strategic competencies (macro-competencies). This basically consists of drawing up a list of the current competencies of the company, and in parallel, producing a list of the future competencies that will be required. It is then appropriate to plan a process for the reconfiguration of the competencies or their development, learning through cross-fertilisation, and so on. The company-specific macro-competencies will need to be designed and built progressively.

Different pilot groups can do this work, but in all cases it must be directed and supervised by management. It quickly becomes clear that this work is an extremely important opportunity for the players and it may become the central vector for collective intelligence such as that of the strategic reconfiguration of the company.

3. Work on the key processes. In some cases, it may be interesting to move on to the redesigning of one or more of the company's key processes. For example, if during a strategic diagnostic exercise it emerges that development of new products and/or services does not match the demands of the market and the competition, it will be appropriate, if need be, to restructure the company's product design department.

4. The generalised triggering of different support processes by managers, agents for change within and outside the different entities. This will call for research and design groups as required, individual coaching, team building, study and progress groups, groups to resolve inter-group conflict, ad hoc groups, and so on.

Institutionalisation

Institutionalisation does not mean the end of the process of deployment or a return to square one. It is rather a question of maintaining the dynamic, and eventually providing further impetus where necessary.

We suggest two criteria that describe the stage to which the institutionalisation phase must lead.

■ An acknowledgement, established from a shared feeling, and also from an objective assessment of previously defined indicators, that the dynamic has reached a point of no return, even if some breaks prove necessary in one or another area or operation.

■ An acknowledgement that the representation systems, the beliefs and the values of the collective intelligence have been integrated by the players in the company, not only into their behaviour (the visible part), but also into the attitudes (the invisible part made up of the person's beliefs). Things can no longer be 'as before', and the company has taken on a new spirit. This is often linked to an event, such as a restructuring, the arrival of a new chief executive or a take-over, and one can speak of a new era for the company, like Hewlett Packard's 'H-P Way'.

This institutionalisation may take various forms, such as a charter of values, action principles, a project or new company agreement. It does not really matter. It is simply sensible to see that two elements are maintained:

■ Permanent organisational processes, supported by a political will and the example shown by management, on the one hand, and through suitable budgets, on the other. Once the deployment phase is over, these two elements sometimes happen to be missing through simple negligence or ignorance of managers who 'forget' that this dynamic needs to be constantly maintained.

■ Generalised learning processes with testing phases, which must be maintained on a voluntary basis; because they are not widely known or habitual, they are at risk of disappearing into the moving sands of organisational homeostasis.

Conclusion

Our goal was to bring together some aspects that appeared to us fundamental for a company to be able to call itself an advanced company.

We hope that at the end of this account, it is apparent that it implies something more than a methodology, a set of techniques or the implementation of a new approach to management subject to a passing fad, but much more an attempt at formulating and assessing parameters that belong to a dynamic that is in continual evolution. The collective intelligence must always be built and, like the horizon that recedes as one advances towards it, it remains in the sphere of the possible.

While it rests on specific actions that require, on the part of the players, a special competence in the different vectors chosen, this implementation of the collective intelligence presupposes an approach that is both global, integrating the paradigm of complexity and above all necessitating a thorough reconfiguration of the culture (soft) and the organisational systems (hard).

Moreover, the collective intelligence cannot survive without the collective taking of a decisive step towards a community. In other words, the players will only be bound together when, having surpassed the excellence of their expertise, they will know how to become united to a certain extent, as well as more caring for the common good. The spirit and the hand belong to the same body only if the heart beats for all.

Ethical reflection will be the condition for the survival of this collective intelligence, for it will be the only guarantee that the essential can be experienced at the heart of the important.

The Stakes in Training for Coaching[1]

Introduction, the Practice of the Profession

The profession of coach is practised in four different ways depending on the context in which the coach finds himself:

- a person with responsibility whom we shall call a manager,
- a coach within the company,
- a coach outside the organisation.
- a person who does not necessarily have the status of a coach, but who holds the position and assumes the role vis-à-vis his director, someone in a cross-company post, or someone inside or outside the company.

Training: What are the Techniques?

When considering the training of a coach, it is appropriate first to specify what coaching practice we are discussing then describe the reference framework of the skills to be acquired.

Specific or Basic Training

When one refers to a specific type of coaching or training being pursued, reference is often made to a specific practice, such as training an internal coach or training a 'manager coach'; each has its terms and identities that include its own characteristics and the unavoidable ambiguities linked to them.

As an example, one can use the title 'manager–coach' even though the semantics of the two terms seem irreconcilable. The manager is in fact, to a great extent, the person who directs, evaluates, controls, sanctions and consequently shoulders the pressure of the stakes in the operational life of the organisation, whereas the coach creates the conditions that allow his client to develop his own approach and find his own solutions.

If one wants to train a manager and give him the dimension of coach or 'a man of resources', it will for example, be necessary to make him aware of the problems in the learning curve for his staff and to teach him to generate learning processes even though his position as manager and assessor infers his lack of neutrality so far as the results are concerned, thus making the task more difficult. One can therefore easily appreciate that it is by no means the same profession to be coach or manager–coach, the latter being first and foremost a manager. Can he lay claim to being a coach? He can certainly, at times, adopt the position of a coach, but basically the ambiguity is too great and, in the end, the managerial role carries the day. However, its unique quality lies in the fact that it can offer room for professional development by making use of operational opportunities.

For the external coach, there is also the characteristic of being outside the 'goldfish bowl', as he is outside the system, which has its advantages and disadvantages. The status or position of the external coach gives him a freedom, albeit relative, but distinctive in comparison with the internal coach, who is caught up in other unavoidable ambiguities.

It therefore seems pertinent for there to be specific types of training. Nevertheless, I shall begin by first examining the basic aspects of training for coaching, including the competencies that govern all coaching professions and which lie ahead of their applications.

Characteristics of Basic Training

Three elements characterise basic training in coaching:

- Training in relationship to assistance with the specificity peculiar to coaching, which is not the same as that of the therapeutic or other professions whose basis is in relationship to the other person.

- The capacity, specifically relating to the coach, of developing while at the centre of a complex situation, both from the conceptual point of view (knowing what complexity is) and from the operational point of view (knowing how to manage complex situations).

- A fundamental choice that is both the provision of an unavoidable, basic reference framework (in terms of content) and the deployment in space and in time of training that must be the opportunity for each trained person to find his specific identity.

Since it is a question of producing competent people who are capable of finding their own solutions, training to coach, par excellence, must be highly differentiated according to each individual. Training coaches is clearly not an exercise in cloning, where each coach would be the copy of his colleague or of the teacher!

Beyond the transfer of knowledge, beyond the learning about practice, and so on, this training must be basically the 'space time' during which the person comes to recognise himself, to succeed in sketching out his personal identity and his specific professional position so that he can finally plough his own furrow while conforming with his aspirations and embark on his own activity.

In the process of this training, the person progressively learns how to 'handle the cursor' on the continuum that extends from his particular expertise, which he gradually abandons, up to what we describe as 'internalised coaching' (see Figure A4.1).

We underline the fact that initial experience, the first side of the cursor, is absolutely necessary and has been acquired through the practice of one profession or another, and then through some managerial job. In this respect, the training process aims to ensure that, by relying on his expertise, the person finds sufficient support to become convinced

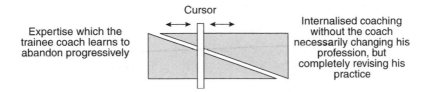

Cursor

Expertise which the trainee coach learns to abandon progressively

Internalised coaching without the coach necessarily changing his profession, but completely revising his practice

Figure A4.1 From expertise to internalised coaching

of his competence and, through being recognised internally (by himself) and externally (by others), able to progressively abandon it and have no further need for it in order to prove his own competence. This is required in order to be open to the development of the other person's competency, an attitude and behaviour that is a basic requirement for the coach. Therefore, an accountant who becomes a coach does not give up his knowledge of accounting, but he may provisionally refrain from referring to it in order to be of service to the client he is coaching. Similarly, a coach may refrain from giving external signs of his expertise by putting forth solutions that he can offer in order to make himself completely available to the solution found by his client.

The second side of the cursor is what we describe as 'internalised coaching'. When people come to me and ask the question 'Will I be a coach in two years with your training?' this indicates that they see this training as an identity change and that they will be able to put the word 'Coach' on their business card. I always reply: 'The stakes of training have nothing to do with that. There is certainly the question of whether in one or two years you will have changed your profession, job or position, but it may perhaps be that nothing changes externally and you prepare yourself to live your activity completely differently on the inside. For example, you may still be a communications consultant, but instead of completely devoting your professional activity to media plans, as a speech writer, or writer for newspapers or whatever else you do, you will assist the development processes of people, manage team-building operations to achieve, among other things, a consensus on communication. You will perhaps still be officially a consultant in communication with that on your business card but, internally and operationally, it will no longer be the same profession.' The idea is precisely that of interiorising the approach to coaching. Of course, the cursor can go in either direction. It may be appropriate for the coach to make use of his previous experience on one occasion or another, or at some other time to keep quiet about it and change his approach. This for me is a basic approach to training. We now examine what a coach is, and what his qualities and competencies are.

Being a Coach: Qualities and Competences

The Four Essential Qualities

The qualities that I outline here come directly from my training in bioenergy with Lowen and Pierrakos.[2] The four qualities of the competent coach are, for me, as follows:

- The quality of being (ontological security, simple confidence in oneself, radiant energy, inspiring trust, etc.).

- Competence in managing relationships.

- A capacity for understanding problems and what is at stake.

- Technical qualities (one practice or another, one language or another, the transactional analysis type of approach, neuro-linguistic programming, etc.).

Obviously, training must lead to the development and fulfilling of these qualities. However, in my view, it must be accomplished in the order that is described above. This is the true ranking of the qualities of a coach; technique, however important, comes second, not secondary – it comes after all the rest in terms of importance.

The client's choice of a coach must include the four preceding elements grouped together as the qualities of a coach, to which should be added two other criteria: references and regard for the persona. Concerning the latter criterion, one speaks of 'fit', and this is suggestive for the client to provide his own answer to the question 'Do I feel at ease with this coach?'. However irrational and subjective it might be, this criterion is completely essential. As for the reference criterion, we are thinking of the notoriety, training qualifications and what the prescribers who have helped you in your approach have told you.

Competencies of the Coach

What exactly are the competences of the coach? What is it that is going to make up the global competency of the coach, make him recommendable and give him legitimacy, apart from the technical competencies that we have already described?

Age
The first aspect is age. Although a child can sometimes be the most effective of coaches, to comfort his mother or his grandfather, age has nothing necessarily to do with this capacity for a comforting relationship with another person, this is certainly not the case in the world of business. One needs to have spent at least five to 10 years experiencing the business world to be a coach. I would therefore say that for someone less than 35 it would be hazardous, if not ineffective, and occasionally present a credibility problem.

Experience
The second point is experience. On the one hand, what is required is organisational experience, with knowledge of the day-to-day problems of work; on the other hand, experience of management or of a support relationship in a company that, for example, allows the consultant to understand problems, restraints, resistance to change, and so on. For these first two criteria (age and experience), a few grey hairs won't hurt!

Personal Development
The third competency that may prove quite decisive in comparison with the two preceding criteria is obviously personal development. There are people who simply through their existential, spiritual or historical experience, have lived through breakdowns, changes and ordeals that have brought about the building of their identity and their quality of being. The course of their existence has positioned them in a fundamentally new attitude towards life, in the sense that they have opened up to themselves,

to their own limitations, have made their choice of values and irrevocable personal choices. I am thinking in particular of a marketing consultant with whom I found myself teaching in a business school in 1973 or 1974. This man had an inner breathing and radiated an astonishing sense of inner peace. When I asked him about the origin of this peace, he confessed that he had been a fighter pilot and had had a flying accident that caused him to spend six months confined to a hospital bed without being able to move. 'This event transformed my life and gave me another outlook on life', he said. Some people have had a Near Death Experience and have returned. For them, the world is no longer the same. There are many such examples, and I stress this idea of personal development as a sometimes essential factor for growth.

Therapeutic work
A metaphor that I used a lot, when I was a therapist, in order to enter the mystery of personal development and therapy, is that of the Japanese soldier. In 1975, some Japanese soldiers were found on a Pacific island; they believed that the Second World War had not ended. They were returned to their country and received like national heroes. I compare these Japanese soldiers with personal development in the sense that it is only after 30 years after the war has ended that one accepts to surrender one's arms. One needs to be at least in one's thirties to be able to embark on true therapeutic work, that is, when one stops telling one that problems are caused by others. Up to the age of 30, it is the others who have the problem! But after 30 to 35 one begins to notice that situations recur and that perhaps it has something to do with oneself. One begins to discover that one possesses an armour and an enclosing 'life scenario', and one wants to leave all that, clean one's spectacles and surrender. I therefore think that one can only be a good coach when one has escaped from the syndrome of the Japanese soldier.

A characteristic, common to all coaches, is to have led a solitary life spread over a certain period of time. One does not hear a four-year-old say 'When I grow up, I'm going to be a coach'. Firefighter or pilot, but not a coach. It is not yet a sufficiently identified profession for that to be possible. One becomes a coach because one has recognised one's limitations, because one takes a step towards humanity. The competence developed here is the opening to therapeutic work and personal development that is precisely the space where a person who has emerged from the Japanese soldier syndrome has begun to empower himself and take his destiny in hand.

Training
Obviously, when considering competencies, it is important to take into account the education and training that the person has received. Nowadays, there are many courses available, with some schools in France focused on therapeutic and personal work, and others concentrating on the organisation and action of the company. On the other hand, there are the Anglo-Saxon schools whose attitudes and approaches are oriented more towards the achievement of results and make more use of the methods of coaching that follow this path.

Support: Supervision and Control
Controlling authorities are necessary for the acquisition of competencies in the long term and in order to prevent possible errors and lapses. There must also be a pace to the supervision that allows the implementation of processes to enrich, enlighten and validate the work of coaches, guiding them in the pursuit of their own professional development.

Requirements of Transformance

As the director of Transformance, when I select participants for training in coaching, I keep the following two main requirements in mind:

■ Adequate professional experience, either of management, or of an assistance role. In other words, people who wish to follow the programme must have had to manage relationships and not simply have pursued solitary or purely scientific or technical occupations. A minimum knowledge of one of the tools of communication, such as TA,[3] NLP,[4] PCM,[5] TMS[6] or other, is a valuable asset, although its absence is not an obstacle. The participant can always arrange to take a supplementary course on one of these techniques during training, and this is often the case.

■ Some therapeutic work. Here I do not mean that the person has at the very least begun therapeutic work, has learnt about the importance and need for time for training for the future practice of his profession. Rather, I show a preference for and advocate the integration of work in a group and individually, and an approach that integrates aspects that are analytical, corporeal, emotional and relational.

Training Proposed by Transformance

Principles of Transformance Training

The training that I set up and have carried out since 1989 is partly the result of my own training, as consultant, therapist and educator, integrating some 15 approaches to the provision of assistance, analysis and humanist psychology, even though my status as transactional analyst was my first qualification. I believe that the training offered by Transformance is based on the following principles that integrate and go beyond acquiring operational grids, techniques and various learning processes:

■ The principle of complexity. To train for complexity it is necessary to propose a complex system and thus train people to live in complexity. This will be expressed in the group through ambiguity (am I a participant? am I the coach? am I the leader? am I being coached? am I an observer? etc.) and in the continual changing of positions. The ambiguity continues between content, process and meaning (knowing how to give up the content at any moment, if necessary, should the process no longer be judged as a sound one or if the values and meanings have shifted, learning how to reposition all that is in the meaning to overcome opposition of a logical nature, and so on). It is a question then of training oneself to continually evaluate the complexity of a situation because therein lies the skill of the coach that the participant will experience in future. The coach does not know a priori in a training exercise whether he will be the manager's crutch, the leader, whether he will be inside or outside the team he works with, whether he is there to assure some function that fosters permission or some prescriptive function that fosters protection. It is necessary to be constantly making choices and learning to position oneself.

■ The second principle is that of auto-organisation. The players will be invited to constantly take themselves in hand, to bring forth their own situations, to intervene, to function in groups and in pairs and to consider themselves competent from the beginning. This is carried out in practice, through a variable geometry in the task: the individual task, in pairs, in threes, in groups of 10 to12 people, in plenary session of 40 to 45 people.

▪ This practice in relating 'one-to-one' or 'one-to-many' exposes the participant to an internal flexibility that is indispensable in this profession.

▪ The third principle is work based learning using the model of the learning business, as NONAKA defines it, with the matrix in which the first axis corresponds to the implicit/explicit relationship and the second to the individual/collective relationship and the eight vectors of work: internalisation, individual and collective clarification, and so on. The four faces as represented in Figure A4.2 are gradually visited by each according to the eight vectors moving from one dial to the next.

The following examples are noted for clarification:

▪ The movement from C1 to C3 corresponds to the vector for internalisation (or to the metabolic changes of knowledge) according to the process of enactment (one x exogenous requires four x endogenous)

▪ That being professional is knowing how to theorise about the practice and practice the theory. In other words, it demands that as a first step, it be explicit that the individual experience is, by definition, implicit (movement from C3 to C1) then to explain it to others (passage from C1 to C2) (see Figure A4.3).

▪ The fourth principle is holomorphism.[7] Each party holds the whole and the shape of the whole. Each learns progressively to navigate and to feel at ease with the complexity of true reality: recursive causality. The training is in the person and the person in the training. The participant generates the dynamic of the training, which, in return, nourishes him. The whole is in the part and the part in the whole. Thus each moment of the training, whether it is experienced individually or collectively, can contribute to building or blocking the process.

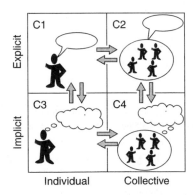

Figure A4.2 Nonaka matrix

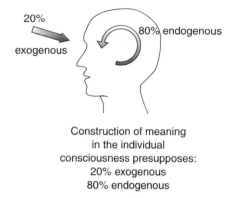

Construction of meaning
in the individual
consciousness presupposes:
20% exogenous
80% endogenous

Figure A4.3   The process of enacting (according to Varela)

- The fifth principle reveals an attitude that consists of considering the person competent from day one, and therefore already a coach. This has practical implications such as the fact that from the first day, the first morning, a participant is designated as coach for half the day.

- The sixth principle is that of supervised auto-evaluation. It is not the seminar organiser who evaluates the others, but people who have learnt to auto-evaluate themselves with the help of supervision that allows them to define standards, norms, and allows them to regulate, and so on.

- The seventh principle arises from putting into practice the processes that contribute to the identity building of the participants, such as restitution, enactment, inclusion, work on beliefs, and so on. The group offers each participant the opportunity to project and introject a new 'family constellation'.

Three Levels of Training

Following here are some principles governing training that I have developed and which I am still developing with the Teachers in Training (TT or 'EEF: *enseignant en formation*') I supervise. This training, which concentrates on identity development and the reconfiguration of professional competencies, consists of three programmes:

- The initial programme CT® (Coach and Team) that allows entry into this culture and the means of acquiring the necessary and unavoidable fundamentals, together with a certain amount of experience.

- An in-depth programme, the Master CTIC® (Master Coach and Team for the deployment of the Collective Intelligence) that aims at the full mastery of the different concepts and the capacity to experience permanently the different logical levels of meaning, the identities of the players, the company, and so on. It aims

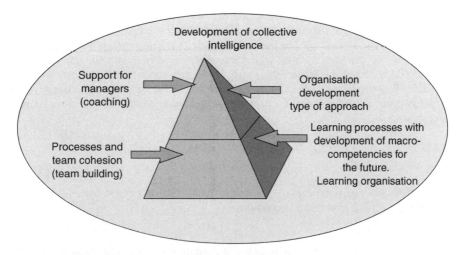

Figure A4.4   Collective intelligence as a meta-system

at training those professionals who are already confirmed in the practice of coaching and team building, intervening in the logic of the development of collective intelligence (see Figure A4.4).

■ The training of EEF instructors that will not only make the person capable of being a successful coach but also of being a supervisor and an instructor assuming all the functions of a developer. This latter function consists of knowing how to create in another person the conditions for the emergence of his identity through the nine levels of the 'spinal column of meaning' by helping him to reveal it within his life scenario. The aim is still to focus on the growth of the Prince (or champion) or Princess that is in each of us.

– In coaching, the work lies in achieving coherence in the levels of what is important (organisational, managerial and professional).

– The developer, for his part, works in the order of the essential contained in each of the nine levels of the spinal column of meaning.

Training that Opens the Way to a Professional Code of Ethics

Through its processes and the rules that govern it, this training allows the participant to be receptive to the ethics of the coaching profession, that is, the principles for working with a company and its rules. The ethics will not descend on a practice from above but emanate from within that practice, which is something quite different. One decides not to do one thing or another because one knows that it will provoke an undesirable effect within the training body. Alternatively, one adopts a particular approach because one knows that it results in efficiency and rigour and is a factor for emergence.

Strengthened by our experience and in order not to be forced to retrench a practical approach, we have established rules that allow time to be saved and which protect the training area. These rules, part of the ethics of the coaching profession, are gradually internalised by the participants, who themselves in turn come to practice these ethics. The elements of these ethics are numerous and of three types: vis-à-vis oneself, vis-à-vis clients (those coached), vis-à-vis the organisation (usually the sponsor of the coaching operation or of implementation of the company's collective intelligence).

Vis-à-vis oneself (as coach)
There are three aspects:

▫ The three prerequisites, namely (1) training and company experience, (2) work on oneself and (3) a place for supervision.

▫ Confidentiality.

▫ Obligation of means. The coach does not commit himself to obtaining results, but instead to the implementation of means.

Vis-à-vis the client
There are three aspects:

▫ Respect for the person. The art of coaching is not based on the use of techniques that aim to motivate others. It is based on the capacity to help them to (re)discover their own source of motivation and act from that.

▫ Protection. The person is accepted unconditionally as he is. In personal coaching, the person is always more important than his objectives, and one of the coach's roles is to help him to discover who he is, find his way and discover what motivates him. But for all that, it is the clarity of the limits (permissions and protections) combined with the respect for the other and a strongly positive stimulation that gives strength to coaching and to any educational process.

▫ Development of his responsibility. Each of us is the first to be responsible for the results we obtain. We do not accuse others, nor do we blame the circumstances.

Vis-à-vis the organisation
There are two aspects:

▫ The triangular contract (see Figure A4.5). It is a question of making the relationships between the different parties coherent, that is, the sponsor (the company), the client (the person coached) and the provider (the coach). This work clarifies and contributes to the success of the operation.

▫ Protection of people vis-à-vis the hierarchy. Of course, the coach does not accept mediocrity, neither for himself, nor for his clients. He expects them to give it their best and does likewise. However, the coach cannot be the right hand of management, hence the importance of setting up contracts such as mentioned above.

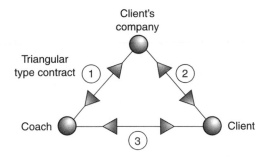

Figure A4.5 The triangular contract

Conclusion: Uniqueness of Training in Coaching

Training in coaching is unlike any other type of training in that it is not a programme that aims to provide a supplement of skills (another layer), but it is in itself an original construction in complexity, a development that is cross disciplinary, as Edgar Morin would say, located at the interfaces of a whole set of professions, such as therapy, the sociology of organisations, psycho-sociology, economics, systems operation, and so on. This training borrows from all these disciplines and leads the coach to live a cross-disciplinary life at the centre of which he can build his identity.

This training belongs to an area of professional and organisational development and it basically opens the door to a humanisation of individual players as well as the human community. This humanisation step is not conceived for the building of supermen or invulnerable beings, but on the contrary, to build beings who become more human, in that they are more open to their own limitations.

The grandeur of training in coaching is that it will occupy a level that includes and integrates, and I would even say that it accomplishes therapeutic work. Becoming a coach presupposes that one is ready to take account of the levels of reality that include epistemological leaps, since one passes from the depths of psychology and psychotherapy, to psycho-sociology, sociology, and so on. As a consequence, one touches upon the whole mystery of the human being and, through that, one finds oneself in contact with the infinity of being while at the same time dealing with objective realities that are extremely concrete, economic and organisational, something that the therapist cannot always achieve.

Finally, this profession is located at the heart of complexity. The coach is invited to take into account the individual in his unique dimension and as such separated from the rest of the world, then put him into a relationship with the teams, with the organisation and with the environment in its entirety. It is the holomorphic dimension of the individual in the organisation that is especially interesting for the coach and which constitute the uniqueness of this profession. It is not a question of seeing the person as one would see him for example in therapy with a completely protected and isolated silhouette, but on the contrary to consider him as a complex whole, who can consequently only be won over with the tools of complexity.

A

Adult, integrated
A transactional analysis term. The Adult Ego State integrating the positive aspects of the Parent and of the Child.

Agitation
A transactional analysis term. Passive behaviour in which the person channels his energy towards some pointless repetitive activity and not towards solving a problem.

Alliance (therapeutic or for change)
Bilateral commitment between coach and coached person to sustain mutual trust and maintain the relationship despite the inevitable frustrations. In other words, the alliance is a mutual commitment not to break the relationship despite the possibly extremely high level of frustration involved. The alliance is based on mutual trust and on shared objectives and (sufficient sharing of their minimum cultural envelopes).

Aquarium
Live coaching situation where a participant under training plays the role of coach, while another represents the client and the remainder of the group are observers. The situation reminds one of two goldfish in a bowl.

Attribution
A transactional analysis term. A message coming from one person to another (receiver) concerning his identity. This may generate in the receiver an identity envelope or a 'fate' in which he may entrap himself, constituting or strengthening his 'scenario'.

B

Behaviour, passive
A transactional analysis term. One of the four modes of behaviour (do nothing, over-adapt, be agitated, disable oneself or become violent) that results from a discount.

C

Change (types of change)

- Type 0: Intervening on elements in the manager's environment: strategy, system, structure and organisation.

- Type 1 (corresponding to change category of the Palo Alto School): Conducting a change in managerial behaviour. The elements to be found in this category can for example be the client's management style, his listening and his method of communication, his capacity for working in a group, his managerial identity (Manager as order giver, Resource manager, Manager as carrier of meaning).

- Type 2 (In the Palo Alto School, type 2 change embraces what in the CT school comes under levels 2, 3, 4 and 5): Conducting a change in the attitudes, beliefs, values and representation systems. This type of change often leads to questioning of one's own scenario and a re-decision (type 3).

- Type 3: This change affects the person's deeper structure. It includes the identity elements of the person, such as his defence system, injuries, history, unconscious, his body and emotions. Type 3 belongs to the field of therapy and must not be handled in coaching.

- Type 4: Develops the positive part of the person. From the humanist viewpoint, one speaks of the growing prince who constantly wishes to develop.

- Type 5: From a Christian (St Paul) perspective the person splits into two, the old man and the new man. Type 5 development corresponds to making the divine grow within us; the new man welcoming the salvation of God offered by Jesus Christ through his death and resurrection.

Child, Adaptive Submissive
A transactional analysis term. Subdivision of the Child in the functional model, showing how an individual uses this Ego State in order to conform to the rules and demands of society.

Child, Free
A transactional analysis term. Subdivision of the Child in the functional model, showing how an individual uses this Ego State to express his feelings and his needs without censoring them and without concern for rules or social demands.

Child, Adapted Rebellious
A transactional analysis term. Method of expression of the Adapted Child in which an individual rebels against the rules instead of conforming to them.

Circuit of trust
This is a spiral process that is constructed in time with a team in order to allow an initial collection of individuals to become an effective team.

Clarification of representations
A technique that aims at identifying the frameworks of reference of the people present and allowing them to create a higher level of communication by unmasking the misunderstandings, disagreements and the real zone of agreement.

Coaching
Coaching is both an assistance and a collaborative construction offered to a person (or team) through a time-limited intervention or, more often, as support spread over a period of time.

This assistance and co-construction is in keeping with a professional situation, and/or a managerial and/or organisational situation.

The aim is to create conditions for the person (or coached team) for them to find and build their own solutions.

The approach is to achieve the prompt solution of the problem with a view to a lasting and global development.

Compass, trainer's
(Expression credited to Nicolas Schilfarth, CT15, EEF)
Conceptualisation of the training approach introduced at the Danone company for action based on the individual's level of awareness of his competence or incompetence.

Conscience, clear
A transactional analysis term. The capacity to experience impressions that are purely sensory and emotional, in an uncontaminated way, like a newborn child, without interpretation.

Consensus
Agreement between parties. One can define three types:

1. Symbiotic consensus, characterised by a narrow hierarchical relationship. It is the result of a directorial management style and implies two Ego States (Parent and Adult) in the one and one in the other (Child), the other Ego States being excluded from the relationship.

2. Partial consensus or compromise. The two parties mobilise the same Ego States (PP or AA or CC). If the relationship is of type P/P, the individuals agree on the values but they neglect reality (A) and their real feelings (C). If the relationship is of type A/A, the persons rationalise from real elements but exclude values and their true feelings. Decisions made in this context do not stand up to crises. If the relationship is of type E/E, the persons are enthusiastic and make a decision based on their emotions (C), but this consensus does not withstand the test of objective reality (A) or values (P).

3. Shared consensus. A consensus that mobilises all Ego States of both participants.

Contamination
A transactional analysis term. Part of the content Child and Parent Ego States that the individual confuses with the content of the Adult.

Contract
A transactional analysis term. An explicit bilateral agreement aiming at a well-defined programme of action. An Adult commitment vis-à-vis oneself or another to conduct a change.

Definition suggested by V. Lenhardt: the agreement between two parties on the objectives, the means to achieve them and a process (i.e. objectives to be achieved and the roles of each person). The contract consists of three dimensions (Jet Meininger, TA Business):

- The business contract: defines the fees, conditions, objectives and methods of operation.

- The relational contract: an informal contract that contains all the practical details stated and unstated that will condition the whole relationship between the protagonists.

■ The secret contract: the psychological and relational stakes of the two protagonists, which are partly preconscious and partly unconscious.

According to Fanita English, the form of contract often introduces a third pole, namely the institution (this is why one speaks of a triangular contract). The contract may be many sided (e.g. coach, course members, internal trainer, training manager).

The contract is a very useful clarification tool to restrict symbiotic relationships, avoid game playing and empower client and coach.

Transactional analysis has developed a corpus around the contract through the major contributions from Claude Steiner and Holloway.

Counter-injunction
A transactional analysis term. Scenario messages emitted by the Parent of the parent and stored in the Parent of the child.

Counter-scenario
A transactional analysis term. Set of decisions taken by the child to obey the counter-injunctions.

Cultural Envelope, Minimum Shared
Minimum Shared Cultural Envelope. Made up of six elements: 1. values; 2. operational objectives; 3. mutual knowledge; 4. professional shared experience; 5. shared skills; 6. common language.

Culture of a company
The type of relationships in a company, the methods of decision-making, the hierarchical structure, and so on. There are three classic types of company culture in all organisations:

1. Taylorian culture. Companies organised as pyramids in which the type of consensus tends to be symbiotic.

2. The matrix culture. The company is organised in matrix form and ambiguity reigns between hierarchical and operational lines. Procedure and normalisation are keywords to resolve the paradoxes and the ambiguities in this type of organisation. Consensus tends to be partial or based on compromise.

3. The network culture. This often leads to the multicellular culture. There is a multiplicity of interpersonal relationships and the classic type of consensus tends to be shared.

D

Decision
A transactional analysis term. Conclusion about oneself, others or life, most often adopted in early childhood, as the best means available for survival and satisfying needs. Restricted by a very incomplete level of information and conditioned by a magical way of thinking and facing reality typical of a child at this age.

Degree of evolution
An assessment of the cultural maturity of a person, group or institution in order to establish the best way of working with the coach.

Questions that should be asked are:

- Have the participants already experienced coaching, or working with a consultant?
- Are they ready to be called challenged?
- What experience do they have of other cultures, change and personal development?
- Do they know how to assess the frustration that must be undergone in managing an organisational change?
- Where do they stand in the model of the levels of autonomy?

Diagnosis-Diagnosis (putting forward a diagnosis-diagnosis in coaching)

This relates to the need for the model-for-action grid.

Competencies. To confirm a diagnosis-diagnosis, the coach must have:

- A representation system or reference framework for the levels of development (DPI-personal, DMI-managerial, DRI-relational, DTI-team, DCI-cultural).
- Real experience of the business world, of training, of personal therapy and of serious communication skills.
- An integrated knowledge of the management theory and of Berne's organisational theory.

The diagnosis is the result of:

- an evaluation of the needs and stakes of the entity coached.
- an intuition.
- an ability to evaluate the unsaid.
- a free creativity.
- a faculty for adapting optimally to the situation.
- an ability to manage ambiguous processes (capacity for instinctive diagnosis and improvisation).
- an integration of the 15 parameters.

Diagnosis, behavioural
A transactional analysis term. Judging in which Ego State an individual is located by observing his behaviour.

Diagnosis, historical
A transactional analysis term. Judging in which Ego State an individual is located by gathering factual information about his parents or parental figures and his childhood.

Diagnosis, phenomenological
A transactional analysis term. Evaluating in which Ego State the person is located from what he relives of his own past. It refers to an intra-psychical diagnosis made by the person in regard to himself.

Diagnosis, phenomenological and social
Evaluation made by the coach of the person's Ego State by analysing what one feels in one's Child or Parent (analysis of the counter transfer).

Diagnosis, social
A transactional analysis term. Judging in which Ego State a person is located by observing the Ego States used by others in their dealings with the person.

Dialogic (Cf. *Manager dans la complexité*, D. Genelot)
Term created by Edgar Morin, corresponding to the co-existence of two logical systems of different nature and type, each having its own life.

DCI
Development of Cultural Identity. The way of integrating the following three levels: the relationship of the team to its institutional structure, the relationship of the structure to the environment and the relationship of the team to the environment.

DMI
Development of Managerial Identity. The development of some specific competencies of the manager, including stress management, motivation, decision-making, time management, the stages of development (professional expert, manager and leader), the identity envelopes.

DPI
Development of Personal Identity. It involves both therapeutic work and personal development work.

DRI
Development of Relational Identity. It refers to developing the manager's capacity for relationships, bearing in mind that 70 per cent of his time is devoted to relating (telephone, interviews, meetings, etc.).

DTI
Development of the Team Identity. This is the area for the specific application of team building. It involves assessing the team's level of development and identifying what it needs in order to develop.

Discounting
A transactional analysis term. Unconsciously neglecting information that is appropriate for the resolution of a problem.

Distortion (of reality)
A transactional analysis term. Exaggeration of an aspect of reality through discounting.

Driver (or restrictive message)
A transactional analysis term. One of five categories of behaviour occurring over a period of half a second as the functional manifestation of a negative counter-scenario.

Dual control
Live coaching situation in which a training participant plays the role of coach, another plays the role of the client, the course leader or a staff member acts as resource and supervisor for the coach to whom the coach can appeal if the situation becomes blocked. The supervisor can intervene at any time that he sees fit, by 'freezing the frame'. The remainder of the group acts as observer.

E

Economy of recognition signs (strokes)
A transactional analysis term. Set of restrictive Parental rules concerning signs of recognition.

Egogram
A transactional analysis term. Column diagram (conceived by Jack Dusay) that shows the intuitive evaluation of the importance of each subdivision of the functional model of the Ego States in an individual's personality.

Ego State
A transactional analysis term. A coherent set of thoughts, feelings and emotions and experiences directly associated with a corresponding coherent set of behaviours.

Elastic
A transactional analysis term. Point of similarity between a here and now situation of stress and a painful childhood situation relived by the person, generally unconsciously and to which the person will probably react by going into his scenario.

Elements of transfer (transferential elements)
Three aspects needs to be identified:

- The transfer from the client to the coach. The client will fantasise about the personality of coach 1 based on figures from the past whom the client has 'introjected' (like the bad father, i.e. transfer < 0; like the ideal parent, the saviour from whom one expects magical solutions, i.e. transfer > 0; based on his own image (the client will imagine that the coach is like him)). Cf. the two types of transfer identified by Carlo Moiso.

- The coach's counter transfer. The coach needs to know how to manage the emotional reactions activated by the client's transfer onto him.

- The transfer from the coach to his client. Everything that the coach fantasises about his client because of his own introjections or his unconscious perception of himself.

Enaction
Process elicited by Francisco Varela who specifies that for a person to be able to integrate what is explained to him, he needs four times more energy (endogenous process) than that used by the person who explains (exogenous process). The formula is: 'for every "x" exogenous, it requires "4x" endogenous'.

Episcenario
A transactional analysis term. Negative scenario message that a Parent sends to a Child in the magical hope that, thereby, he will be freed from the burden of this message.

Exclusive (Ego States)
A transactional analysis term. Ego State that remains operational when the other two are excluded.

Exclusion (Ego States)
A transactional analysis term. Absence of use by the individual of one or more Ego States.

F

Feeling, authentic
A transactional analysis term. Original uncensored feeling, which an individual has learnt to hide in childhood through an interfering feeling.

Feeling, Racket
A transactional analysis term. A habitual feeling that has been learnt and encouraged in childhood, experienced as an adult means of resolving a problem in many varied and inappropriate situations of stress.

G

Gallows laugh
A transactional analysis term. A communication in which an individual smiles or laughs while talking about something painful.

Game
A transactional analysis term. A process that consists of doing something that has a hidden aim that: 1. Is outside the field of awareness of the Adult, 2. Only becomes explicit when the protagonists engage in role reversal and 3. Results in everyone feeling confused, misunderstood and wanting to accuse the other.

Grandiosity
In the corpus theory developed by the Cathexis Institute (a classic transactional analysis school) grandiosity is the name given to the erroneous conscious or unconscious belief that serves as justification for all the elements governing passivity (the discounting which is the internal mechanism resulting from grandiosity, the relational problem of symbiosis, and the different behaviours related to the different levels of passive behaviour).

I

Identities, managerial
The identities that the manager endorses progressively and according to the situation to be managed: manager as order-giver, resource manager and manager as carrier of meaning. A second approach also suggests identities in terms of expert technician, manager and leader.

Identity envelope
A model that aims at pinpointing the historical stages of the person's identity (rather as if one studied the growth rings of a tree trunk). The elements that constitute the envelope include, among others:

- The person.

- His education for his profession and his professional practice developed in the field throughout his different jobs.

- His job in the current organisation.

- What he carries from his organisation.

Illusion
A transactional analysis term. Contamination of the Adult by the Child.

Incongruity
A transactional analysis term. Discrepancy between the explicit content of a communication and the behavioural signs shown by the communicator.

Information, useful
Information likely to alter the contour of a group or important for its existence.

Injunction
A transactional analysis term. Negative and restrictive scenario messages emitted by the Child of the parent and stored in the Child of the child.

Integrated identities
A conceptualisation that helps chart the action of the individual and team coach on different vectors: the development of the manager's personal identity, his managerial identity and his relational identity, and the development of the team's identity and of the company's cultural identity.

Intervention plan
Means and stages of intervention and alternative strategies. The complete set of means and stages that will go to make up the range of interventions made by the coach. This implies that the coach has:

- Measured the time required (number of stages, meetings, etc.) for the intervention.

- Developed an alternative strategy.

- Considered the tactical approaches to 'preparing his improvisations' during the sessions (creativity without losing sight of the group's destination and orientation).

Intimacy
A transactional analysis term. Method of structuring a time in which people express one to another authentic feelings and needs without censoring them.

L

Layers of personality (Cf. *Transformational Leadership*, A. Godard and V. Lenhardt)
Concept established by John Pierrakos (bioenergeticist) that structures the person in three concentric layers: the mask (social protections), the negative self (defensive injured part) and the positive self (positive part). In the CT lectures, V. Lenhardt refers to the combined mask and negative self as the 'frog' and to the positive self as the 'prince'.

Level of autonomy
The stages of dependence, counter-dependence, independence and interdependency.

Level of meaning (grid)

The grid for the levels of meaning identifies nine levels of reality with their own stakes. This grid in particular allows a diagnosis of where the difficulties lie by analysing inter-personal transactions.

For example, if the person has not found his identity nor the ontological security of someone who knows who he is, a parasitic interaction will occur, in which the identity (level 9), being insufficient, leads the person to invest desperately in a power level (level 8) that is nurtured by at least seven levels of reality: the psychological unconscious (level 1), the psychological conscious (level 2), the operational level (level 3), the level defining the job (level 4), the company level (level 5), the environment level (level 6) and the meta-meaning level (level 7). This implies that, within the company, the entire operational dimension (level 3) is interfered with, even blocked, by the energy invested in the other levels of meaning.

Level of discount

A transactional analysis term. Concerns a discounting relating to the existence, signification, possibilities for change or personal capabilities.

Logical level of vision (Cf. *Transformational Leadership*, A. Godard and V. Lenhardt)
The vision comprises six levels: vocation, ambition, values, management principles, strategic priorities and action plans.

Logics based on OR, AND, BECAUSE
See monologic, dialogic and teleologic.

M

Matrix, scenario
A transactional analysis term. A diagram in which the transmission of messages is analysed in terms of Ego States.

MCM
Manager as Carrier of Meaning

Message, psychological level
A transactional analysis term. A hidden message, generally sent by non-verbal signs.

Message, restrictive
A transactional analysis term. Synonym of **driver**.

Message, scenario
A transactional analysis term. A verbal or non-verbal message sent by parents, from which the child draws conclusions about himself, others and the world during the process of developing his scenario.

Message, social level
A transactional analysis term. Explicit hidden message, generally sent through verbal content.

Meta-communication (Cf. Palo Alto School, E. Marc and D. Picard)
The art of communicating about communication (the way in which one communicates). Term created by the Palo Alto School (Gregory Bateson).

Misreading (misunderstanding)
A transactional analysis term. Unconsciously neglecting information that is appropriate
for the resolution of a problem.

Modelling
Examples shown by the coach to his client through his behaviour, which are self-
introjected and then reproduced by the client.

MOG (Cf. *Transformational Leadership*, A. Godard and V. Lenhardt)
Manager as order-giver.

Monologic (Cf. *Manager Dans la Complexité*, D. Genelot)
The only existing logic that excludes all others. One also speaks of 'OR' logic (reasoning based on 'OR') or non-differentiation ('hard' logic), in contrast to 'AND' logic
(dialogic).

MR (Cf. *Transformational Leadership*, A. Godard and V. Lenhardt)
Manager as Resource.

Mine, yours, his, ours, mine
A model that allows the coach to take three dimensions into account (himself, the other,
the team) in pursuing the work of the team and choose his intervention level. Is this
problem mine, his, yours, ours or mine? This model is representative of systemic and
holomorphic thought for each team member.

N

NLP
Neuro-Linguistic Programming.

O

OK, OKness
Someone who has given meaning to his life is OK. This OKness inspires work in four
specific domains:

- In relation to myself. To be OK, is to accept oneself unconditionally, to know that
  one is lovable, unconditionally. I am OK because I have within me sufficient strength
  for healing, growth and love for me to seize my freedom and the responsibility for
  my growth.

- In relation to others. To be OK with others, is to see there is a Prince in everyone,
  and to accept the limit of the relationship. To be OK with someone is to be ready to
  take on a commitment with this person even if he/she collapses. It is to accept the
  other person in his/her unavoidable ambiguity and at the same time accept that if
  I cannot put up with that person, the coaching relationship is not possible.

- In relation to griefs. Griefs over my sexuality, griefs over my all-powerfulness
  (out-of-place seizure of power), of the therapeutic relationship if I am in a business

environment, accepting to be potentially challenged in my behaviour whilst retaining sufficient stability.

▪ Having come to terms with one's relation towards money as a means of evaluating one's OKness at a personal level (ontological security) and at a professional level (has the coach found his managerial identity, i.e. internal and external recognition, his 'skin'). If this identity adjustment has not been made, the coaching relationship may be racketeered or hijacked.

William Schutz in particular has developed this concept in his various books, and especially in *The Human Element*. The concept of OKness will be considerably enriched by the concept of self-esteem.

ORT model (Operations, Regulation, Training)
The model highlights that every team-building operation is focused simultaneously on team operations (from vision to production), regulation (from adjustment of representations and processes to conflict management) and training (technique, management, culture). According to one's understanding of the situation, the weight of each polarity can be adjusted.

Over-communication
Once one has communicated and possibly meta-communicated (communicate about the way one has communicated), it is necessary to over-communicate, that is, to check that the communication and feedback loops have indeed succeeded, especially if several people are involved.

P

Parallel process or 'hot potato'
A concept originally put forward by Fanita English (Transactional Analysis) relating to a situation in which the person (generally the client) transmits his own problem to another person (generally the coach).

Parent, Controlling or Criticising
A transactional analysis term. Subdivision of the Parent in the functional model, indicating how an individual uses this Ego State to control, direct or criticise.

Parent, Nurturing
A transactional analysis term. Subdivision of the Parent in the functional model, indicating how an individual uses this Ego State to nurture, care for or help.

Passivity
A transactional analysis term. How people do not do things or do not resolve problems that present themselves.

Paths, spiritual
The different spiritual paths are present consciously or unconsciously at the heart of everyone's finality. There are five pathways:

▪ Humanist: agnostic, atheist, open and syncretist.

▪ Pagan: non-Judeo-Christian.

- Esoteric: emphasising knowledge as Man's means for self-realisation.

- Monistic and ascetic: as are the major oriental approaches.

- Biblical: Jewish, Islamic, Christian, aiming at sainthood, that is, opening to the grace of God, the creator who deifies what Man has humanised, and as a result of his work, becomes co-creation.

Permission (in the scenario)
A transactional analysis term. Positive and liberating scenario messages sent by the Child of the parents and stored in the Child of the child.

Persecutor (in the drama triangle)
A transactional analysis term. Person who humbles or humiliates others.

Position, life or existential
A transactional analysis term. Fundamental beliefs that a person has about himself and others, and which serve to justify decision and behaviour. The fundamental position that a person adopts on an intrinsic value and grants to himself and to others.

Procrastination
The set of components and the process that lead the person to delay the resolution of a problem or any outcome.

Programme
A transactional analysis term. A set of scenario messages send by the Adult of the parent and stored in the Adult of the child.

R

Racket
A transactional analysis term. Set of scenario behaviours unconsciously aimed at manipulating the environment, and implying that the person harbours a parasite or 'racket' feeling.

Re-decision
A transactional analysis term. The replacement of an earlier restricting decision, taken with regard to oneself, by a new decision that takes account of the fullness of adult resources within the person.

Redefinition
A transactional analysis term. A distortion of the perception of reality by an individual in the way that it fits with his own scenario.

Reference framework
A transactional analysis term. A structure of associated reactions that integrate the different Ego States reacting to particular stimuli. It provides the individual with a global whole that enables him to perceive, conceptualise, feel and act and with which he defines himself and defines others and the world.

Request
This designates what the client asks for in a coaching session. There are seven types of request: the anti-request, the non-request, the counter-request, the confused or ambiguous request, the explicit request and the latent request. In every case, the coach will have to clarify and identify the content request (what is being discussed and the results that

one expects) and the process request (the client's and the coach's contribution and the nature of their interaction).

S

Saviour (in the drama triangle)
A transactional analysis term. A person who suggests helping others from a position of superiority, believing that 'they are not sufficiently competent to help themselves'.

Scenario of life
A transactional analysis term. Unconscious life plan developed in childhood, strengthened by the parents, 'justified' by subsequent events and culminating in a foreseen outcome.

Signs of recognition or strokes
A transactional analysis term. A unit of recognition: a verbal or nonverbal sign, positive (agreeably felt by the person who receives it), conditional (concerns action) or unconditional (concerns being), and essential to the psychological survival of the individual.

Spinal column of meaning
Ways of presenting the different identity levels (9) and of envisaging the action of coaching either in the domain of the important (levels 2, 3 and 4) or of the essential (levels 5 to 9). The coach's role is always to create conditions so that the person can make levels 2, 3 and 4 coherent (organisational, managerial and professional levels).

Each identity level in the 'spinal column of meaning' corresponds to a specific 'logical level' endowed with its own coherence. Working like a kind of osteopath of meaning, the coach's task is:

- To accept the relative levels of meaning.

- To focus on levels 2, 3 and 4 (organisational, managerial and professional) while ensuring that the essential lies at the heart of the important.

Stages of development of the manager
A manager's development goes linearly through three stages:

1. Expert in a job. The focus is on technique and content (what and how it is done).

2. Hierarchical manager. The focus is on relationship and processes (what and how to get it done).

3. Leader. The focus is on strategy and meaning (why have it done and for what).

Stages of team development
There are two models for the growth of teams. The first offers six development stages, the second offers three (collection of individuals, cohesive group, effective team).

Structure of the relationship in coaching
This includes the following set of elements:

- The business contract (written down and covering legal aspects).

- The methods of meeting (place, means, communicating via the telephone, the mail, etc.) or the relational contract.

■ The characteristics of the relationship (spontaneity, client/coach partnership) or the secret contract.

Structured time
A transactional analysis term. Passive behaviour in which the person submits to what he believes to be the wishes of others, without checking and without considering his own wishes.

Symbiosis
A transactional analysis term. A relationship in which two or more individuals behave as though, together, they form a single person and therefore do not fully use their other Ego States.

T

TA
Transactional Analysis

Teacher in Training
Third cycle of training course designed and led by V. Lenhardt.

Teleological (Cf. *Manager Dans la Complexité*, D. Genelot)
A logic focused on aims (from the Greek, telos, end, purpose).

TMS
Team Management System.

Transaction
A transactional analysis term. Basic unit of social discourse: a transactional stimulus then a transactional response.

Transaction, blocking
A transactional analysis term. A transaction in which one avoids raising a question by showing one's disagreement about the very definition of this question.

Transaction, complementary or parallel
A transactional analysis term. A transaction in which the transactional vectors are not parallel or in which the targeted Ego State is the one that responds.

Transaction, crossed
A transactional analysis term. A transaction in which the transactional vectors are not parallel or in which the targeted Ego State is not the one that responds.

Transaction, hidden
A transactional analysis term. A transaction in which an explicit message and a hidden message are sent at the same time.

Transaction, tangential
A transactional analysis term. A transaction in which the stimulus and the response affect different points or affect the same point but from a different perspective.

Triad
A live coaching situation, involving three people, in which one participant plays the role of the coach, another is the client and the third acts as observer.

Triangle, drama
A transactional analysis term. A diagram that illustrates how people in turn adopt one of the roles of the three scenario positions (Persecutor, Victim, Saviour).

Trust (Cf. *Transformational Leadership*, A. Godard and V. Lenhardt)
Trust is a complex conviction that implies five zones of support: the hierarchy, oneself, others, the situation, life or its major referent. If one of these is missing, the virtuous circle of trust may become blocked.

V

Valley of despair
A key stage in the process of the growth in competencies where the person has passed from being unconscious of his incompetence to being conscious of it.

Victim (in the drama triangle)
A transactional analysis term. A person who considers himself to be inferior, worthy of belittlement or incapable of escaping from this state without help.

Violence
A transactional analysis term. Passive behaviour in which the person channels his destructive energy towards the outside to try to force his environment to resolve a problem.

Vision (Cf. *Le Manager Intuitif*, M. Le Saget; *Transformational Leadership*, A. Godard and V. Lenhardt)
Often promoted by a company's CEO or the leader who was able to capture the collective intuition and perceive the future needs of the market, the vision is not a fixed state or a photograph to be put into a frame and then forgotten. It is a dynamic of progress.

Visioning is a living dynamic that allows a company to become aware of its purpose, its ambitions, its strengths and weaknesses, but also to become aware of the ways that help it to achieve, among the many domains of its daily life, the desired standards of excellence. This process of discovering and asserting an identity comes as an advanced and very powerful response to every CEO's concern for strategy planning.

The vision consists of six logical levels that line up on the continuum of the stakes in play. Starting with the stakes, there are sequentially the vocation (the raison d'être), ambition (the challenge), values (organisational, cultural and ethical), management principles (the translation of values into management systems), strategic priorities (choices for resource allocation in time) and action plans (tactics: actions and schedules). The task will be to nurture each of these logical levels and to make their respective content coherent (through alignment).

Y

Yo-yo, managerial (Cf. *Transformational Leadership*, A. Godard and V. Lenhardt)
This is the approach that the manager has to adopt when he translates his vision on the six logical levels of any vision (1. vocation, 2. ambition, 3. values, 4. management

principles, 5. strategic priorities, 6. action plans). He must permanently navigate between the different logical levels that spread over the continuum stretching from the stakes (the top of the yo-yo) to action (the bottom of the yo-yo).

Z

Zones, identity
Four zones define identity: internal recognition, external recognition, my skin (D. Anzieux), referents or parental figures.

Zones, intervention
A model that allows the coach to identify at least eight zones in every coaching problem brought to him by his client. This model allows the coach:

1. To put his client's situation in context and not 'get his hands dirty' prematurely (by dealing with the problem), by identifying the interfaces and separating out the problems.

2. To prioritise the problems to be dealt with by suggesting to the client that he choose the area for intervention in the time available for the session.

3. To develop a plan of work for the long term (these areas will be dealt with, that one left out, etc.).

4. To help his client position himself in relation to the different interfaces.

5. To identify the presence of any possible parallel process.

6. To check that his identity problems are taken into account.

7. To secure the client's autonomy.

8. To reassure or re-establish his OKness and his self esteem.

Preface

1. According to a remark made by a consultant friend, Dominique Christian.
2. See the article in the CNAM journal, June 2001, 'New Support for Change. Coaching and Team Building, A Fad or A Serious Trend?'
3. From 'holes', the whole and 'morphos' the form.
4. Jaques Hervet, coach of tennis champions, in a personal communication.
5. Key People, 12 rue de l'Église, 75015 Paris.
6. 'Oser la Confiance', INSEP CONSULTING Éditions.
7. *Transformational Leadership: Shared Dreams to Succeed*, Palgrave Macmillan 2000 (English translation of 'Engagements, Espoirs, Rêves' Village Mondial.
8. Such as Collins and Porras ('Built to Last', Harper Business Essentials, 1994), Bartlett and Goshal ('The Individual Corporation: A Fundamentally New Approach to Management', Harper Collins Publishing Inc.), Dominique Genelot ('Manager dans la complexite – Réflexions à l'usage des dirigeants', INSEP CONSULTING Éditions), Edgar Morin, William Schutz ('The Human Element', John Wiley and Sons Ltd) to cite just a few.
9. In their book 'Built to Last', Harper Business Essentials, 1994.
10. Organisation development: this is an approach which is both internal and external to the organisation based on a process of education and support that allows the players to solve their problems progressively.
11. Cf note 3.
12. See article that appeared in the July 2001 issue of Management et Conjoncture Sociale: La dimension personnelle du développement du dirigeant.

Introduction

1. 'Managers as Carriers of Meaning. A Seminar on Coaching and Team Building, The Two Tools of The Manager.' Éditions Sonothèque Média.
2. Olivier Lecerf: 'The risk of winning. The director's profession.' Conversation with Philippe de Woot and Jacques Barraux. Éditions de Fallois, pp. 183–7.
3. François Varillon, *Joie de croire, joie de vivre*, Centurion, Paris, 1975.

Chapter 1

1. By 'impostor complex', I mean the internal thoughts of the manager who takes up a new post or assumes a new responsibility. It often happens that the person asks himself rightly whether he has not taken a step too far. His self-questioning might be: 'Up until now, on certain matters I knew nothing, but I was the only one to know. Now that I am taking on this new responsibility, everyone is going to know it.' This situation occurs frequently and is something that coaching can handle quite specifically. It allows the manager to think about and develop this question and receive feedback from a competent person who gives him an opinion that is both objective and subjective. Furthermore, the coach will help the manager by helping him to measure the importance and the need to transform a more or less rational and opportunistic decision into a strategic decision for identity development balanced against the risks.

Chapter 7

1. We begin with level 3 because that is the habitual starting point in a company and sometimes the only one that people are 'conscious' of; the other levels correctly belong to the 'unsaid'.
2. Cf. *The Human Element*, Jossey Bass, 1994.

Chapter 9

1. In AAT (Actualités en Analyse Transactionnelle), vol. 3, 12, October 1979.

Chapter 11

1. This chapter draws its initial inspiration from an idea of Pierre Nicholas and Jacques Turbé, expressed in 'The Management of Meetings', an organisation memo, as well as the writings of Hubert Landier on 'The Multicellular Company'.
2. For definitions of pyramid, matrix and multicellular companies, see Appendix 2, pp. 185–8 of Engagements, espoirs, Rêves, interview with Jean-René-Fourtou, extract from *Le Monde Affaires*.

Chapter 13

1. The structure and dynamics of organisation groups, Grove Press, New York, 1966.

Chapter 20

1. This chapter is developed from an idea briefly put forward by Pierre Nicholas in his book, 'Le temps, c'est de l'argent et du plaisir' (InterÉditions) ('Time is money and pleasure') and during a personal conversation.
2. In his *A Force for Change, How Leadership Differs from Management*, The Free Press.

Chapter 26

1. Which led to the book Oser la confiance, INSEP CONSULTING Éditions, 1996.

Appendix 1

1. Article in the CNAM Review, June 2001.

Appendix 2

1. Article published in *Management et conjuncture sociale*, June 2001.

Appendix 3

1. Article published in the journal *Management et Conjoncture Sociale*, January 1998, written in collaboration with Manfred Mack.
2. Manfred Mack has more than 25 years' experience of advising on strategy and organisation, the first 10 of which were spent with McKinsey & Co. Inc., in New York and London.
3. Vincent Lenhardt is head of a consulting firm, a trainer of consultants and lecturer to business associations, universities and institutions of higher education.
4. Charles Handy, Le temps des paradoxes...
5. Cf. the principle of the 'vision on the abyss' and the famous Escher drawings (the hand that draws the hand, etc.).
6. *Holos*, the whole and *morphos*, the form.
7. See the book, 'Oser la confiance', by Bertrand Martin, Vincent Lenhardt and Bruno Jarrosson, INSEP CONSULTING Éditions, 1996.

Appendix 4

1. Article published in *Management et Conjoncture Sociale*, July 2002, special issue on coaching for a specific course on coaching at Lyon's 'Ecole de Management'.
2. Alexander Lowen and John Pierrakos are the founders, in the line of Wilhelm Reich, of the therapeutic approach called 'bioenergetic analysis' or 'bioenergy'.
3. Transactional Analysis.
4. Neuro-linguistic Programming.
5. Process Communication Model.
6. Team Management System.
7. From 'holos', the whole and 'morphos', the form.

BIBLIOGRAPHY

ABURDENE & NAISBITT, *Coup d'état dans l'entreprise*, InterÉditions.

ATHOS A.G. & PASCALE R.T., *Le management est-il un art japonais?*, éditions d'Organisation, 1984.

AURIOL Philippe & CORNET Virginie, *Le parler vrai*, ESF, 1985.

BAILLEUX Jean-Marie & CARDON Alain, *Pour Changer*, éditions d'Organisation, 1998.

BAUMARD Philippe, *Organisations déconcertées: La gestion stratégique de la Connaissance*, éditions Masson, 1996.

BENNIS Warren G., *Organization Development*, Addison-Wesley Publishing Company, 1969.

BENHAYOUN Raphaël, *Entreprises en Éveil*, Entreprises modernes d'éditions.

BLAKE Robert, *Spectacular Teamwork – How to Develop the Leadership – Skills for Team*, John Wiley & Sons, 1987.

BLANCHARD Kenneth, CAREW Donald & PARISI-CAREW Eunice, *The One Minute Manager, Builds High Performing Teams*, HarperCollins Business, 2000.

BLANCHARD Kenneth & WAGHORN Terry, *Anticiper le changement*, Dunod, 1997.

BRILMAN Jean, *Les meilleures pratiques de management*, éditions d'Organisation, 1998.

BUCHHOLZ Steve & ROTH Thomas, *Creating the High-Performance Team*, ed. Kären Hes, Wilson Learning Corporation, 1987.

CARDON Alain, *Décider en équipe*, éditions d'Organisation, 1992.

—— *Le manager et son équipe*, éditions d'Organisation, 1986.

—— *Profils d'équipes et cultures d'entreprises*, éditions d'Organisation.

—— *Jeux Pédagogiques et Analyse Transactionnelle*, éditions d'Organisation.

COLLINS James, *Good to Great*, HarperCollins Business, 1994.

COLLINS James C. & PORRAS Jerry I., *Built to Last, Successful Habits of Visionary Companies*. Harper Business Essentials, 1994.

COMTE-SPONVILLE Alain, *Valeur et Vérité* (*Essais cyniques*) (chapitre: *Le capitalisme est-il moral?*), PUF, 1994.

COVEY Stephen R., *Seven Habits of Highly Effective People*, 1990.

CROZIER M., *L'entreprise à l'écoute*, InterÉditions, 1994.

—— *La crise de l'intelligence*, InterÉditions, 1998.

De ROSNAY Joël, *L'homme symbiotique*, Seuil, 1995.

DELIVRE François, *Le métier de coach*, éditions d'Organisation, 2002.

DEVILLARD Olivier, *La dynamique des équipes*. Dunod, 2000.

—— *Coacher*, Dunod.

DHERSE Jean-Loup & MINGUET Dom Hughes, *L'éthique ou le chaos*, Presses de la Renaissance, 1998.

DRUCKER Peter, *Le Leader de demain*, Village Mondial, 1997.

DYER William G, *Team-building – Issues and Alternatives*, second edition, Addison Wesley OD series.

FABER Emmanuel, *Main basse sur la cité*, Hachette Littératures, 1992.

FAUVET Jean-Christian & FOURTOU Jean-René, *La Passion d'entreprendre*, éditions d'Organisation, 1985.

GENELOT Dominique, *Manager dans la complexité – Réflexions à l'usage des dirigeants*, INSEP CONSULTING Éditions, réédition 2001.

FRANKL Viktor E., *Man's Search for Meaning: an Introduction to Logotherapy*, 1984.

GHOSHAL Sumantra & BARTLETT Christopher A., *The Individualized Corporation: A Fundamentally New Approach to Management*, HarperCollins Publishing Inc.

GIBSON Rowan, *Rethinking the Future*, Nicholas Brealey Publishing Ltd, 1996.

HALL & HALL, *Guide du comportement dans les affaires internationales*, Seuil, 1987.

HAMAL Gary & PRAHALAD C.K., *Competing for the Future*, 1996.

HANDY Charles, *The Age of Paradox*, Harvard Business School Press, 1994.

HERSEY Paul, *Management of Organizational Behaviour: Leading Human Resources*, ed. Prentice Hall, 2001.

JARROSSON Bruno, *Invitation à une philosophie du management*, Calmann-Lévy, 1991.

JONES & STEWART, *Manuel de l'Analyse Transactionnelle*, InterÉditions, 2000.

KATZENBACH Jon & SMITH Douglas, *The Wisdom of Teams: Creating High Performance Organizations*, Harvard Business School, 1993.

KERJEAN Alain, *Hors Limites*, Albin Michel

—— *Les nouveaux comportements dans l'entreprise*, éditions d'Organisation, 2000.

KINLAW Denis C., *Coaching for Commitment – Managerial Strategies for Obtaining Superior Performance*, University Associates.

LECERF Olivier, *Au risque de gagner*, éditions de Fallois, 1991.

LE SAGET Meryem, *Le Manager Intuitif*, Dunod, 1992.

MACK Manfred, *L'Impératif Humain*, Masson Éditeur, 1992.

—— *Co-évolution, Dynamique Créatrice*, Village Mondial, 1997.

MALAREWICZ Jacques-Antoine, *Systémique et Entreprise*, Village Mondial, 2000.

MARC Edmond & PICARD Dominique, *L'école de Palo Alto*, Retz.

MORIN Pierre, *Le développement des organisations*, Dunod.

MOUTON Jane S., *Success*, éditions John Wiley & Sons.

OUCHI William, *Theory Z*, Addison-Wesley Publishing Company Inc., 1981.

PETERS Tom, *Liberation Management*, A.A. Knopf Inc., 1992.

SALMON Robert, *Tous les chemins mènent à l'homme*, InterÉditions.

SALMON Robert & de LINARÈS Yolaine, *L'Intelligence compétitive*, Economica, 1997.

SALOFF COSTE Michel, *Le management du 3ème millénaire*, 1990.

SAUCET Michel, *La sémantique générale aujourd'hui*, Courrier du Livre, 1987.

SCHUTZ William, *The Human Element*, San Francisco, Jossey Bass, 1994.

—— *Profound Simplicity*, WSA.

—— *The Truth Option*, Ten Speed Press, 1984

—— *Joy: Expanding Human Awareness*, Grove Press Inc., 1967.

SENGE Peter, *The Fifth Discipline*, Doubleday, 1994.

—— *The Dance of Change*, 1999.

SERIEYX Hervé, *Le Big Bang des Organisations*, éditions Calmann-Lévy, 1992.

—— *Le zéro mépris*, InterÉditions, 1999.

—— *La nouvelle Excellence*, éditions Maxima, 2000.

SINGER Edwin J., *Effective Management Coaching*, Management Paperbacks.

STRATEGOR, *Stratégie, structure, décision, identité, politique générale de l'entre-prise*, InterÉditions.

TICHY Noël, *Control Your Destiny or Someone Else Will*, New York, Doubleday Currency, 1993.

—— *The Leadership Engine*, Harper Business, 1994.

TISSIER Dominique, *Le management situationnel®*, INSEP CONSULTING Éditions, réédition 2001.

TOFFLER A., *Powershift*.

ZARKA Michel, *La stratégie réinventée*, Dunod.

TRANSFORMANCE S.A.

Transformance S.A., is a consulting company founded by Vincent Lenhardt, its current president. Transformance concentrates on two activities:

- Corporate assignments to coach senior executives and management teams as well as to professionalise agents of change through training or professional support within companies;

- Professionalising agents of change by conducting specific inter-organisational seminars and long-term training.

These activities give rise to a variety of publications and conferences as well as interventions within executive clubs and major business schools.

Through its approach, Transformance aims to be a place of growth, of resource and of change management for executives within 'advanced' companies.

An Advanced Concept of Organisations

Transformance considers organisations to be living entities, intelligent and constantly learning, where the players and management teams together discover and construct the corporate goals and form capacities to reach these goals.

This task, as exciting as it is difficult owing to the complexity of our times, demands mobilisation of all of the intelligence and goodwill available within the company. It is therefore essential to encourage the Development of Collective Intelligence. This can be done through instituting learning processes and building teams into cohesive groups of players interconnected through a common vision and who continually share their goals and sense of meaning.

The Know-how

A successful coaching relationship is centred on the development of individuals, teams and the organisation. The Transformance team is made up of experienced consultants, with many years of experience in consulting and coaching. Since 1988, Transformance has pioneered in France the fields of: individual coaching for Executives ('Coaching'), creating cohesive, high-performance teams ('Team Building'), and has, from the beginning, organised conferences and published material on these subjects. Transformance's unique training approach for agents of change (consultants, trainers and managers) includes a 20-day programme spread out over the year, which earned an instant success and has allowed some 600 consultants to benefit from the training since 1989.

By starting with the management team, the entire organisation can be taught to become co-responsible: The Managers, or 'Order-Givers', learn to position themselves as 'Resource Directors' and thus facilitate processes by creating meaning for the players.

Building a Corporate Vision

Transformance brings to management teams its competence for leading a strategic reflection, specifically by contributing to a co-elaboration of a strategy with the different organisational players, by enlarging the vision to include a larger scope. This global vision includes all of the company goals: its vocation, ambitions, values, management principles, strategic priorities and action plans.

Transformance emphasises the fact that elaborating the Vision is only meaningful if it leads to the combination of its effective deployment within the entire organisation coupled with an Alignment of all management systems (evaluation interviews, remuneration, training, recruitment, etc.). This systematic implementation cannot be completed without specific attention to the Exemplary nature shown by the principal players involved or without carefully piloted coaching processes carried out conjointly among managers, in-house change agents and external partners.

The combination of these approaches leads to the Development of collective intelligence which has become Transformance's specialty, knowing that the implementation of each management tool (coaching, for example) has this Collective Intelligence as a goal without which the organisation cannot be assured of its staying power and growth.

Training of the Transformance Players

Transformance spreads its training among different companies and within individual organisations. These include both specifically tailored programmes and long-term consultant training ('CT+' training: 20 days spread out over a year in the form of one seminar every two months and ending with a certification) and brief and concentrated seminars ('Resource Director', for example, initiation to Collective Intelligence, and 'Resource Manager', initiation to the role of manager/coach).

Resources

A team of high-level consultants, most of whom have cross-cultural or international experience and a record of specific personal development. A network of consultants trained by Transformance in France and in French-speaking countries allows for the formation of teams working on national and international levels.

A few of our publications

Oser la confiance by Bertrand Martin, Vincent Lenhardt, Bruno Jarrosson, INSEP CONSULTING Editions, 1996.

L'impératif humain by Manfred Mack, Masson, 1992.

Co-évolution: dynamique créatrice by Manfred Mack, Village Mondial,1999.

Engagements, Espoirs, Rêves, Alain Godard and Vincent Lenhardt, Village Mondial, 1998.

Transformational Leadership, Alain Godard and Vincent Lenhardt, Palgrave (London 1999).

L'analyse transactionnelle, concepts et procédures, bioscénarios, perspectives spirituelles, éditions Retz.

Analyse transactionnelle et bio-énergie, in collaboration with J.-M. Fourcade, éditions Universitaires.

Analyse transactionnelle, outil de communication et d'évolution, in collaboration with A. Cardon and P. Nicolas.

TRANSFORMANCE – 90 rue Anatole France – 92300 LEVALLOIS-PERRET
Tel.: 33 (0) 1 47 48 18 19 – Fax: 33 (0) 1 47 57 19 99
http://www.transformance.fr
E-mail: secretariat@transformance.fr

INSEP CONSULTING *Editions* is a department of INSEP CONSULTING.

INSEP CONSULTING aims at improving the overall performance of companies through the development of individuals and organisations.

We coach our clients in situations of change (mergers, restructuring, shifts in productivity, integration of information systems, professionalisation of management) and provide all skills required for their success: diagnosis, consulting, engineering and production of training courses, coaching, realisation.

Our interventions revolve around three main fields:

- *Development of management*: professionalisation of managers, strategic deployment, change management, coaching.

- *Development of human resources*: skills evaluation and management, assessment, training engineering.

- *Organisational development*: process, function and project re-organisation, innovation, knowledge management, customer relations.

Our clients are leading industrial or service companies, whether large or average sized, which have taken leadership in their respective markets.

In France, we have 90 consultants.

On the international scene, INSEP CONSULTING conducts management consulting operations for large groups, in collaboration with the Oxford Group and other partners in Europe and the United States.

Through the publications of INSEP CONSULTING *Editions* and its website (www.insep.com), all have access to the professional principles and methods that make it successful.

INSEP CONSULTING
18 bd Malesherbes – 75008 PARIS
Tel: +33 (0) 1 42 68 0101 – Fax: +33 (0) 1 42 68 11 44
E-mail: consulting@insep.com
www.insep.com